THE UNIVERSITY OF
WINCHESTER

JOURNALISM AND REALISM

Medill School of Journalism
VISIONS *of the* AMERICAN PRESS

GENERAL EDITOR
David Abrahamson

Selected titles in this series

HERBERT J. GANS
Deciding What's News: A Study of "CBS Evening News," "NBC Nightly News," "Newsweek," and "Time"

MAURINE H. BEASLEY
First Ladies and the Press: The Unfinished Partnership of the Media Age

PATRICIA BRADLEY
Women and the Press: The Struggle for Equality

DAVID A. COPELAND
The Idea of a Free Press: The Enlightenment and Its Unruly Legacy

MICHAEL S. SWEENEY
The Military and the Press: An Uneasy Truce

PATRICK S. WASHBURN
The African American Newspaper: Voice of Freedom

KARLA K. GOWER
Public Relations and the Press: The Troubled Embrace

TOM GOLDSTEIN
Journalism and Truth: Strange Bedfellows

NORMAN SIMS
True Stories: A Century of Literary Journalism

MARK NEUZIL
The Environment and the Press: From Adventure Writing to Advocacy

JOURNALISM AND REALISM

RENDERING AMERICAN LIFE

Thomas B. Connery

Foreword by Roy Peter Clark

MEDILL SCHOOL OF JOURNALISM

Northwestern University Press

Evanston, Illinois

Northwestern University Press
www.nupress.northwestern.edu

Printed in the United States of America

10 9 8 7 6 5 4 3 2 1

Library of Congress Cataloging-in-Publication Data

Connery, Thomas Bernard.
    Journalism and realism : rendering American life / Thomas B. Connery ;
foreword by Roy Peter Clark.
      p. cm. — (Medill School of Journalism Visions of the American press)
    Includes bibliographical references and index.
    ISBN 978-0-8101-2733-3 (pbk. : alk. paper)
    1. Journalism—United States—History—19th century. 2. Reportage
literature, American—History and criticism. 3. Journalism and literature—
United States—History—19th century. 4. Realism in literature. I. Title. II.
Series: Visions of the American press.
  PN4864.C66 2011
  070.430973—dc22

                                       2011000504

For my family

CONTENTS

FOREWORD

Roy Peter Clark

WHEN NOTHING IS REAL

My title comes from the John Lennon song, "Strawberry Fields Forever," the psychedelic anthem of a world where "nothing is real," but it doesn't matter because you don't need to "to get hung about" anything.

The *American Heritage Dictionary* defines realism as

1. An inclination toward literal truth.
2. The presentation in art or literature of objects, actions, or social conditions as they actually are, without idealization or presentation in abstract forms.

In the history of philosophy, the word *realism* has been used to describe two antithetical notions: that abstractions are real aside from thought, and that things in the world are real whether perceived or not. So that freaking tree in the freaking forest does make a freaking sound after all.

It was that great Biblical postmodernist, Pontius Pilate, who asked of Jesus the still relevant question "What is truth?" By the time I got to college in 1966, the Dominican Friars at Providence College, wearing the robes of Thomas Aquinas—who believed that universals existed outside the human mind—seemed to have answered Pilate's question by the prominent publication of the college's motto: "Veritas," the Latin word for "Truth." Make that Truth with a capital V. How easy it was to stick that decal on the back window of our '66 Mustang.

At Providence College I was an English major, and I remember my surprise at Plato's banishment of poetry from his Republic. Why ban poets? Because, writes Plato in "Poetry and Unreality," a chapter of *Republic*, "they are two generations away from the throne of truth." For Plato, the real exists not in the world of things but in the world of ideals. The flower I pick is but a shadow of the idea of the flower. And when the poet writes words that claim to represent the flower, he creates nothing more than a shadow of a shadow—two generations from the throne of truth.

Let's travel forward in time from Plato to Poland circa 1985. American poet Peter Meinke lives in Warsaw for a year on a Fulbright Fellowship and notices a profound cultural difference between America and Eastern Europe. He picks up the newspaper, as is his habit in America, but he is told that the newspapers are "nothing." Everyone knows they are propaganda tools of the Communist Party and are widely disdained. Peter attends a poetry reading in a stadium filled with Poles who want to hear the banned word of Nobel Laureate Czesław Miłosz. "In America," Meinke told a group of reporters, "newspapers are everything, but a poet is lucky if he can attract ten people to a reading. In Poland, the newspapers are nothing, but the poets can fill a stadium." Something in the poetry *is* real.

Peter Meinke once wrote a Christmas sonnet sequence titled "Mendel's Laws," in which the narrator speaks to his wife, who is expecting a child: "And in the code that Mendel labored on/our child will be deciphered." Peter and his wife Jeanne turned the poem into a Christmas card. Peter got messages back that read, "Hey, old man, way to go. We had no idea that Jeanne was pregnant!" Of course, she wasn't. The poet, using the rungs of the real world, was climbing toward a higher truth.

Careful with that "higher truth" business.

It is January 2006, and I am a guest on one of the most memorable Oprah Winfrey shows of all time. I sit in the first row watching Oprah, once a journalist, eviscerate an author named James Frey. The young writer—who wrote his book, *A Million Little Pieces,* as a novel—was persuaded to turn it into a memoir, a book that became a choice of Oprah's Book Club, making the author both wealthy and the object of scrutiny.

A group of investigative reporters fact-checked the book and discovered that it was full of fabrications and exaggerations. Under interrogation by Oprah, who had to that point continued to endorse the book, Frey admitted that he had not spent three months in the clink, but only, maybe, three hours. As one scene after another was defrocked, Oprah's audience, mostly women who had given Frey a standing ovation when he entered, began to murmur and hiss, collectively disappointed and disillusioned. An unwritten contract between author and audience had been violated. The author promised readers that his story was real.

It was not the case that nothing in the book was real. But when a reader learns that a piece of a memoir, however realistic, has been fabricated, that reader begins to doubt everything in the memoir. And if one memoir turns out to be rotten, skepticism can turn to cynicism, the belief that every work of nonfiction is somehow tainted. And what damage is done when a memoirist fabricates stories about the Holocaust, or about persecution of Native

Americans, or about gang culture in Southern California—all of which have happened?

In 1977, Annie Dillard won a Pulitzer Prize for nonfiction for her book *Pilgrim at Tinker Creek*. I doubt that book would win today. I served as the chair of the Pulitzer jury for nonfiction books in 2007 and can attest that standards have tightened considerably in the thirty years since Dillard wrote

> I used to have a cat, an old fighting tom, who would jump through the open window by my bed in the middle of the night and land on my chest. I'd half-awaken. He'd stick his skull under my nose and purr, stinking of urine and blood. Some nights he kneaded my bare chest with his front paws, powerfully, arching his back, as if sharpening his claws, or pummeling a mother for milk. And some mornings I'd wake in daylight to find my body covered with paw prints in blood; I looked as though I'd been painted with roses.

That old tom cat is so important to Dillard's reality that she brings him back for an encore at the very end of the book. The cat provides a good and powerful image. Something to see, smell, and feel, those bloody paw prints on her body, looking like roses.

If only it were true. At a literary festival, Annie Dillard told an adoring audience that she borrowed that story of the cat, with permission, from one of her students. I assume that's true. But who knows? Maybe she should give back the prize. Dillard's writing seems very realistic, which only demonstrates that realism and truth are not coterminous.

The reality scales are not in balance.

On one side we have objectivity, neutrality, disinterest, nonpartisanship, evidence, empiricism, truthfulness, representation, mimesis, realism—all noble pillars of epistemology, to be sure.

But check out the other side: subjectivity, bias, slant, spin, propaganda, opinion, bullshit, point of view, agenda, lies, deception, fabrication, plagiarism, social construction, take, postmodernism, argument, partisanship, ideology, marketing, advertising, image makers, what Stephen Colbert calls "truthiness."

We're outnumbered.

In a scene that offers a flash of insight into Shakespeare's directorial philosophy, Hamlet coaches the traveling players on how to perform the play that will expose King Claudius's murder of Hamlet's father:

> Speak the speech, I pray you, as I pronounced it to you, trippingly on the tongue; but if you mouth it as many of your players do, I had as lief the town-crier spoke my lines. . . . Suit the action to the word, the word to the action, with this special observance, that you o'erstep not the modesty of nature. For anything so o'erdone is from the purpose of playing, whose end, both at the first and now, was and is to hold as 'twere the mirror up to nature.

Hold a mirror up to nature. The performance should represent the real world in a way that the audience would recognize it.

Objectivity, as media scholar Jay Rosen has described so well, is a word that stands for several different ideas, depending upon the speaker or writer. While journalists may have long overstated their exclusive handle on the truth, who can deny that there is a degree of pragmatic empiricism in their methods? Melvin Mencher describes it as a rough parallel to the scientific method: that a reporter begins with a hypothesis, a preconception of what the fire at the morgue will look like, a notion that must be tested against the evidence provided by his investigation.

Jim Dwyer of the *New York Times* describes journalism as a discipline of "reproducible results." The reporter may not be a rocket scientist, but he or she gathers evidence, draws conclusions, and presents what is most important to the reader. By examining sources, any reasonably smart person should be able to retrace the steps of the reporter and, if Dwyer has done his job, reach similar results.

In a now famous essay that appeared in the *Yale Review,* "The Legend on the License," John Hersey rags on the New Journalists of the 1960s for what he describes as their distortion of the truth. Hersey, the author of *Hiroshima,* draws an important distinction in his essay about two different forms of reportorial distortion. A reporter gathers a thousand details and uses only ten, a subjective distortion by subtraction. It is when the reporter distorts by addition that he steps over a line that should not be crossed. The legend on the license of every journalist should be that nothing in the book was made up.

That would seem like a voice of conscience drawing a stark line in the sand, except for the fact that there is good evidence that Hersey was a "compulsive plagiarist." It comes from Anne Fadiman in her book *Ex Libris,* a chapter of which describes the manner in which Hersey ripped off Fadiman's mother in writing the book *Men on Bataan.* She interviews Laurence Bergreen, who testifies to instances in which several authors complained about being plagiarized by Hersey. "He borrowed repeatedly," writes Fadiman, "he left extravagantly obvious clues, and—what a gifted writer he was!—he didn't need to do it."

• • •

"The essence of journalism," write Bill Kovach and Tom Rosentiel in *The Elements of Journalism,* "is a discipline of verification." When the concept of objectivity evolved, they write, "it was not meant to imply that journalists were free of bias. Quite the contrary. The term began to appear as part of journalism early in the last century, particularly in the 1920s, out of a growing recognition that journalists were full of bias, often unconsciously. Objectivity called for journalists to develop a consistent method of testing information—a transparent approach to evidence—precisely so that personal and cultural biases would not undermine the accuracy of their work."

In a *New Yorker* piece from April 26, 2010, Richard Rayner reports on the fabrications embedded in the work of historian Stephen Ambrose on the life of Dwight D. Eisenhower. Detailed records reveal that Ambrose met with Ike on only three occasions for a total of less than five hours and always with someone else present. These facts contradict Ambrose's embellished testimony that he and the former president had spent "hundreds and hundreds of hours" in interviews from 1964 to 1969. "I felt ill" when these revelations appeared, wrote Garrison Keillor. "I admired the man."

No one could argue that the narrative histories of Ambrose are not realistic. In fact, the techniques we associate with realistic fiction are employed liberally through his use of scenes, dialogue, and careful characterization. He creates what appears to be a real world into which the reader can enter. But how real?

Most of us grow up believing that the forms of journalism and literature that exist now have existed forever. In fact, they were created at a moment in time to serve a society's new needs, influenced by politics, demography, ethnicity, and markets. Professor Tom Connery does us a great favor by taking us back in time a century or so to take a look at the cultural changes that came to emphasize realism as a way of telling stories and reflecting the world. He calls this movement from the romantic and ideal to the real as a shift to "the paradigm of actuality."

We need to know this story, how realism became a dominant mode of representational art in the nineteenth century, and how it began to fall apart in the twentieth. We are left at the beginning of the twenty-first century on very unsteady ground. Annie Dillard still has her Pulitzer Prize for nonfiction. Some memoirists defend her work in the interests of a "higher truth." James Frey is writing novels, but *A Million Little Pieces* continues to sell, in spite of a long mea culpa in a new edition testifying to the distortions in the story. Television is now dominated by "reality" programming, a reality that is shaped, scripted, cast, revised, and sensationalized for added entertainment value. Millions of people have become leading men and women in the exaggerated stories they tell about themselves on social networks such as Facebook.

The exercise of craft without a noble purpose is an empty gesture. The goal of a realistic craft, as Connery's subtitle suggests, is to "render" America, not to "rend" it as so many of the fabricators have done. Journalism, as James Carey taught us, is, in the end, an expression of culture. Connery is tuned in to that tradition. "Journalism matters," writes Connery, "because in its accounts of people, places, events, and activities it carries cultural meaning, values, ideals. And in the 1800s its overriding, broad cultural message was that the actualities of life being lived were important in knowing and understanding America."

Something is real after all.

PREFACE

Recently I picked up my local newspaper, a large urban daily, and read a front-page story about how elderly Hmong immigrants were getting the kind of food they want and need, prepared at a Hmong store and delivered by an organization that helps immigrants settle in Minnesota. About the same time, I read in a news magazine an excerpt from a new book, *Working in the Shadows: A Year of Doing the Jobs That (Most) Americans Won't Do*, by Gabriel Thompson. Thompson, whose work has appeared in several magazines, also wrote about immigrants in *There's No José Here: Following the Hidden Lives of Mexican Immigrants* (2007). The local newspaper article and the books and magazine writing of Thompson are examples of what I call cultural reporting, or writing that documents the lives of those living among us, that provides meaning and insight, often simply by treating its subjects with respect and dignity, but also by going beneath the surface so that we can see people in their environment and hear them speak in their own voices.

Other examples of newspaper cultural reporting go well beyond the Hmong example in getting readers inside people's lives, giving us more than facts and straight information. In November 2008, for instance, the weekly alternative newspaper in Minneapolis, *City Pages*, caught my attention by pulling me into the life of a recently murdered Somali college student. By immediately setting the scene at the home of the student during Ramadan, the article allows us to very quickly get a taste of cultural and religious ritual, not as something odd but as a part of the rhythm of Muslim life:

> On Monday, September 22, Asha Hagi-Mohamed woke her 20-year-old son Ahmednur up at around 5:30 A.M. so that he could pray. Asha had busied herself in the kitchen preparing *suhoor,* the meal eaten before daybreak during the holy month of Ramadan to prepare for the fast. Asha offered the food to her son, her husband, and the other five members of the household, and then the family prayed. It was during the last 10 days of Ramadan, the holiest time of the Muslim holy month, when the gates of hell were closed.
>
> After the *fajr,* the dawn prayer, Ahmednur Ali returned to bed, where he dozed until the last possible moment. Around 8:30 A.M., Asha heard her son rise again and ask his father for lunch money. Then Ahmednur left with his older sister, who drove him from their Columbia Heights home to Augsburg College, where he had just begun his third year as an international-relations major.[1]

Regardless of their form or structure, such articles and books that document life being lived all are part of a type of journalism that both expresses and shapes culture and has a rich history and deep roots in the American realism tradition. These writings reach back through time to the many portrayals of the poor and marginalized, of immigrants and African Americans, of people of all types chasing the American Dream and its middle-class status while they struggle to get by and overcome stereotyping and prejudice. Thompson's *Working in the Shadows,* for instance, is a current version of Walter Wyckoff's *The Workers: An Experiment in Reality,* an account of his 1891 walk across the United States doing unskilled labor. Thompson's story of immigrants, built around the tale of Enrique, a Mexican cab driver and his family in Brooklyn, connects Thompson to Ted Conover's story of undocumented Mexican farm workers (*Coyotes*), and to Tracy Kidder's first literary journalistic attempt (*The Road to Yuba City*), while Conover's *Rolling Nowhere: A Journey Across Borders with America's Illegal Migrants* anticipates *Coyotes* and connects to *The Road to Yuba City*. They all reverberate back to Josiah Flynt's accounts of riding the rails and tramp life in the late 1880s and early 1890s, while Adrian Nicole LeBlanc's remarkable story of love and life in a Bronx ghetto, *Random Family*, reminds us that many of the human conflicts and urban problems that were documented in Jacob Riis's *How the Other Half Lives* still resonate a hundred years later.

It was in a master's seminar at Ohio State University in the early 1970s that I first became intrigued by journalism as literature, which was a central theme of Professor John Clarke's course, "Literature and Journalism." Tom Wolfe's essays and his anthology *The New Journalism* had yet to be published, but we read several of the writers that would appear in that volume, including Gay Talese, Truman Capote, and Wolfe himself. But we also read John Steinbeck and Sherwood Anderson, with Clarke clearly linking journalism and realism, and we read a 1958 lecture by the poet Archibald MacLeish called "Poetry and Journalism" in which MacLeish declared that journalism and poetry "are both recreations, different in degree but not different in kind, for the material in each case is our human experience. . . ."[2] Nicely complementing MacLeish's insight were excerpts from a 1968 report written by James Carey in which, while assessing a journalism curriculum at the University of Iowa, he perceptively explored the relationship between journalism and the novel and, in the process, the cultural significance of the New Journalism. It was all exciting stuff that stayed with me, influencing my own newspaper writing as I toyed with scene-setting leads and more descriptive narrative, but also sparking a desire in me to learn more, to investigate and discover more about journalism as a form of literary and cultural realism.

After working as a journalist for several years, I returned to the classroom and searched for the roots of the New Journalism and, building on what I heard from Clarke and learned in his seminar, identified and defined a literary journalism that thrived in the late 1800s. In my research, it became clear that journalism wasn't merely linked to realism; it was part and parcel of a realistic movement with repeated attempts to record life observed. It seemed that all forms of expression and communication—fiction, art, journalism, poetry—insisted on the primacy of observation. I wanted to know more. Occasionally in a conference paper or presentation I touched on what I suspected: that is, not only was this type of writing that some of us called literary journalism clearly in the realistic tradition, but journalism of all types and forms had not simply served as a vehicle for realism—although it did that—but by its fascination and constant, repeated attempts to feed the curious reading public with depictions, accounts, and stories about themselves and many types of Americans, this type of reporting helped mold what *Century Magazine* in 1897 would call the age of "recording realism."[3]

In other words, if society exists in its various forms and practices—such as music, dance, art, storytelling, poetry, filmmaking, and so forth—it also exists in its journalism, which is another of its forms and practices. Journalism matters because in its accounts of people, places, events, and activities it carries cultural meaning, values, ideals. And in the 1800s its overriding, broad cultural message was that the actualities of life being lived were important in knowing and understanding America.

This book confirms the journalism-realism relationship by exploring connections among representative writers, editors, and publications from the 1830s through the turn of the century, connecting to and building upon the research and ideas of a number of scholars, thereby continuing an intellectual journey that for me started so many years ago in John Clarke's seminar. I will be forever grateful for that opportunity to study with and learn from him.

Over the years I have benefited from support and encouragement from many, but especially Norm Sims, Nancy Roberts, John Pauly, and Linda Steiner. Finally, this book never would have happened had it not been for David Abrahamson. David, the general editor of the Visions of the American Press series for the Medill School of Journalism and Northwestern University Press, helped shape the book's thesis, allowed me to roam wide for its content, and demonstrated deep patience and knowledge to go with his keen editing skills.

JOURNALISM AND REALISM

ONE

A PARADIGM OF ACTUALITY

In 1871, Bret Harte, a writer and magazine editor living in California and writing very popular short stories about mining camp characters, slick Western gamblers, and heart-of-gold dance hall girls and prostitutes, among others, decided to go East where his star was particularly bright. Harte's journey caused quite a stir. Mark Twain said Harte "crossed the continent through such a prodigious blaze of national interest and excitement that one might have supposed he was the Viceroy of India on a progress, or Halley's comet come again after seventy-five years of lamented absence."[1] That popularity was mostly due to those Western short stories as well as the poem "Plain Language from Truthful James," also known as "The Heathen Chinee," both of which first appeared in the *Overland Monthly,* the magazine Harte founded and edited. Harte's stories and poem were well received in the northeast and reprinted in newspapers, and in 1870, the same year he published "Plain Language from Truthful James," his stories that had been published the previous two years in *Overland Monthly* were collected and published as the book *The Luck of Roaring Camp and Other Stories.*

For many readers, Harte provided sentimental but real tales of the California gold country; he seemingly gave them actual characters and captured the distinct way they talked, thought, and behaved, all characteristics of what came to be called "local color" writing, or a regional realism. But as Wallace Stegner has written, whatever "virtues" Harte's stories possessed, "they were not the virtues of realism." Stegner, a Western writer of repute, went on to say that "there are a hundred firsthand accounts that give a more faithful picture of life in the mines than his stories do."[2] As true as that may be, it doesn't matter. Because Harte was telling tales about an actual place—the California Gold Rush area—and because he was a California writer who appeared to be familiar with the place and its people, the popularity of his work guaranteed that his version contributed to a Western "reality" regardless of its accuracy. Harte's stories had the ring of authenticity. Rather than fully depicting the common and actual, Harte used a few basic characteristics and phrases of speech to create some predictable Western mining camp types whose language was peppered with "It's agin justice," "this yer young man," "Just you go out ther and cuss, and see," or "Rastled with it, the damned little cuss."[3]

Of course, at least thirty years before Harte, readers of many American newspapers and magazines were reading local and regional dialect and slang that supposedly made the people talking that talk real and believable. This meant that despite their weak claim to being "realistic," Harte's tales were *perceived* as such, particularly in the Northeast and in England, where Harte lived the last part of his life. Several of the stories were repeatedly anthologized and the area he wrote about became "Harte Country" and a tourist destination, thereby validating Harte's version of reality, a reality and popularity made possible by magazine and newspaper journalism.

Although Harte's depictions of a slice of California were infused with sentimentality, his literary ascendancy points to the central, crucial role that journalism played in depicting "actuality" and presenting versions of reality as it expanded and solidified its role in rendering American life, often far more accurately than Harte had. Even a cursory review of the evolution of journalistic style and content in newspapers and magazines reveals that journalism, as one of many cultural forms of expression, was fully participating in and being influenced by realism's ascendancy in the nineteenth century. Journalism did this, of course, by publishing articles and drawings about contemporary people, places, and events, recognizing and often promulgating regional differences and tensions. But journalism also served as a vehicle for the move toward a more realistic fiction that focused on American people and types, themes, and topics, particularly as they applied to emerging class and race issues. As one literary scholar has put it, for writers realism meant "capturing the special immediate American reality in the familiar American dialect," which newspapers were doing on a daily basis.

While this may seem obvious and self-evident, too many histories and cultural studies of the nineteenth century, including those done by journalism historians, fail to acknowledge the centrality of journalism's role even when it is assumed or minimally acknowledged. I thought as much years ago when I presented a paper at an American Journalism Historians Conference that pointed out the interplay between local color characteristics and stories in the daily newspaper, thinking at the time that the journalism-realism discourse was actually much larger, that journalism's role in expressing and shaping an important cultural sensibility was far grander than using some slang and dialect to connect with local color. But I did nothing further with it until I was very much reminded of it again when I read David Shi's impressive interdisciplinary study of the cultural rise, impact, and significance of American realism, *Facing Facts: Realism in American Thought and Culture 1850–1920.* Journalism was right in the thick of the overwhelming cultural shift that Shi so thoroughly and convincingly documents.[4]

Although newspapers and magazines for much of the nineteenth century were full of references to realism in various guises, often strongly endorsing the idea, often deploring it, or often simply trying to be more "realistic," today to even raise the concept of realism in the nineteenth century can be problematic. As will be discussed more fully in chapter 2, the claims of realistic writing by writers of the time are often challenged, as is the very notion that such a thing as "realism" exists as it has been defined. The claims of realistic depiction, in whatever form of expression, were misleading and naïve, charge some more recent critics, particularly since the very notion that there is a single reality is no longer accepted. This study makes no attempt to consider the validity of nineteenth-century realism; nor does it assess realism or its impact. First, it explores the role of journalism in participating in this broad, significant cultural shift, and secondly, it considers the ways that journalism both helped create that shift and reflected it with its content and commentary. I call this shift a paradigm of actuality.

By "actuality," I mean actual people and places, incidents, activities, and actions that have actually occurred. The emerging curiosity throughout society about contemporary life and existence, about real people, places, and events, about the present rather than the past, about life being lived rather than life as it should be lived, led to more of it in newspapers and magazines, and that in turn sparked more curiosity about the actual and present. In other words, it cut both ways. Nineteenth-century writers, artists, and thinkers often described this as a turn to the real and a move away from the ideal, seeming to embrace Emerson's declaration in "The American Scholar": "Give me insight into to-day, and you may have the antique and future worlds."[5] This statement also implies concern with the common and everyday, rather than the extraordinary and lofty.

As the Harte example suggests, distinguishing between the real and ideal is not always clear and clean; in fact, throughout the nineteenth century a tension existed between the real and ideal, and just as journalism provided the place and way to cast importance upon the everyday of American culture, it also provided the place where a realism-idealism discourse would be ongoing, particularly in magazines but also in newspapers, whether the discussion dealt with writing, painting, or other forms of expression.

For journalism, this paradigm of actuality essentially involved documenting, in nonfiction and fiction, in drawings and photographs, the perceived reality. Writers and artists, including journalists, were saying, "Come see how people live, how they talk, how they treat one another, what it is they value." Although many thought they could "mirror" life being lived by providing a photographic word picture, others were more concerned with accurately capturing the essence of a moment or scene or person and truthfully recording or rendering what had been observed and heard, frequently providing an interpretation of life in the process. Too often, actuality simply meant depicting—and thereby endorsing—bourgeois values and virtues, or in capturing the bleak or tawdry lives of an increasingly marginalized class in society, thereby providing a means of middle-class voyeurism rather than insight or understanding.

While this study does not delve deeply into arguments over the nature of realism as a concept, it also does not repeat familiar history regarding the social and cultural forces that allowed for a paradigm of actuality. That an assortment of scientific, economic, and demographic developments drastically altered American society in the nineteenth century has been carefully and fully documented. Overall, industrialization and urbanization occurred, but those related developments were marked by new steamships, railroads, commercial expansion and more trade, westward growth and expansion, and waves of immigrants flooding major cities. The consumer culture was born and with it came the extremes of wealth and poverty. On top of that were transformative developments in communication: the telegraph, faster and cheaper printing, improvements in image-making, including reproduction of sketches or drawings and photography. Newspapers, magazines, and books all were more readily available to document changing American society and its hodgepodge of subcultures, each with its own customs, habits, language, and behavior.

Americans were naturally curious about one another and eager for information and descriptions of the many parts of the city and country in which they lived. That curiosity, consisting of both a desire to learn more about one another and a need to understand remarkable change under way, stimulated journalism in all its forms to feed that need and desire. Such curiosity was demonstrated by, for instance, Bret Harte sending "letters," or reports, from California as a correspondent for two Massachusetts newspapers, the *Springfield Republican* and the Boston *Christian Register.* These articles, as with most such correspondence that newspapers ran from correspondents outside their normal coverage area, were typically written from a strong point of view and generally grounded in facts but also filled with opinion and commentary. In Harte's case, readers in Massachusetts read about people and happenings in California, as well as detailed descriptions of the weather and climate, and California fruits, vegetables, and flowers. Such articles fed that national need to better understand and experience the present, as did short works of fiction.[6]

In order to document and elucidate the journalism–realism discourse and its influential and dynamic interconnections, this book places nineteenth-century journalism more firmly and exactly within realism's emergence and rise to prominence, showing how journalism was at the center of this cultural shift, sharing realism's inclinations, its philosophical bent, and its impact. While many journalistic histories tend to look at how newspapers covered major events and people, or at how certain publications served their readers or shaped attitudes toward gender, race, or ethnicity, this study examines and reexamines a selection of writers, journalists, and illustrators in order to connect them to an important development in American cultural history. Daily news writing and reporting were quite naturally expressions of realism and the actual, even when they were exaggerated or sensationalized. Some early penny paper coverage will be discussed in chapter 2, connecting it to common cultural values, particularly in fiction, but otherwise the focus is on some very different attempts at showing people to people, living, often struggling; the manner that it was done was rooted in more literary journalistic impulses.

This study makes no claims to uncovering new knowledge or data. Rather, it takes existing knowledge and research and reconfigures it to produce a different interpretation, what Ernest L. Boyer called the scholarship of integration, or scholarship that brings together in a fresh perspective seemingly disconnected facts and material, making connections and providing new meaning.[7] Thus the reader will find a few odd couplings of representative figures, such as, in chapter 3, journalist and iconic poet Walt Whitman with *New York Tribune* reporter and urban chronicler George G. Foster, who is little known, if known at all, even among journalism historians but readily acknowledged among many cultural and New York City historians and scholars; or the pairing in chapter 4 of one of the best known and most popular American writers, Mark Twain, with only recently rediscovered Rebecca Harding Davis. Chapter 5 introduces the important role of the visual in journalism's attempt to capture real life, with consideration of two major illustrated weeklies along with the depictions of illustrator and artist Winslow Homer and photographer Mathew Brady, among others, while chapter 6 explores the work of Cincinnati reporter Lafcadio Hearn before highlighting major voices and drivers of realism, including the largely forgotten Henry Mills Alden, who was an influential *Harper's* editor from the 1860s to the early 1900s. The book's concluding chapter focuses on the last two decades of the century, a time when the drive to make sense of American society finds expression in several journalistic and nonfiction forms that try to get at the "truth" of American life. Chapter 7 features investigations by Jacob Riis and Josiah Flynt as well as the descriptive narratives and literary journalism of Stephen Crane and Abraham Cahan. Each chapter, however distinct from the others, serves to document journalism's participation in cultivating and advancing the paradigm of actuality. But two additional unifying elements exist: many of the examples deal with the emerging class distinctions and the marginalized working class and the poor, and much of the writing discussed tends to be human interest and even early forms of what we today call literary journalism, or writing that shares several qualities. It generally is characterized by a distinct writer's voice and perspective, and it informs at a level common to fiction, attempting to give not just facts but the "feel" of the facts.

Although this study is representative, it is far from comprehensive; each chapter could be easily expanded into its own book, and chapter 7 would be the thickest among them. Some will object to the emphasis on New York journalism and the northeastern magazine establishment. As Lafcadio Hearn demonstrates, writers and journalists in any number of urban areas, especially in Chicago, Philadelphia, New Orleans, and San Francisco, were also documenting life in their cities. But to broaden would be well beyond the scope of this study, and therefore necessity dictated its narrowness, which nonetheless still validates journalism's essential role in fostering the realistic sensibility while setting the table for additional scholarship.

TWO

SEARCHING FOR THE REAL
AND ACTUAL

Ashcan artist Everett Shinn's 1899 painting, *Cross Streets of New York,* depicts a snow-covered, shabby Lower East Side street, with its buildings and people echoing similar depictions in journalism and fiction, such as Stephen Crane's homeless men standing in a snowstorm, waiting to get into a shelter, or Upton Sinclair's Jurgis Rudkus trudging through snow-covered streets of Chicago, poor, hungry, and in need of shelter and work.[1] The scenes in these works of art, journalism, and fiction do not give us life as it ought to be; in all three depictions, little is idealized or simply imagined. Yet during much of the first half of the century such representations would have been unusual or subsumed in a romantic and idealized context. Of course, the idealizing and romanticizing of life and people, creating a patina of gentility, were still evident at the end of the nineteenth century. But close observation of the surrounding urban spectacle in order to depict life being lived, in order to acknowledge and attempt to recreate that which is actual rather than imaginative, had become pervasive if not dominant. Such attempts to faithfully record or represent reality have been called "realism" but not without some complaint from recent scholars and historians who consider the phrase vague, imprecise, and generally inaccurate in describing what happened in the second half of the nineteenth and early twentieth centuries.

Consequently, literary critics and historians since the 1980s have done their best to debunk or significantly qualify the notion of a genuine American realism in the nineteenth and early twentieth centuries.[2] They claim there's no real evidence of a "movement" in the true sense of that word, as there was, for instance, in nineteenth-century France. They point out that much of the writing and many of the writers identified with American realism retained romantic impulses and touches. Much so-called realism, they further claim, never really went beyond mere surface imitation, which too often simply contained listings of details and facts rather than a more sophisticated and complex level of impression and interpretation of those details and facts that artistically moves closer to the truth, or at least to genuine understanding. Finally, some maintain, there is no common, single, objective reality to reproduce or depict.

These claims and criticisms may have merit. Yet they should not mask the clear historical evidence of a shift during the nineteenth century in the focus and nature of American cultural forms of expression of all types: in poetry and fiction, art and architecture, and photography and journalism. This shift, which occurred from around 1850 to 1900 or so, can be treated as a new cultural paradigm, a *paradigm of actuality,* one that is defined by a focus on the actual and real, on people, events, and details that are verifiable and based on observation and experience. It includes common things and common people, but also can deal with daily concerns, experiences, and relationships, both cultural and personal, of the emerging middle and commercial class. This paradigm stands in contrast to the more romantic one—previously overwhelmingly dominant—that focused on the ideal, one whose depictions were ideational and weakly representational and at the same time mostly unrecognizable in the rapidly changing American social and demographic landscape.

While some of those writing and creating images believed that they could genuinely fully recreate reality, what they produced were *versions* of reality that provided a range of cultural interpretations. The bottom line is that this paradigm of actuality did indeed reflect a realistic impulse, a realistic sensibility, in that it was based primarily and essentially on the *observation* of life being lived, and not created in a more abstract fashion from the imagination while ensconced in the confines of the study, with its comfortable chair and stacks and rows of books, or by going outdoors and away from human activity to quietly observe—and romanticize—the supposed grandeur of nature. As the century unfolded, observation involved looking, seeing, and documenting the urban landscape, which became central to the paradigm of actuality.

It is important that this be recognized as a genuine *cultural* paradigm and not simply a literary proclivity. Of course, fiction also was pulling away from the romantic and ideal (although never completely abandoning that inclination), and a range of writers have been acknowledged as realism's advocates and practitioners; prominent among them were Mark Twain, William Dean Howells, Hamlin Garland, Henry James, Stephen Crane, and Theodore Dreiser, who all became established in the second half of the century. It is significant, however, that the sensibility was just as strong in other forms of communication and artistic expression. For instance, the architect Louis Sullivan, known for his declaration that "form follows function," called for "exact observation," while an architectural critic noted that artistic realism was generated by "the habit of observation."[3] As early as the 1860s, a new art publication, called *The New Path,* published by the Society for the Advancement of Truth in Art, pointed out two contrasting schools of art: "One is sentimental, dreamy and struggling after that it calls the ideal. The other is hard-working, wide awake, and struggling after the real and true." In its inaugural issue, the editors of *The New Path* called for "pictures that will give us a right to rejoice in the present" and urged young painters to "turn their backs deliberately and without ceremony upon the rubbish of the past."[4] About the same time, a writer who had a strong romantic bent himself produced what one literary scholar calls an "unheralded manifesto for a realism based on utility and joy."[5] Writing in 1862, Charles Godfrey Leland used the term "realism" in declaring that a "higher art" would be attained through a "dusty, steam-engine whirling realism."[6] He directly addressed writers, calling for a focus on the "Actual of life," on "reality," and on "facts":

> Young writer, young artist, whoever you be, I pray you go to work in this roaring, toiling, machine-clanking, sunny, stormy, terrible, joyful, commonplace, vulgar, tremendous world in *down-right earnest . . .* you will find your most splendid successes not in cultivating the worn-out romantic, but in *loving* the growing Actual of life. . . He or she is best and bravest among you who gives us the freshest draughts of reality and of Nature. It lies all around you—in the foul smoke and smell of the factory, amid the crash and slip of heavy wheels on muddy stones, in the blank-gilt glare of the steam-boat saloon, by the rattling chips of the faro table, in the quiet, gentle family circle, in the opera, in the sixpenny concert, the hotel, the watering-place, on the prairie, in the prison. Not as the poor playwright and little sensation-story grinder see them, not as the manufacturers of Magdalen elegies and mock-moral and mock-philanthropical tales skim them, but in their truth and

freshness as facts, around and through which sweep incessantly the infinite joys and agonies, the dreams and loves and despair of *humanity.*[7]

Although Leland never mentions Whitman, his enthusiastic tone of celebration and his list of common, everyday places suggests, as we shall see, Whitman's *Leaves of Grass,* first published in 1855. But even prior to writing his "manifesto," when he was editor of *Graham's Monthly* magazine in the 1850s, Leland urged writers to break away from convention and "write about what you *see* and not what you read" and to give him writing that contained "keen appreciation and observation of life."[8] Eventually, it wouldn't be only artists and writers who would embrace the real and actual. Even Ralph Waldo Emerson, the "sage" at the center of an American romanticism called transcendentalism, recognized that a genuine picture of life had to include "odious facts." He declared, "Let us replace sentimentalism by realism."[9] During the last quarter of the century, for example, influential thinkers such as William James and John Dewey argued that thought should be considered an instrument of concrete action rather than abstract speculation. James said that "An idea becomes true when it is made true by events."[10]

One way to illustrate this cultural shift is by comparing two poets and two painters. First, consider a landscape painting called *Kindred Spirits.* The scene depicted in the painting is rather simple: a wild American landscape and, just off-center, almost swallowed by the surrounding nature are two hikers, standing on a ledge, enjoying and contemplating the grand picture before them. But these aren't just any hikers. One is Thomas Cole, America's first important landscape painter and the artist generally noted for founding the Hudson River School—the nineteenth-century artistic movement, launched around 1825—and the other is Cole's good friend, William Cullen Bryant, the poet and newspaper editor who as a poet wrote of nature with the same sensibility that Cole painted it. The painting was done by Asher B. Durand, who was influenced by Cole and was also associated with the Hudson River School. The painting, a gift to Bryant after the death of Cole, depicts Cole and Bryant doing what they often did together: seeking inspiration and spiritual sustenance in the Catskill Mountains of New York, which provided settings and stimulation for Cole's paintings and Bryant's poetry.[11]

Significantly, the painting's title comes from the English romantic poet John Keats and his poem "Sonnet to Solitude," which celebrates nature's ability to inspire. The words are found in the poem's conclusion:

> Yet the sweet converse of an innocent mind,
> Whose words are images of thoughts refin'd,
> Is my soul's pleasure; and sure it must be
> Almost the highest bliss of human-kind,
> When to thy haunts two kindred spirits flee.[12]

Furthermore, Keats's poem expresses his dislike of the city, made clear in his opening lines: "O Solitude, if I must with thee dwell/Let it not be among the jumbled heap/Of murky buildings." It was just such a jumble of "murky buildings" that would later be depicted by the Ashcan artists, as well as fiction writers, journalists, and photographers.

Bryant, a nature poet strongly influenced by the English romantics such as Keats, but also Wordsworth and Coleridge, was one of the so-called American Schoolroom Poets, which included Whittier, Longfellow, Holmes, and Lowell. His most influential poetry, particularly "Thanatopsis" and "To a Waterfowl," were published

in 1817, but "Green River" and "A Forest Hymn" also share a
sensibility with the paintings of Cole and with the idealized view
that informed such depictions and forms of expression at that
time. Such works saw in the purity of the American landscape a
grandeur that reflected God, revealed nature's harmony with the
human spirit, and provided humanity with hope. In an influential
essay published in 1836, Cole declared that "associations" evoked
from the American wilderness were "of God the creator—they
are his undefiled works, and the mind is cast into the contempla-
tion of eternal things."[13] When Bryant delivered Cole's funeral
oration in 1848, he said Cole had "wandered and studied and
sketched" in the Catskills and they "wrought his sketches into
such glorious creations."[14]

Bryant's journalistic career was significant and considerable. He
was the highly regarded editor of the *New York Evening Post,* a
position he held, beginning at age thirty-five, from 1829 to 1878,
yet his poetry remains better known than his journalism, with
little to connect the two areas of his work and expression. That
is, Bryant's poetry did not inform his journalism, most of which
came after he had written his best poems, and his journalism never
influenced his poetry, although both endeavors were infused by
a strong moral sentiment and a belief in progress and improve-
ment. Both were idealistic to a large degree and designed to uplift;
whether nature in his poetry or politics in his *Evening Post,* both
were "seen at their grandest," as Roy Harvey Pearce put it, with
"Nature" in the poetry being a cure for life's contradictions and
conflicts, while progress and democracy were cures in his literary
and refined journalistic writings.[15]

This poet, Bryant, and this painter, Cole, stand in striking contrast to Walt Whitman and Thomas Eakins, a poet and a painter
who came after Bryant and Cole but whose works represent a

distinct shift in subject matter, perspective, and purpose. Whitman and Eakins were participants in and progenitors of the move
to focus on the actual. Unlike Bryant and Cole, Whitman and
Eakins did not look to nature or the ideal, but turned to the
common and the everyday for inspiration, depictions, and cultural
meaning. Drawn together by shared perspectives on the purpose
of art, Eakins and Whitman, Eakins's senior by twenty-six years,
developed a friendship in the late 1880s. Eakins painted a highly
regarded portrait of Whitman in 1887 and 1888. Although many
of Whitman's friends did not like the portrait, Whitman apparently admired its realism and said that Eakins had set "me down
in correct style, without feathers" and that the painter saw "not
what he wanted to but what he did see."[16] Whitman once said: "I
never knew of but one artist, and that's Tom Eakins, who could
resist the temptation to see what they thought ought to be rather
than what is," while a close friend of Eakins thought that what
particularly appealed to Eakins about Whitman was "the realistic; the observation, the truth, the sense of coming direct out of
life."[17] Significantly, both men had a strong interest in photography, which was considered by many to be the perfect realistic
image. Regular references were made at the time regarding the
seeming ability of photographs to be more than just "images" but
the actual complete. It is no accident that Whitman was completely enamored with photography and was a regular visitor to
photo galleries, where he could leisurely observe many of the
types of people and faces that he had so enjoyed quietly observing as a journalist working for the *Brooklyn Eagle* and the *New
York Aurora*. These same people and faces appeared in his strikingly original volume, *Leaves of Grass,* and Whitman declared that
the poetry there "is literally photographed."[18] Eakins did not just
enjoy photographic works but became a skilled photographer and

painted from his photographs, including several photos he took of Whitman.

The statements by Whitman regarding the need to look at and write about the common and everyday are numerous. In some lecture notes, for instance, he wrote that his ideal of the beautiful was "not the beautiful girl or elegant lady. . . but the mechanic's wife at work."[19] Emerson once predicted that the great American poet would be one who would be "Yankee born" and not someone who would "run from home" to the likes of "feudal keeps, or Arab tents, or Iceland huts underground" but someone who "visits without fear the factory, the railroad, and the wharf," and he then acknowledged that Whitman did just that.[20] Whitman himself indicated his willingness to comply with Emerson's sentiment when in an early notebook attempt to write a new type of verse, he declared, "I am a poet of reality."[21] In his great and seminal poem "Song of Myself," he says, "I accept Reality and dare not question it," and "I believe in the flesh and the appetites/Seeing, hearing, feeling."[22] He backed up those contentions with an incredible variety of images, scenes, and facts, documenting and cataloging the America he saw, and doing so in a style that, though ultimately symbolic and metaphorical, at the same time appears literal, simple, and distinctly journalistic. For instance, consider these lines in the poem's tenth section:

> The boatmen and clam-diggers arose early and stopt for me,
> I tuck'd my trowser-ends in my boots and went and had a
>   good time;
> You should have been with us that day round the chowder-kettle.
> I saw the marriage of the trapper in the open air in the far west,
>   the bride was a red girl,
> Her father and his friends sat near cross-legged and dumbly
>   smoking, they had moccasins to their feet and large thick
>   blankets hanging from their shoulders,

On a bank lounged the trapper, he was drest mostly in skins, his
     luxuriant beard and curls protected his neck, he held his bride
     by the hand,
She had long eyelashes, her head was bare, her coarse straight
     locks descended upon her voluptuous limbs and reach'd
     her feet.[23]

Significantly, in contrast to Bryant, whose poetry was separate and
distinct from his journalism, Whitman's poetry was grounded in
and grew out of his journalism; one fed the other. So many of
the people and places catalogued by Whitman in *Leaves of Grass*
were identified in Whitman's newspaper articles first before being
transformed in his poetry, as will be explored in the next chapter.
In fact, one early biographer called Whitman "very definitely a
product of American journalism."[24]

Eakins was inspired by Whitman's poetry and by his essay
Democratic Vistas. But even as he encountered Whitman, he was
already inclined to tap into the emerging cultural sensibility that
called for depiction of the *actual,* whether the ordinary, such as
men sculling or shad fishing on the river, or the extraordinary,
such as a famous surgeon, scalpel in a bloody hand, performing
surgery. Boxing paintings done in the late 1890s pushed Eakins
into a somewhat grittier realm, one already marked by the Ashcan
School of painters, who depicted all aspects of the urban environment. Two of this group's most significant members, Robert
Henri and John Sloan, became friends in 1892 (the year Whitman
died), when Sloan gave Henri a copy of Whitman's *Leaves of Grass.*
Henri and Sloan appreciated Whitman's "close observation and
ecstatic celebration of the daily lives of all Americans," and one
art historian goes so far as to call Whitman the "prophet" of the
Ashcan artists.[25]

The distance from Bryant and Cole and "the sweet converse

of an innocent mind," through Whitman and Eakins, to the Ashcan artists is considerable and is symbolic of this significant cultural shift. But, as has been suggested, this cultural shift also involved journalism. That was at least partly reflected in 1868 when
Charles A. Dana declared that the *New York Sun* would be "a
daily photograph of the whole world's doings."[26] But years before
Dana, newspaper journalism had led the way in moving toward
writing about, reporting on, and depicting "the warm truth of
real life," as Charles Godfrey Leland put it.[27] In fact, while Leland
and others were calling writers and artists to focus on the real and
actual, newspapers and especially the penny papers that had blossomed in various cities, but most strongly in New York, had been
covering the range of city life, telling tales about real people and
events to the working-class and middle-class urban population
before fiction started to do so.

While journalism historians have occasionally acknowledged
that journalism's style and content were influenced by this cultural
force and at the same time contributed to it, they have mostly
ignored it. Any consideration of journalistic writing has been ap-
propriately coupled with a focus on reporting and emphasis on
coverage of politics, government, and major news events, or coupled with investigations of journalistic performance and methods,
such as yellow journalism or sensationalism or objectivity. Occasionally, one of these narrower studies does consider journalism's
relationship with realism. For instance, Dan Schiller, in his important work, *Objectivity and the News,* notes a journalism-realism
connection, although he focuses on photographic realism and
touches on "literary" realism. He does declare that realism "shared
extensive common ground with journalistic objectivity" and then
he recommends that "students of American literary realism might
do well to study the formal practices of American journalism, with

an eye toward their influence on realistic literature" because, he says, quoting Richard Hofstadter, literary realists had been trained in "journalistic observation."[28] David Mindich's more recent and highly regarded study of objectivity, *Just the Facts: How "Objectivity" Came to Define American Journalism,* also acknowledges a realism-journalism connection in briefly considering society's "bending toward the real" as an influence on the development of journalism's "reverence for facts." Significantly, both of these works present much evidence for the cultural shift toward a focus on the real and actual, or as Mindich puts it, journalism changed along with other parts of the culture toward "a more empirical and 'fact-based' paradigm," grounded in science rather than religion and philosophy, as the century progressed.[29]

Beginning in the 1830s and by the 1840s, "events" in a broad sense were becoming the focus of much urban daily journalism, particularly in New York City, and observation often was part of the mix of the emerging new type of daily newspaper. To a certain extent, the New York dailies were pointing the way toward depiction of the actual by focusing on common and seemingly inconsequential matters. For instance, when Benjamin Day, an experienced printer, started the first penny paper in New York in 1833, he also started running short, light items designed to amuse and entertain as much as inform, with emphasis on local news that Mott describes as "interesting and readable."[30] But it wasn't that "information" was no longer presented, but rather that often such items and articles informed at a different level. For instance, many of these items were culled from police court, and were, as Mott put it, an "amusing, though crude, exploitation of the tragicomedy of drunkenness, theft, assaults, and street-walking" that began the journalistic tradition of police beat reporting in the United States.[31] The police court items appeared in a column consisting of separate cases that took no more than a few sentences and would become a staple of the penny papers. For example, the first issue of the four-page *Sun,* September 3, 1933, printed this brief in a column titled "Police Office": "John McMan, brought up for whipping Juda McMan, his darling wife—his excuse was, that his head was rather thick, in consequence of taking a wee drap of whiskey. Not being able to find bail he was accommodated with a room at bridewell."[32]

Of course, such short snippets from police and courts did not suddenly change the nature of urban journalism. What is obvious from the mix and variety of content in the early days of the *Sun,* as one might expect, is that it did not yet have a distinct identity or purpose. For instance, the front page of the same issue ran a full column in the center of the page, top to bottom, that consisted entirely of a conversation between an "Irish Captain" and a "young student of his acquaintance" who questions the captain about his pistols and his tendency to duel at the slightest affront, with strangers, relatives, and friends alike. The captain brags about his dueling exploits, and presents himself as a man of courage. Near the end, the captain describes a man he had shot in a duel "being carried home in a coach" while the captain marched "from the field of battle." This slice of human interest ends with an ironic touch when the student asks the captain if he has ever been in a battle. The captain admits that he never has and declares that he would give "all the money in the world" to fight in a real battle.

That bit of storytelling, of course, has little or nothing to do with city life; the exchange could have occurred just about anywhere. Nevertheless, it does introduce readers to a character type, to a distinct personality. But another item in the *Sun*'s first issue does contain the specificity missing from the story of the Irish captain, and, perhaps more importantly, connects in a very simple way to the emerging urban issue of poverty, homelessness, and orphans or abandoned children. Here it is in its entirety:

> *The Almshouse Boy.*—a youth who was brought up at the Alms-house was lately into the family of Mrs.___, in Pearl st. to run of errands. The first day he became an inmate of her house, the following dialogue passed between them:
>
> "Are you not sorry, my dear," said Mrs. M___, "to leave home?"
>
> "No," answered he; "I don't care."
>
> "Is there not somebody at home whom you are sorry to leave?" resumed she.
>
> "No," replied the boy, "I am not sorry to leave any body."
>
> "What, not those who are good to you?" joined she.
>
> "Nobody was ever good to me," said the boy.
>
> Mrs.___ was touched with the child's answer, which strongly painted his helpless lot, and the cold indifference of the world. The tear stood in her eye.
>
> "My poor little fellow," said she, after a short pause. "was nobody ever good to you!—have you no friend, my dear?"
>
> "No, for old dusty Bob, the rag-man, died last week."
>
> "And was he your friend?"
>
> "Yes, that he was," replied the boy, "he once gave me a piece of gingerbread!"[33]

Sentimental, mawkish, and certainly intended to engage the reader emotionally, this very brief account nevertheless contains urban signposts such as "Pearl st." and the "Almshouse," as well as the practice of placing unwanted children at the disposal of a family, all adding authenticity and immediacy and implying veracity. Very basically, the article gave a glimpse of the city to its readers, so that in a small way at first a penny paper connected readers to their urban environment. In the coming years, articles containing recognizable points of reference would become common and expected. While the penny papers did have a number of "firsts" that were developed over time, these new versions of the daily newspaper were still cultural forms of expression and as such were cultural products of their time and not simply or only "real" newspapers, or even new moneymaking machines.[34] The penny papers were attempts to depict urban life, but as with all journalism, they did so in a highly selective way and largely by embracing existing cultural narratives and themes, even while shocking or offending readers with content. In the penny papers, readers got a presentation of the city that "gives life an overall form, order, and tone," as Carey has put it, regarding the basic role of the newspaper.[35] The penny papers carried in their content the familiar, sense-making narratives of the antebellum period, but occasionally—and more and more frequently—also carried the tensions, fears, and confusion reflected in a changing society. This perhaps is best illustrated by considering the penny papers' coverage of the highly sensationalized and enduring Jewett-Robinson murder case of 1836.

As the success of the *Sun* became clear, other penny papers followed, including Bennett's *New York Herald,* first published in 1835. When New York's penny papers captured the attention of a mass of the city's readers in 1836 with intense and detailed coverage of the murder of a prostitute, Helen Jewett, it both titillated and shocked readers, and Bennett essentially guaranteed the success of the *Herald* with his own reporting of the Jewett murder. Jewett was a beautiful prostitute allegedly murdered by Richard Robinson, a young clerk from a prominent Connecticut family. Jewett's killer took an ax to her head and then tried to burn the body. The case became the talk of the city in large part because of Bennett's detailed and sensational accounts, which he ran on his front page for days. A highly emotional account appeared in the *Herald* the day after the murder, but two days later the *Herald* carried a story by Bennett in which he described a visit he had made to the scene of the crime. His article included a lengthy description and commentary on Jewett's corpse, and a description of the room:

> "Here," said the Police Officer, "here is the poor creature."
>
> He half uncovered the ghastly corpse. I could scarcely look at it for a second or two. Slowly I began to discover the lineaments of the corpse as one would the beauties of a statue of marble. It was the most remarkable sight I ever beheld—I never have, and never expect to see such another. "My God," exclaimed I, "how like a statue! I can scarcely conceive that form to be a corpse." Not a vein was to be seen. The body looked as white, as full, as polished as the purest Parian marble. The perfect figure, the exquisite limbs, the fine face the full arms, the beautiful bust, all, all surpassed in every respect the Venus de Medici according to the casts generally given her.
>
> "See," said the Police Officer, "she has assumed that appearance within an hour."
>
> It was the first process of dust returning to dust. The countenance was calm and passionless. Not the slightest appearance of emotion was there. One arm lay over her bosom—the other was inverted and hanging over her head. The left side down to the waist, where the fire had touched was bronzed like an antique statue. For a few moments I was lost in admiration at this extraordinary sight—a beautiful female corpse, that surpassed to her horrid destiny by seeing the dreadful bloody gashes on the right temple, which must have caused instantaneous dissolution.

I then looked around the room. It was elegant, but wild and extravagant in its ornaments. On the drawers was a small library, composed of light novels, poetry, and monthly periodicals. There hung on the wall a beautiful print of Lord Byron as the presiding genius of the place. The books were Byron, Scott, Bulwer's works and The Knickerbocker.

A work table in a state of disorder, stood near by. It was covered with fragments,—pen, ink, paper, crayons, pamphlets, etc. etc. Above the mantel piece hung several theatrical fancy sketches.[36]

Extensive coverage, with endless detail, of the murder of a prostitute was uncommon and the Jewett murder drew readers to the *Herald*. But perhaps what is striking today is not the coverage of the event but rather how the tone, style, and point-of-view romanticized this actual event, even to the point of declaring Byron, the embodiment of English romanticism, as the "presiding genius" of Helen Jewett's room, and, perhaps, of her life as well, or so Bennett wanted readers to think. On the one hand, Bennett was making this prostitute more human and more understandable to readers, but on the other he was idealizing her in death, with a Poe-like absorption in the body, making her purer and lovelier in death than she had been in life, but before Poe's tales appeared.[37] Thus, in order to lend significance and meaning to the murder of a common person, Bennett turned to the familiar narratives of his time, employing in form, tone, and theme not one but two well-known narratives. That is, while Bennett appeared to be treating Jewett first as the fallen angel, a victim, he soon shifted narratives and then depicted Jewett as the evil siren, a temptress and a victimizer. With the latter depiction, he championed Robinson's case, while Bennett's competitors favored treating Jewett as the victim of Robinson.

Regardless of the literary form employed by Bennett, his articles contained descriptive scene-setting as well as revealing detail that played to the readers' emotions and imaginations. The *Herald* and other penny papers gave readers a tragic tale of a misguided and beautiful young woman, perhaps led astray by the melancholy and passion of Byron and the improbabilities of Sir Walter Scott's novels. In addition, Bennett gave them the unfortunate tale of a handsome young man with a bright future falling prey to an evil woman in a house of sin and depravity. And this familiar and entertaining story was available to all for a penny a day. To a large extent, this type of writing and reporting resembled the conventions in the popular pamphlets that told stories of actual crimes, but it also resembles the conventions of the sentimental novel of the early nineteenth century. Bennett's account, for instance, was similar to novels that used the subtitle "A True Story."[38] The best-selling work of fiction in America had been *Charlotte Temple: A Tale of Truth,* a cautionary tale of seduction first published in 1794, followed by more than two hundred editions that were published well into the 1800s. The author, Susanna Rowson, opens her preface with this declaration: "For the perusal of the young and thoughtless of the fair sex, this Tale of Truth is designed; and I could wish my fair readers to consider it as not merely the effusion of Fancy, but as a reality."[39] But Rowson's claim that her tale was true was not simply read by "the fair sex." Examination of inscriptions of hundreds of copies of the book reveals that "copies were given by mothers and fathers to their sons as well as to their daughters, by brides to their new husbands or by young men to their fiancées, by sisters to brothers and by brothers to sisters, and even by a grandmother to a grandson who, in 1872, affectionately recorded in his calf-bound copy of *Charlotte Temple* that he had received this special gift over forty years earlier in 1830."[40] The books were also read across the nation, north, south, east, west, by people on the range of the socioeconomic scale. *The Coquette* by Hannah Foster, first published in 1797, another novel of seduction and betrayal, was nearly as popular as *Charlotte Temple*.[41]

The Jewett-Robinson case remains "enduring" in the sense that while it still receives some attention by journalism historians and focused investigation by one—Andie Tucher in *Froth and Scum*—it also attracts historians and American studies scholars who use the crime and its coverage as a way of exploring manners, mores, and issues of class and gender. Perhaps the most detailed, impressive, and thoroughly researched cultural and historical study of the crime is *The Murder of Helen Jewett* by historian Patricia Cline Cohen. Tucher's intent is to investigate claims of journalistic objectivity by comparing and contrasting how "an array of truths" were uncovered or proffered by the press in the Jewett murder and in another murder that occurred five years later. Significantly, however, although Tucher's focus is on press performance, she also suggests how the Jewett-Robinson case ultimately was about "the possibility of justice, the privileges of power, the inequities of class, the consequences of sin, and the nature of evil; it was about the need to figure out who one was and where one fit into a community riven by change."[42] Cohen focuses on these issues and more specifically on the "raw dynamics of class and sex privilege in American society," in the process providing a rich and varied cultural context for the nature of the press performance, clearly demonstrating just how journalistic expression is indeed part and parcel of the cultural fabric.[43]

Because journalism was naturally a part of the broader culture that was still suffused with and dominated by the romantic sensibility, including women as prey to the lies and seductive arts of men, it only follows that some newspapers would make sense of events by framing them with these familiar narratives. The facts alone provided no help for the reader trying to understand how such an ugly crime could occur, or as Tucher puts it, "The facts explained nothing about tragedy or violence or suffering or fairness," or the fallout from "the ultimate combustion of sex and death," and the facts didn't fully explain who was to blame and why it happened.[44] Consequently, the penny papers "introduced a new fluidity between literary and journalistic forms in the daily newspaper."[45] Furthermore, this fluidity reveals a mix of fact and fiction in imaginative writing *and* in journalism. Building on Tucher, Roggenkamp claims that Bennett's coverage of the Jewett murder "was a narrative that took as much license as a purely imaginative work," and she notes how publications of the time, including the popular *National Police Gazette,* were "mingling information and poetic license" or blending "solid fact and titillating entertainment."[46] Certainly, the newspaper editors gamely enhanced this "fluidity" with their willingness to publish hoaxes and cover "humbugs" and even admit to their inability to verify various claims, as Day of the *Sun* did when he reprinted book excerpts but said his paper could not "vouch for the truth of the appalling disclosures." He wrote: "They may be true or they may be false; they may be partially true or partially false; and we have no better means than are possessed by every reader to decide upon their truth or falsehood."[47]

A crucial difference exists, however, between the "true" but sentimental stories told in the novels and magazines of the time and the tale of prostitution and murder told by the *Herald* and the other penny papers: *it did indeed actually happen.* It was a story of the city, a murder that was carried out in a specific place on a specific street, the City Hotel at 41 Thomas Street, a place where readers could walk by and gawk. Readers would also eventually gather near the courthouse to see the accused killer, Richard P. Robinson, a clerk whose employer was publicly supporting him, or they could actually attend the trial. Reportedly, young clerks sympathetic to Robinson walked the streets dressed in "Robinson" cloaks and "Robinson" hats, while women sympathetic to Jewett wore a "Helen Jewett mourner" hat consisting of white fur and black crepe ribbons.[48] Even if Bennett and the others applied their imaginations to the presentation of detail and fact, thus giving the incident a narrative shape, it remained a recent tale involving actual people whose friends and families and coworkers were available to share insight, information, and opinions about the tale's two main characters, Jewett and Robinson. But perhaps more importantly, besides entertaining the masses, this story of the city was a tale of class and changing, clashing morals and values. Robinson was from a respected and well-connected Connecticut family and the fact that he was a regular visitor to one of the city's upscale brothels was part of readers' fascination in the case, especially among readers "who saw him as an example of the new breed of young men whose licentious, antidomestic lifestyle had begun to pose a troubling challenge to the city's middle class," as one scholar notes.[49] But Jewett also was "intriguing" because she challenged middle-class definitions of gender and sexuality and because she was depicted as intelligent and talented and not necessarily as a tawdry or decadent lowlife. Furthermore, casting Jewett as a woman of charm was not far-fetched. Certainly, the books, magazines, and decorative items in her room suggested as much, as did her letters to Robinson and other clients who were addressed as lovers on high-grade stationery in a handwriting that Bennett described as "uncommonly beautiful—a neat running hand."[50]

By going to the scene of a crime, Bennett clearly pioneered the notion of seeking out the news. What the evidence also shows, however, is that the emergence of such journalism was indeed an important step toward increasing coverage of the "actual," and in this sense the penny papers were both participating in and stimulating the broader cultural shift that was just getting under way during this period. The general perspective on events and the narrative framing of these events may not have been fresh, original, or without embellishment; real characters, such as Jewett and Robinson, or the sad and poor boy from the almshouse, were symbolic and even mythic types. But the firsthand reporting combined with descriptive writing was a significant push into that different direction. Rather than staid and often stuffy accounts of political goings-on and somewhat more lively reports about faraway places and distant people, the focus was becoming more local and immediate. As with the Jewett case, such journalism tended to be sensational.[51] Bennett was not the first and would not be the last to feed "his readers a steady diet of violence, crime, murder, suicide, seduction, and rape in news reporting and gossip," as one historian put it, but in no way was all the reporting and writing in the *Herald* or the other penny papers sensationalized.[52] But whether the writing and documentation would be more restrained or more sensational, it all reflected this desire to write about real people and real events, from a perspective that reflected the issues, concerns, and fears of the time and place depicted.

Of course, New York City wasn't alone in gingerly moving toward a focus on the actual and real. On the one hand, newspapers all across the country published penny paper accounts of the Jewett-Robinson affair as part of a newspaper exchange. But in other small ways, communities and regions began to occasionally move beyond the lists of community notices and legislative and political coverage to portray a greater sense of a region or state. It is worth noting one particular example because it demonstrates what one Southern newspaper was willing to publish at the same time that the penny papers were getting started in Northern cities.

In Georgia in 1835 Augustus Baldwin Longstreet published *Georgia Scenes, Characters, Incidents, Etc., in the First Half Century of the Republic,* which came to be known simply as *Georgia Scenes.* The book contains a series of "realistic sketches" that ran in two newspapers, starting in the *Milledgeville Southern Recorder* in 1833. In 1834, Longstreet purchased the *North American Gazette,* changed its name to the *State Rights' Sentinel,* and started publishing the *Georgia Scenes* pieces in his own paper.[53] The scenes—with titles such as "The Dance," "The Horse Swap," "The Gander Pulling," "The Fox Hunt," and "The Shooting Match"—depict the manners and behavior of the people of Georgia, most of them from the country, and always written with a bit of humor and often with dialogue, dialect, and slang, with the narrator occasionally translating certain words or phrases for the reader. In the book's preface, Longstreet acknowledges the mix of fact and fiction in his short tales, saying the book "consists of nothing more than fanciful *combinations* of *real* incidents and characters; and throwing into those scenes, which would be otherwise dull and insipid, some personal incident or adventure of my own, real or imaginary, as it would best suit my purpose—usually *real,* but happening at different times and under different circumstances from those in which they are here represented . . . Some of the scenes are as literally true, as the frailties of memory would allow them to be." He felt compelled to apologize, however, for some of what he depicted, explaining that such details or talk would have been excluded if they had been "merely the creations of fancy" but since they were true and happened, he included them. Furthermore, he says that those "who have taken exceptions to the coarse, inelegant and sometimes ungrammatical language" should keep in mind that such language fits the person speaking.[54] Of course, when the sketches appeared in the newspapers, they did not contain such apologies and explanations, yet were still very popular with readers.

What Longstreet was doing was not the same as the penny papers' more immediate depiction or reporting of crime and city types. Nevertheless, his sketches illustrate still another step toward realism and more specifically toward the local color writing that would blossom in fiction after the Civil War but that was already under way in newspapers across the country. That Longstreet's sketches ran regularly in two newspapers suggested a different role for newspapers, involving documenting and depicting life with a narrative point of view just as accounts in the penny papers did. Longstreet's sketches showed what was possible and at the same time revealed a public desire to see its own people depicted and interpreted. And they had an impact and audience beyond Georgia. After a glowing review of *Georgia Scenes* by Edgar Allan Poe in the *Southern Literary Messenger* in 1836, Harper and Brothers came out with a second edition in 1840, which stayed in print until 1860, and a Mississippi man published *Mississippi Scenes* and dedicated it to Longstreet.[55]

Longstreet and his writing are often placed in the category of Southern and southwest humor. While that categorization fits to a certain extent, it may be limiting. Longstreet believed his sketches were preserving the present and recent past, and literary scholars who considered his work early in the twentieth century recognized the realistic detail and themes, with one describing *Georgia Scenes* as "consciously realistic" and "the first realistic interpretation of Southern character," and another stating that Longstreet's goal was "realistic portrayal." Reviewers of *Georgia Scenes* also found the book both amusing and realistic, recognizing "Longstreet's Georgia as the Georgia they knew."[56] When too many readers seemed to consider the scenes mere tales designed to entertain, Longstreet wrote a second preface for the book in which he insisted that his goal was not to merely entertain but rather to "supply" readers with "the manners, customs, amusements, wit, dialect, as they appear in all grades of society to an ear and eyewitness to them" and to capture "the ways of the common walks of life, in their own dialect."[57] He insisted again on the general veracity of his sketches: "The scenes which I describe—as, for instance, 'The Gander Pulling'—actually occurred at the very place where I locate it. The names of the persons who figure in it are such as were well-known in Richmond County at the time, and the language which I put in the mouths of my actors was just such as was common at such exhibitions."[58]

These very different samples of the shift to depicting the common and the actual clearly reveal the role of newspapers in contributing to a general shift in an overall cultural sensibility. They indicate not only that news publications were fully participating in this paradigm shift right from the start; the samples suggest also that these publications' contribution to the shift to realism may have been especially significant because they employed it in so many types of writing—news reporting, essays, sketches, and fiction.

THREE

STIRRINGS AND ROOTS: URBAN
SKETCHES AND AMERICA'S FLANEUR

In 1842, a young newspaper editor wrote a short commentary on "The Penny Press" in which he declared the penny papers to be "common schools" that "carry light and knowledge in among those who most need it." Specifically, he wrote, the penny papers "disperse the clouds of ignorance; and make the great body of the people intelligent, capable, and worthy of performing the duties of republican freemen." He added that the penny papers would eventually lead to the death of "the large papers," or the papers that sold for six cents, and he claimed that the penny papers were not just for "the lower and middling classes" but also could be found among the "wealthy and proud." In fact, he said, "Every where is their influence felt." He concluded by stating that the "only sensible move" of President John Tyler since assuming office was his "currying of favor with the penny press."[1]

Because this young newspaper editor, Walt Whitman, became such a pivotal figure in defining and advocating for a focus on the common and became, many critics maintain, the archetypal American poet, and because of his connection to the penny press, which was an early participant in depicting and covering the real and actual, it is worth taking a close look at the poet's journalistic roots, specifically at his urban sketches. As noted in chapter 2, in writing *Leaves of Grass,* Whitman put into his lines of verse the people, sights, and sounds he had observed closely on the streets of New York as a journalist. About the same time that Whitman was a journalist, George G. Foster was writing urban sketches for the *New York Tribune* and for widely circulating books. Whitman and Foster were two very similar yet different versions of an American flaneur, writers who roamed the city, observing, recording, and commenting, explaining the city and the ways of its urban dwellers, who were all a part of it, in newspapers, magazines, and books. These urban strollers became urban chroniclers. In bringing all aspects of city life to readers, the flaneurs, including Whitman and Foster, were saying: "Here it is. This is the way it is in the city. Here's how people behave." They gave readers verbal snapshots of city life and versions of urban actuality, often with accompanying illustrations.[2]

WHITMAN

When twenty-three-year-old Walt Whitman wrote that editorial on the penny press, he had been editor of the *New York Aurora* for about a month. As already noted, Whitman was not simply a "poet"—although many consider him the first great American poet—but one of the major cultural and literary figures of the nineteenth century, someone who influenced other artists with both the content and style of his poetry but also with his ideas of what should be the intent and subject matter of art and literature. Yet his journalism career was surprisingly extensive, involving printing, editing, reporting, and writing from 1831 to 1854. During that time, he edited eight newspapers, coedited one, helped edit another, contributed articles to or wrote for about a dozen additional publications, mostly newspapers, and contributed essays to at least a half-dozen journals and magazines.[3] What journalism provided Whitman was easy exposure to the actual and the common. By strolling daily through the streets of Manhattan and Brooklyn, Whitman absorbed the urban spectacle and regularly shared his wonder and pleasure at this passing parade of people and activity while editing the *New York Aurora* (1842) and the *Brooklyn Daily Eagle* (1846–48). That urban spectacle contained the same people and ideas that would later appear in "Song of Myself."[4] Whitman took his readers to a range of shops and activities, including auction houses, butcher shops, boardinghouses, and the people who work and reside in them, but also to churches, synagogues, a home for delinquents, the waterfront, theaters, schools, and city parks. In an editorial, he would claim that the penny papers and especially the *Aurora* were giving readers "pictures of life as it is."[5] With Whitman, readers might witness a game of marbles involving a group of "fine, healthy, dirty, bright eyed, mischievous little devils."[6] They could take a look inside a boardinghouse at breakfast time and see the landlady, "the fleshy, red cheeked, good looking woman at the head of the table."[7] Or they might join him for a visit to a food market and have "burst upon" their eyes the "array of rich, red sirloins, luscious steaks, delicate and tender joints, muttons, livers, and all the long list of various flesh stuffs," which, he adds, hang there, "tempting, seductive—capable of begetting ecstasies in the mouth of an epicure."[8]

The visit to the market, "Life in a New York Market," written for the *Aurora,* is worth a closer look. The piece opens with Whitman telling readers that rather spontaneously on a recent Saturday he decided to "take a stroll of observation through a *market.*" From the outside, the market is a "large, dirty looking structure." But then he says, "We entered," and once inside Whitman changes to the present tense, creating a sense of immediacy as he becomes the readers' eyes and ears through a narrative point of view that is personal and subjective, directly addressing readers as if they were simply walking along with him. For instance, in the following passage he points out people he sees on his stroll and he directly addresses the reader by saying "There comes" and "Notice that," and specifically points to "That fat, jolly featured woman" as though the reader were standing right next to him looking over at the woman. These paragraphs appear in the article right after the description of the "luscious" hanging meats:

> There comes a journeyman mason (we know him by his limy dress) and his wife—she bearing a little white basket on her arm. With what an independent air the mason looks around upon the fleshy wares; the secret of the matter is, that he has his past week's wages in his pocket, and therefore puts he on that devil-may-care countenance. . . .
>
> Notice that prim, red cheeked damsel, for whom is being weighed a small pork steak. She is maid of all work to an elderly couple, who have sent her to purvey for their morrow's dinner. How the young fellow who serves her, at the same time casts saucy, loveable glances at her pretty face; and she is nothing loth, but pleased enough at the chance of a little coquetry. Cunning minx! she but carries out the foible of her sex, and apes her superiors.
>
> With slow and languid steps moves along a white faced, thin bodied, sickly looking, middle aged man. He is dressed in a shabby suit, and no doubt will look long and watchfully before he spends the two ten cent pieces to which his outlay is limited. Poor fellow! he is evidently a member of one of those trades which require a

man to stay cooped up in the house in some constrained bodily position. The healthy air, and the pleasant sunshine, and the delicious influences of the outer world, have not been showered upon him; and here he is, fast sinking into the grave. What a mockery of the benefits of civilization!

That fat, jolly featured woman, is the keeper of a boarding house for mechanics, and every one else who chooses to take up with good solid accommodations, for a moderate price. She is foraging for her Sunday dinner. What is it to be? She has piece after piece taken down from its hook, but none seem to suit her. She passes on.[9]

He then declares that those "who compose the bustling crowd" are "a heterogeneous mass," and he again runs through one of his lists—or catalogs, as they have come to be called in his poetry—one that emphasizes the range and diversity of the crowd, which is an early play on the one-in-many theme that would be a central motif in *Leaves of Grass*. He concludes by urging readers "to take a stroll, now and then, in the mazes of these miniature worlds" where "pictures of life" will be seen and "lessons may be learnt there."[10]

Whitman's narrative consists of thin sketches of scenes of regular folks, especially working-class New Yorkers, doing what they all do, buying food for their tables. He is showing, in a small way, life being lived, depicting actual people engaged in a common activity, and he does so without quoting a single person, relying through it all on observation and speculation based on experience.

Occasionally, Whitman would resort to a more typical storytelling approach, such as when he related for *Aurora* readers how a boardinghouse keeper at "one of the most fashionable boarding houses just north of the City Hall" had been swindled by a young man from the "country" who had been lured into a gang of thieves. The piece, "The Clerk from the Country," has a traditional storytelling structure, with a beginning (a handsome young man who says he is a clerk, becomes a resident at the boardinghouse, and becomes a favorite of all), middle (a valuable gold watch turns up missing and the landlady suspects the clerk), and end (the clerk confesses to the landlady, helps her get the watch back, then disappears and is "heard from no more"). Whitman's story is a "telling" and not a "showing." It doesn't have much concrete detail and its shape and tone are much like that of a "Did you hear about . . . ? Listen to this" kind of yarn that might occur between acquaintances passing on the street or sharing dinner conversation, perhaps after they have read about it in a newspaper or heard about it from a friend. The story is not sensationalized in the least and is explicitly presented as a cautionary tale. Whitman ends that piece not with the tale's end but with a bit of moralizing common to the times. He feels obligated to point out to his readers the lesson to be learned and he testifies to the veracity of the story:

> We have given this long story, every syllable of which is true, partly as an exposure of what vicious tricks there are going on among us, and partly as a caution to parents in the country. Hundreds of young fellows are lost by the carelessness of people in letting their sons be placed where temptation surrounds every side, as in the case of the youth whose history has been given.
>
> Very likely, the villainous swindlers have him in their clutches again, and will effectually prevent a second relapse into virtue. The lady in question learnt not sufficient of his history to be able to tell where his parents or relations reside; consequently, she cannot, as she anxiously desires to do, give them information upon the subject by letter.[11]

The shape of the story and its ending have Whitman participating in a standard country-city narrative in which the country naïf is tempted and led astray by the evil city types, coupled with the good-hearted person being duped by the charming, apparently handsome youth.

Most of Whitman's identified journalism does not consist of reporting or covering the types of events and incidents that would come to define "news," such as robberies and murders or other crimes, court proceedings, official announcements, legislative, government, and business activity and policy decisions, tragic accidents such as a ferry sinking, or untimely deaths. He regularly expressed strong, often biting, opinions in editorials on a host of issues, including politics and political parties, legislative matters, schools and education, patriotism, music and art, capital punishment, the importance of good manners, slavery, and a host of other topics. But his coverage of a fire for the *Aurora* is worth noting because of how his coverage differs from that of the larger penny papers. Whitman's account does not contain names, addresses, or a description of how the fire spread, or statements and explanations from police, fire marshals, building appraisers, and so forth, all of which appear in the accounts in the *Herald* and the *Tribune,* for example.[12] Perhaps what is most striking about the article is that Whitman appears to have talked to no one. As with the stroll through the market, he is an observer, a witness—not just of working people doing a normal, everyday task, but of a dangerous and destructive event as it occurs. Whitman essentially lets readers know what it is like to be at the fire, just as he told readers what it was like to be in the market. Whitman tells of the "squads of people hurrying," including "women carrying small bundles—men with heated and sweaty faces—little children, many of them weeping and sobbing." Besides the scurrying people, he sees "stacks of furniture upon the sidewalks and even in the street; puddles of water, and frequent lengths of hose-pipe . . . the hubbub, the trumpets of the engine foremen, the crackling of the flames, and the lamentations of those who were made homeless."[13] The article's next four paragraphs demonstrate, as Fishkin puts it, just how Whitman "was able to see, hear, feel, and imagine" the fire.[14]

It was a horrible yet magnificent sight! When our eyes caught a full view of it, we beheld a space of several acres, all covered with smouldering ruins, mortar, red hot embers, piles of smoking half burnt walls—a sight to make a man's heart sick, and keep him awake at night, when lying in his bed.

We stood on the south side of Broome street. In every direction around except the opposite front, there was one compact mass of human flesh—upon the stoops, and along the side walks, and blocking up the street, even to the edge of where the flames were raging. The houses at our right were as yet unharmed, with the exception of blistered paint and window glass cracked by the strong heat over the way. We looked through those windows into the rooms within. The walls were bare and naked; no furniture, no inhabitant, no signs of occupancy or life, but every thing bearing the stamp of desolation and flight!

Every now and then would come a suffocating whirlwind of smoke and burning sparks. Yet we stood our ground—we and the mass—silent, and gazing with awful admiration upon the wreck and the brightness before us. The red flames rolled up the sides of the houses, newly caught, like the forked tongues of serpents licking their prey. It was terribly grand! And then all the noise would cease, and for many minutes nothing would break in upon silence, except the hoarse voices of the engines and their subordinates, and the hissing of the fire. A few moments more, and the clatter and clang sounded out again with the redoubled loudness.

The most pitiful thing in the whole affair, was the sight of shivering women, their eyes red with tears, and many of them dashing wildly through the crowd, in search, no doubt, of some member of their family, who, for what they knew, might be buried neath the smoking ruins near by. Of all the sorrowful spectacles in God's world, perhaps no one is more sorrowful than such as this![15]

As with many if not most of Whitman's articles, he finishes this one with a sweeping and sentimental declaration, common in the antebellum period, designed to leave the reader with a positive spin, with something idealistically uplifting. To get there, Whitman describes what he saw when, upon leaving the scene of the fire, he stopped into a temperance hall and listened to speakers and singing. Except for a reference to "a company of fine looking young firemen" this last part of the article seems disconnected from the first part in both content and tone. The article's final paragraph stands in distinct contrast to the "crumbled ashes" and "sorrowful spectacle" he had just documented: "As we left the house, we could not help wondering at the mighty enthusiasm which all there, men, women and children, seemed to be imbued with. Success to the cause! May the blessings that have followed in its path, thus far, be but a harbinger—a shadow of the hundred fold glory that is coming!"[16]

Despite such endings, these snapshots of the city's people, sights, and sounds essentially documented, even if in a rather limited way, everyday life, and through such writing and reporting we see early evidence of the paradigm of actuality. Fishkin claims that unlike other New York newspaper writers and reporters who "mapped the surface of city life, Whitman tried to chart its depths."[17]

Whitman, however, provided little depth but did provide a different journalistic view of the city and its people with his impressionistic reports and their first-person point of view. Fishkin probably is closer to the mark when she claims that Whitman seemed to be exploring a new "mode" of reporting. Whitman is "seeing" the city and sharing what he sees, and more often than not it is the ordinary that catches his eye rather than the sensational. He clearly was enamored by the ordinary—whether people or an everyday street scene. His writing, however, treated them as extraordinary by their very nature, but never in a sensational way. Whitman, enamored with democracy and America's potential, was celebrating America and Americans, the one in many.

The fire and market articles, as well as some of his accounts of walks through the city, bear a basic resemblance to the many newspaper and magazine sketches and "studies" that became more prominent as the nineteenth century progressed. In the 1890s, these types of newspaper stories became common not just in New York but in other cities, especially Chicago. Later writers such as Stephen Crane were indeed "documenting contemporary social history" in much of their journalism, as Fishkin claims Whitman did in his journalism.[18] For instance, Crane's "The Broken-Down Van" or "When a Man Falls, a Crowd Gathers" display the same personal perspective as that of Whitman as well as a preference for depicting city types. In these and other articles, Crane is an observer who talks to no one, who gathers no facts or details from others but merely records his impressions, shares what he sees and hears, and presents it all with a distinct point of view. In Whitman, we are introduced to the butcher, the maid, the firemen, the young wife, the stylish man, the fashionable lady, the mason, the clerk, and others; in "The Broken-Down Van" Crane gives us the van drivers, a "trunk-strap man," a "Division-st. girl," a policeman, a barber, and poor children of various ages. One could argue, as Fishkin has regarding the fire article, that Whitman's facts, or the who, what, where, and when, were different for Whitman than most other reporters. She puts it this way:

> For them the "who" means names, the "what" means figures of property damage and numbers left homeless, and the "when and why" mean a fire marshal's explanation of the principles of combustion. For Whitman the "who" means staring hard at faces and movements and trying to fathom from these images a sense of the pain, the pathos, the dread, the frustration, and the bewilderment that lay behind them. For Whitman "what" means the visual and aural images of flames and firemen, of cracked glass and crushed dreams. For Whitman, "where" is simply "Broome and Delancey Streets" and "when" is simply the hour, between seven and eight o'clock, that Whitman visited the scene of the fire.[19]

Similarly, in "When a Man Falls, a Crowd Gathers" Crane notes that when a man collapses in a fit, voices from the crowd that gathers about the fallen man ask the man's name and where he lives, essentially asking for the who, what, where. Crane said those calling for such information had "magnificent passions for abstract statistical information," thereby suggesting that such supposedly useful and concrete details were actually meaningless in understanding the man and his situation.[20]

Whitman's journalism, whether a new "mode" of reporting or not, is somewhat of a precursor, a hint of what might be once the push to write about the real and actual bloomed more fully. In many respects, Whitman's writing/reporting is an early, rough, and unfinished version of early literary journalism. Many of the 1890s urban sketches, however, and most of Foster's writings as well, are a bit edgier and grittier than Whitman's accounts and observations. In fact, while Whitman might depict the misery caused by a fire or the sadness of a man who barely can purchase food for that day, he seems to shy away from depicting the genuine poverty, crime, and misery of so many city lives, or even that which might be generally unseemly. For instance, when Whitman reviewed a book by "one of the most attractive writers of the age," W. Gilmore Simms, he declared that some of the characters were "in exceedingly bad taste," and contained "coarse and indelicate" details. The last chapter of the book, *The Wigwam and the Cabin,* Whitman found "particularly objectionable" because of a "revolting drunken scene."[21] This same sense of decorum may have influenced his opinion of James Gordon Bennett's thriving penny paper, the *Herald.*

In 1842, Whitman wrote an editorial in which he provided a "short sketch" of New York's leading newspapers. He began by touting the *Aurora,* doing so, of course, "without vanity," declaring it to be "by far the best newspaper in the town."[22] The *Post* was the next best paper, according to Whitman, principally because of its editor, "the refined poet" William Cullen Bryant, but Whitman said no one should infer from his placement or praise of the *Post* or Bryant that it was "what a newspaper ought to be." He pulled no punches regarding a number of other papers: the editors of the *Journal of Commerce* were "hypocritical," the *Express* was a "rather stupid affair," the *Courier and Enquirer* was "a violent and vindictive partisan print," and the *Standard* "a rickety affair, which nobody ever sees." Of the leading penny papers, he called the *Tribune* "a tolerable paper" and said the *Sun* "has its merits" but is of "no great spirit" although the best known. But Bennett's *Herald* was the worst, "a paper which nothing that we can say can convey our opinion more strongly of it. It is a scandal to the republic." For Whitman, Bennett's sensationalism was extreme. But if Whitman's journalism provided the material for his own eventual achievement in writing a distinctively American poetry grounded in a full range of the country's common people, Bennett and the other penny papers were also part of this early stirring of the move toward capturing reality, even though their actuality, their sensationalized versions of reality, often focused on aspects that demeaned rather than enhanced common dignity.

FOSTER

That "tolerable paper," Horace Greeley's *Tribune,* regularly ran urban sketches by George G. Foster from 1848 to about 1850. Foster hoped for literary fame as a writer of more "imaginative" literature, but while his jaunts and strolls around Manhattan produced no pathbreaking poetry, it did produce two relatively popular collections of nonfiction sketches, a final collection of Manhattan sketches, and a more reflective history of New York, with commentary and description. Foster described himself as a "dreamy poet" in his teen years growing up in the Hudson Valley, between New York City and Albany, but after "many and bitter rebuffs, humiliations . . . and disappointments," he became "the patient worker at the laboring oar of every-day journalism."[23] He was probably only about twenty, five years older than Whitman, when in 1834 he became editor of the *Oswego Democrat* in upstate New York.[24] After a year, he moved around, writing a friend from Pittsburgh once and ending up in Alabama where he edited a weekly country newspaper for a short time. He eventually landed in St. Louis where he worked as a reporter and editor for the *St. Louis Bulletin* before purchasing a small-circulation newspaper,

the *Pennant.* While he at first built up the *Pennant's* circulation, he also built up debts and the paper failed in 1842. He then went to New York and tried to get on a magazine or two and even proposed starting his own magazine, but nothing materialized. That's when he returned to newspapering, taking a job at the *Aurora* "writing squibs and paragraphs" just a few months after Whitman had left the paper.

It isn't clear whether Foster knew Whitman, but when Foster started wandering about the city for his articles—which fell under the standing head, "New York in Slices"—it was as though he had heeded Whitman's call to "stroll" and observe the city and its people. He went beyond the routine, straightforward descriptions he had done at the *Aurora,* and it could be argued that he led the way at the *Tribune* toward a livelier style of city coverage. The exact length of his tenure at the *Tribune* isn't known, but he appears to have been there as a city reporter from 1844 to 1847, although he wrote his "New York in Slices" pieces during a three-month period in 1848. But shortly after becoming a *Tribune* reporter, the *Tribune's* "City Intelligence" and "City Affairs" columns were combined into a "City Items" which, according to Blumin, "took both the reporter and the reader beyond the courts and official meeting rooms to fires, militia parades, concerts, arrivals of famous people, and any number of other events that could be found on the streets of the city."[25] In his fourth, final book, *New York Naked,* Foster reflected on his journalism experiences in the book's introduction, where he noted the range and nature of his reporting and writing in the *Tribune's* "City Items" column.[26] But it was in his selected "New York in Slices" articles for the *Tribune* as well as in several of the sketches in Foster's third collection, *Fifteen Minutes Around New York,* that Foster intersected most closely with Whitman as chronicler of the city. The "Slices" were published in book form in 1849 under the title, *New York in Slices: By an Experienced Carver: Being the Original Slices Published in the N.Y. Tribune, Revised, Enlarged, and Corrected by the Author,* and Foster would later claim that many of these sketches were reprinted in newspapers all over the country.[27] Although a few of the sketches are quite different in the book, most are very much the same as the originals that ran in the newspaper. *Slices* the book did very well, with a press run of 20,000, and Foster followed that with another book of sketches, *New York By Gas-Light: With Here and There a Streak of Sunshine,* in 1850. *Gas-Light,* consisting of slices of the gritty and seamy nightside of the city, was even more popular than *Slices* (with about 200,000 in circulation), thereby, as Blumin notes, transforming the emerging urban newspaper sketch into a nationally circulating book.[28] *Fifteen Minutes,* published in 1854, didn't do as well as either *Slices* or *Gas-Light.*[29]

Foster's sketches, both the "Slices" and those of the *Gas-Light,* could be characterized today as journalism as descriptive commentary in that they mix detailed descriptions of his observations with a palpable point of view, often coupled with strong subjective judgments on the people and places depicted. He was as interested in the emerging architecture of the city as Whitman, but perhaps not quite as infatuated by the parade of people. Several of his "Slices," for instance, focus on streets: Broadway, Chatham Street, Wall Street. Those pieces are full of shops, buildings, and goods, with little mention of the people there, except as broad generalizations, such as when he writes that "Broadway in its glory" is at 6 P.M. when "you will see New York's possible in the way of beautiful women, scrupulously-dressed dandies, and pretty children."[30] In that sense, Whitman and Foster are in keeping with the more standard pose of the flaneur, who passes through and provides a broad, sweeping, often panoramic view of the city. The similarity is particularly evident when Foster, like Whitman, visits a market. In "The Markets," Foster even declares in his first sentence that most readers "doubtless had 'slices' from the Markets before now" but suggests they are worth another visit because "they furnish abundant mental food as well as physical, to one who has learned the great secret of eating with his eyes."[31] He then gushes over the "varieties of human nature" in markets, where "every face you meet is a character, every scene affords a piquant contrast." Then, as with Whitman's market visit, he runs through some of the types who can be found there, indulging in a bit of speculation, which he then undercuts by poking fun at his own writing:

> [T]he old huckster-woman who implores you in all weathers to buy her vegetables, although she has a handsome house at home and fifty thousand dollars out at interest, (we hope not in Moonshine Insurance Company,)—the pretty, bare-armed girl who comes to buy breakfast for the mistress and must av coorse have the best of every thing—the modest mechanic's wife, who survey's the aristocratic turkey and the lordly sirloin with a sigh, and then, with a timid glance at the little stock of change, is fain to put up with a lean joint for dear John's dinner. But then it will be cooked by her own hands, and she herself will shell the peas and boil the potatoes and dress the baby; and if the mutton itself is a little tough, her glance of love as her husband enters the door, will be so tender, and will speak a heart so true, that handsome John will not miss the stall-fed luxury that his earnings would not procure, while he owns so much hearty happiness which wealth could not buy and the world cannot take away. Whew! what a sentence![32]

Foster also gives readers a look at "the dainty cit, his boots so nicely black, and his shirt-bosom so impeachably white" who has "an instinct in the selection of asparagus," and the hurrying "Hotel-keeper, fearful that somebody has brought something to market which he shall not see," as well as a much more detailed look at "a thin, meager, sick old lady, meanly clad, and haggard from care and anxiety," who, Foster says, has a private boarding-house whose interior he specifically describes, from its mahogany chairs to its faded "Brussells carpet." Interestingly, in his last book of sketches, *Fifteen Minutes Around New York,* his articles have far less information about a topic, far less social commentary, but more vivid descriptions of types, and overall they are more lively stylistically and more forward-looking. For instance, in "A General Dash at the Ferries," he describes different people entering the waiting room for the ferry, including a "lady" who "is dressed in one of those chocolate-colored, unrevealing, linen-and-cotton out-door night-gowns" and "a shirred barege bonnet of a similar hue, with a thick green veil . . . a thin, intellectual-looking woman, of thirty-five" who is not "old-maidish" but "on the strong-minded womanish order" and "thin, but not meager . . . looks as if she worked hard, and still knew how to enjoy life in her own independent way . . . a nervous old gentleman, who is always afraid of being too late, and looks into the room timidly . . . he advertised yesterday morning in the Herald for a wife."[33]

Perhaps more importantly, Whitman and Foster intersect by both having recognized, depicted, and even celebrated a central characteristic of the burgeoning metropolis and that is the range and diversity of its residents, its inherently democratic nature, or Whitman's one-in-many notion. That, of course, is partially the point of the market sketches of both men, and that was a prime motivation of the flaneur: to stroll through and gaze in public spaces, observing the human spectacle made possible by the urban milieau. "We scarcely know where so much and such varieties of human nature can be encountered as in a walk through the Markets," Foster declares in "The Markets."[34] Foster notes this "one in many" so often that it can be considered a recurring theme in his sketches. For instance, in one of his *Gas-Light* pieces, "Bowling and Billiard Saloons," he notes the natural mingling of class and background among the men:

> But whether we treat of them as saloons, alleys, or simply rooms, the billiard and bowling establishments with which the city abounds are well worth a night's attention, as being frequented by a greater diversity of strongly-marked characters than almost any other class of public places of resort. Here the gay and reckless southerner, the half-frightened and half-fuddled country merchant, the watch-stuffer, the green-horn, the blackleg and the clerk, the editor and the genteel pick-pocket, meet and mingle on equal and familiar terms.[35]

He makes a similar observation in one of his "daylight" *Slices,* "The Omnibuses":

> The omnibus is an excellent school for studying human nature. . . . Each division of the day has it distinctive class of omnibus-riders. . . . All is perfect equality in the early omnibus.
>
> The clerk of Jones, Smith, Brown & Co. is not a whit bigger man than the prosperous house-builder in his straw hat and lime-colored *blouse.* Each pulls the strap and pays his six-pence with the same air of absolute independence and equality. The distinction between *ouvrier* and *bourgeois,* if it exist at all, does not reach the sunrise omnibus. If there be an aristocrat about the establishment it is unquestionably the driver.[36]

But if there are similarities between Whitman's and Foster's journalistic sketches in their depictions of their flaneur's journeys around the city, there also are significant differences both in style and content. As suggested by the previous examples, while Foster's content acknowledged the urban "many," as did Whitman's, Foster also repeatedly and meaningfully highlighted the differences among the many, the "greater diversity," the "varieties," the class differences, and the extreme poverty made possible by the burgeoning metropolis. Stylistically, Foster employed far more narrative devices, such as injecting humor as well as a somewhat satirical or ironic tone, which are nearly absent in Whitman's sketches. But Foster also employed far more storytelling devices appropriate to capturing the moment for his readers than did Whitman, including using bits of conversation or dialogue. For instance, consider this excerpt from one of the *Slices,* "The Pawnbroker's Shops":

> Whom have we here? A very pale, timid-looking little man—thin to diaphony, and with large lustrous eyes that seem like jets welling up from some deep-hidden source. He staggers in under a load of books.
>
> "I want a little money on these books, Sir. They are invaluable to me, and I shall be sure to redeem them as soon as my book is out."
>
> "Don't want books, my good fellow—they don't pay."
>
> "But, Sir, here is Byron, and Shelley, and Bacon, and Jeremy Taylor—"
>
> "Who ish Cheremy Taylor? If it was Zachary Taylor, now!"[37]

To show how expensive jewelry came to a pawnbroker's shop, in the same sketch he includes a conversation between an affluent woman and a gentleman in need of money who is willing to take the "splendidly-attired" woman's valuable jewels and pawn them for cash.[38] In a *Gaslight* sketch, "Mose and Lize," he distinguishes between a Broadway dandy and a "b'hoy"—a young man commonly referred to as Mose from a tough lower Manhattan neighborhood—by contrasting an exchange between the dandy and a young woman with an exchange between Mose and his girlfriend, commonly known as Lize:

> "Do tell me all about your fine parade with the Hoosah troop yethterday, Mither Thmith," lisped a young lady of the Upper Ten to a danday Hussar, the other evening at a party in the Fifth Avenue.
>
> "Oh I assure you, we had a most chawming time, my deah madam—perfectly chawming."
>
> On the same evening Mose returned from a grand fireman's parade and target-excursion, and was met by Lize at the door.
>
> "Well hoss, what kind of time'd ye hev—say?"
>
> "Well now yer'd better *bleeve* we had a gallus time! Give us a buss, old gal! Guess I seen ye lookin' out er ther winder this morning—I did."
>
> "Oh git out—*you* Mose!"[39]

Besides conversation, Foster often employed detailed scene-setting and concrete descriptions of people, at times combining a sense for the moment or the feel of an activity with rather vivid descriptions of types as well as relatively sophisticated use of dialogue, especially in the *Fifteen Minutes Around New York* sketches. The comical "A Plunge in the Swimming Bath," for example, begins with "Plop! goes the fat man . . . with his face red as the full moon, and his whole man appearing about to melt." The man "stripped in marvelous quick time, and glided into the water like a large lump of warm fat," compared to a "lean man" who "splashes and splutters about in the water like four sticks tied together." Sprinkled throughout the sketch are snippets of conversation, such as this one between a "stalwart Californian" and an "Old Fogy":

> "I say, old feller—give us a chor o'terbacker, will yer?"
>
> "Tobacco, sir!" exclaims Old Fogy, Esq., aghast. "Tobacco! Do you mean to insult me?"
>
> "Well, I shouldn't mind, old hoss! Jest you come into this here small tin pan full of water, what they calls a simmin'-bath in these small-potatoe diggings, and ain't no objections to takin' a turn with you. Whooray! Who's afeard?"
>
> Old Fogy looks, reflects a moment, slips on his boots and trowsers, and muttering something about the "encroachments of democracy," disappears.[40]

Similarly, in the sketch on the ferry he begins with "Hurra! There goes the bell! give us the change—run—jump—dash—here we are! Thanks to a quick eye, a pair of tolerably long, if not handsome legs, and considerable practice in the sharp work of getting about and around New York."[41] Foster also would occasionally try something very different to get that "feel" of the moment, of actuality as it occurs, as he did in trying to capture the "spirit" and atmosphere of an eating-house "at high tide" by running together words and phrases to create the near-chaotic sense of motion and speed, anticipating Tom Wolfe's attempt to capture the moment in his opening to "Las Vegas (What?) Las Vegas (Can't hear you! Too noisy) Las Vegas!!!" more than a hundred years later:

"Beefsteakandtatersvegetabesnumbertwenty—In*jin*hardandsparrow-grassnumbersixteen!" "Waiter! Waiter! Wa-y-ter!" "Comingsire"—while the rascal's *going* as fast as he can! "*Is* that beef killed for my porterhouse steak I ordered last week?" "Readynminitsir, comingsir, dreklysir—twosixpence, biledamand cabbage shillin, ricepudn sixpnce, eighteenpence—at the barf you please—lobstaucensammingnumberfour—yes sir!" Imagine a continuous stream of such sounds as these, about the size of the Croton river, flowing through the banks of clattering plates and clashing knives and forks, perfumed with the steam from a mammoth kitchen, roasting, boiling, baking, frying, beneath the floor-crowds of animals with a pair of jaws apiece, wagging in emulation of the one wielded with such terrific effect by Samson—and the thermometer which has become ashamed of itself and hides away behind a mountain of hats in the corner, melting up *by degrees* to boiling heat—and you will have some notion of a New York eating-house.[42]

As with Wolfe, and as Crane would do with "The Broken-Down Van" in the early 1890s, Foster was testing the limits of language in depicting reality, pushing words to get as close as he could to give readers the effect of having been there, to see and feel and hear what he had seen, heard, and felt.

Foster's sketches rarely took the form of a traditional tale—with a beginning, middle, and end—but in his last collection, "The Chief of Police—A True Romance of Life in New York" is an exception, being a cautionary tale with a touch of irony since the title's "True Romance" is anything but.[43] Another cautionary tale in a more traditional storytelling form occurs in one of the *Gas-Light* sketches, "The Dog-Watch." This one is a bit closer to Whitman's "The Clerk from the Country," but rather than occurring over weeks, as Whitman's tale did, this story of the country bumpkin being conned by city sharpies happens as the out-of-towner is led through a single night of drunkenness and debauchery. It is also bleaker than Whitman's tale, with the city visitor being tossed into the Tombs, the city's notorious jail, after being found drunk, broke, and disheveled in a Five Points gutter, which points to perhaps the most important distinction between Foster's sketches and Whitman's impressions: the constant presence or sense of corruption in much of Foster's work.[44] Stylistic differences clearly separate Foster from Whitman, but content that reveals neediness, sleaze, and vice provides a more powerful distinction between the two.

Whitman's tone primarily exclaims to the reader, "Isn't all this grand? Look at all the people, the humanity that surrounds us and is a part of us!" Foster also celebrated urban life, but he allowed readers to see "the horrible stench of the poverty, misery, beggary, starvation, crime, filth, and licentiousness that congregate in our Large City," as he put it in the introduction to *New York in Slices,* and the underbelly is especially revealed in the sketches of *New York by Gas-Light.*[45] Just as he did with his "horrible stench" declaration in his *Slices* introduction, Foster makes his intentions perfectly clear in the opening sketch of *Gas-Light.* He begins that sketch, "Broadway at Evening," by declaring that his purpose is "To penetrate beneath the thick veil of night and lay bare the fearful mysteries of darkness in the metropolis—the festivities of prostitution, the orgies of pauperism, the haunts of theft and murder, the scenes of drunkenness and beastly debauch, and all the sad realities that go to make up the lower stratum—the under-ground story—of life in New York!" He speaks for the reader by questioning his motivation "for invading these dismal realms and thus wrenching from them their terrible secrets" and in his explanation he gives his reporting and writing a somewhat noble purpose, using language that clearly ties him to the emerging realistic sensibility: "The duty of the present age is to discover the real facts of the actual condition of the wicked and wretched classes—so that Philanthropy and Justice may plant their blows aright." What he intends to do, he says, is "to seek for and depict truth" and he invites the reader to "look and listen."[46] Of course, implied in this declaration is a belief that one can go out and observe people and their activities and reality—or truth—will be revealed. But what is clear as well, and central to this discussion, is the call to depict the "sad realities," "life," "the real facts," and the "actual condition," and to do so through observation. These words and phrases will be repeated by writers, editors, and critics in the decades to come.

Overall the sketches involve a tour of the "under-ground," as Foster the urban explorer and guide takes the reader from one place of "infamy" to the next: notorious neighborhoods, saloons, oyster bars, billiards parlors, gambling dens, dance halls, brothels, as well as a range of other places where prostitution occurs, and "Model Artist Exhibitions" where men can view naked women under the guise of art. He shows and tells you who might be present at these questionable establishments, but he also passes judgment and points to the hypocrisy. For instance, while Foster makes the claim that the women who "eat, drink and make merry" in one type of late-night establishment, oyster cellars, "are all of one kind" (prostitutes), he notes that in contrast the men include "reverend judges and juvenile delinquents, pious and devout hypocrites, and undisguised libertines and debauchees. . . . Gamblers and fancy men, high-flyers and spoonies, genteel pick-pockets and burglars." When a policeman responds to "the boisterous mirth below" and raps his stick on the pavement, Foster says, he "may be reminding a grave functionary of the city that it is time to go home to his wife and children after the discharge of his 'arduous public duties.'"[47] In this way, Foster consistently brought into focus the role of those better off, especially men, and essentially the place of class, gender, and the environment in contributing to the behavior and living conditions of this lower class.

Blumin is right in recognizing in Foster's work a curious mix of "celebration and indictment."[48] Not only is that evident in many of Foster's sketches, but also in his introductions to sketches, such as the *Slices* introduction when he writes of the greatness of New York but then suddenly says he is leaving "this false magnificence" to "go among the naked and apparent miseries of the metropolis."[49] In other words, he celebrates in order to provide a contrast that will indict. Foster's visit to a night market in "Saturday Night" in *Gas-Light,* for example, bears some resemblance to Whitman's market stroll, beginning with Foster's exuberant "What a squeeze—what a crowd!" But as he continues, rather than capture pleasure in the market and its people as Whitman did, Foster allows readers to experience the crunch of a jammed and jostling market. He tries to give readers the "feel" of the facts, with a touch of humor, as he describes what it was like trying to squeeze through the crowd:

> It is not here mere elbows and knees, and brawny chests and broad stout backs that you are to encounter. Now you stumble against a firkin, and now are overset by a bag. And there is a woman who has somehow—it is impossible to tell how—squeezed through between you and your next neighbor: but her basket, to which she clings with death-like tenacity, appears to be made of less elastic material than herself. It has assumed the position of a balloon, and forms a target for a score of noses pushed on from the rear. There is no chance of its coming through, that is certain; and the woman will *not* let go of it—that seems equally clear.[50]

As he attempts to crawl under the woman's basket, his eyes water from "briny" mackerel in the bottom of the basket and then a "large slice of the fat" from a piece of corned-beef "reposes" on his coat collar. When he finally stands, he sees that he has been "kneeling in a basket of stale eggs," ruining his pants, and causing the owner of the eggs to angrily respond.

> The Irish huckster-woman who owns them, seeing this wholesale destruction of her brood of incipient chickens, pours out a volley of abuse upon your devoted dead, and loudly demands full compensation of her irreparable loss. You gladly pay whatever she requires; and by dint of pulling and squeezing, and being pulled and squeezed, we at length make our way through the lower walk, past the butter and cheese stands, and stalls for carcasses of dead hogs and sheep, now ankle-deep in mud, and so on to the fish-market. If you are any thing of an amateur in smells, you surely may here be gratified to your nose's content. But don't tread on that pile of eels, for they are slippery fellows and would be very likely to bring you "down upon 'em!" And see there! A fine green lobster has caught your foot in his pinchers and will be through the leather directly. You will find him the closest friend you ever had—he'll stick like a burr.[51]

While a reader might laugh at Foster's watery eyes, his collar stained by fat, his pants ruined by broken eggs, and his foot pinched by a lobster, Foster frames the sketch with poverty and want. He calls the Saturday night of the sketch "the poor man's holiday," which includes going to the market once a week for those who "work the hardest and longest, and in labors the most repulsive" and who are often "cramped six days in seven for something to eat," aspects that Whitman ignored. According to Foster, "the laborer and his family, who really hold society together by the work and cunning of their hands, are often without a dinner."[52] Near the end of the sketch, Foster notes that the Saturday night markets and various shops on certain streets are frequented by "the whole world of middle and lower life" who go there "to see and be seen" and therefore are both viewing and participating in this urban spectacle. But just prior to ending with this bland and predictable concluding observation, Foster calls the "powerful, enlightened, wealthy" of the city "utterly disgraceful" for allowing the poor to exist in "squalor and brutality" in which children will "know nothing but how to work, to become thus horribly degraded."[53] Foster regularly provides such social commentary in his sketches when he pokes fun at the dandies and the Upper Ten and those in power generally, as in the piece just noted. He makes his feelings about the moneyed class perfectly clear in the conclusion of his *Fifteen Minutes Around New York* sketch, "Wall Street and the Merchants' Exchange":

> Such is a fair and not overdrawn picture of a type of the money, shop-keeping aristocracy of the New World—a race of beings who, as a natural historian, we under-take to say, have never been equaled on the face of this earth, in all that is pompous without dignity, gaudy without magnificence, lavish without taste, and aristocratic without good manners.[54]

In several sketches in which prostitution appears, Foster depicts the prostitutes as both vixens and victims, making sure his readers understand the role of poverty, alcohol, and men of means in fostering prostitution, almost always depicting the women as fallen but blameless.

To a certain extent, it reflects the times in that his language regularly indicates that what he depicts and explains is at the very least tawdry if not immoral. Yet he tends to find the powers-that-be responsible for the poverty and vice. Two of his darkest sketches in *Slices* involve visits to two of the city's most notorious places, the Tombs jail and the Five Points section. When he takes readers to the "The Tombs," he calls the city detention center a "foul lazar-house of polluted and festering Humanity!"[55] After clearly declaring in a somewhat overwrought tone and language that this Halls of Justice and House of Detention—its official name—poisons the soul and is "a redhot furnace of corruption, bribery, theft, burglary, murder, prostitution, and delirium tremens," he begins his tour by entering through a side door:

> It is within an hour of daylight. A Policeman stands at the low door, and seeing that we are "connected with the press," offers no obstacle to our entrance.—Sometime he may have a "case" which he has been paid for suppressing—and then we may be of use to him. We enter and grope our way with difficulty, stumbling here and there over a sleeping Watchman, and making slowly towards a dim and distant glimmering light. Approaching, we see a dark-lantern held so that its single ray may illuminate the corrugated face and ghastly spectacles of the Police Magistrate who is doing up the loafers and loaferesses in squads. The recesses of the damp unwholesome apartment are filled with drunken men and women found helpless in the street, with the night-brawlers and disturbers of the public peace, and with young boys and girls who have been caught asleep on cellar doors or are suspected of the horrible crime of stealing junk bottles and old iron!—The very lowest and most brutal form of human depravity may here be seen in all its horrors; and the most horrible sight of all is the blear-eyed, drunken woman, arrested for robbing her paramour or for quarrelling with

> her companions on the Points, and waiting her turn, among negro
> men and women, thieves and vagabonds, of every age and quality.[56]

This sensationalized account seems designed to appeal to the worst
fears and expectations of readers, particularly to those who will
never set foot there. A case could be made that Foster is playing to
that common perception about the Tombs and its inhabitants. But
besides depicting the lower-class ruffians, crooks, and prostitutes,
he captures the extensive corruption of those in charge. After all,
as Foster makes clear, this is a place where the reporter is allowed
in as a favor and where, Foster shortly points out, the magistrate
only listens to the watchman's side of the story, not the prisoner's;
children who have been sleeping in the streets or who stole bottles
are thrown in with adults; the person with some money can pay
the watchman and be released. If, however, a prisoner has "neither
money nor friends, Justice is rigid and uncompromising" and he
will be "thrown howling and infuriated into a yard filled with
wretches like himself" where "they aid each other's attempts at
demonism, until the whole place becomes a shuddering hell."
Readers also learn that the women "are crammed into a long
lampless corridor, and lie huddled up in their rags against the bare
stone walls, or rave in hideous fury to and fro, until their strength is
exhausted and they fall prone upon the floor."[57] Along the "more
aristocratic corridors . . . the forgers, murderers, and genteel swin-
dlers . . . are allowed bed-linen and books, and may, if they choose,
keep themselves cleanly and comfortable." Foster, however, stops
short of blaming the women for their state. When they encounter
those accused of "drunkenness and starvation" thrown together in
the "cattle-yard," especially the women, Foster returns to his common refrain and tells readers to "remember that all these monstrous
creatures were born with pure, beautiful womanly souls, and that

the chances are nine hundred and ninety-nine in a thousand that they were driven to their present condition by starvation and the wiles of some heartless man-villain, and they alone are punished while the man goes free—and you have humanity before you in its most demoniac aspect, its most revolting manifestation."[58] After showing how the system works to the benefit of those in charge of processing the prisoners, Foster's final sentence may strike today's reader as ambiguous because it embraces a satirical and critical tone: "It is true that there are very strong complaints made of the manner in which criminal justice is administered in this Court; but we venture to say that they are altogether unfounded."[59]

Foster visited "The Five Points" in both *Slices* and in *Gas-Light*. That section of lower Manhattan would remain of interest to journalists and writers into the 1890s, when it was largely cleaned up through reform efforts. Here is his description of this "foul and loathsome" place, with detail marked by the repetition of words and images of decay:

> The buildings in all that neighborhood are nearly all of wood, and are so old and rotten that they seem ready to tumble together into a vast rubbish-heap. Many of them are furnished with steps, from which half the stairs are missing, and each provided with a decayed cellar-door, broken from the hinges, and ready to precipitate any one who ventures to tread upon it into the cellar below. Nearly every house and cellar is a groggery below and a brothel above. In the doors and at the windows may be seen at any hour of the afternoon or evening, scores of sluttishly-dressed women, in whose faces drunkenness and debauchery have destroyed every vestige of all we expect in the countenance of Woman, and even almost every trace of human expression. . . . Here and there, digging in the foul gutters, or basking in filthy nakedness upon the cellar

doors, may be seen groups of children, from the merest infancy up to the verge of premature puberty—some seeming pretty, some deformed and idiotic, and others horribly ulcerated from head to foot with that hereditary leprosy which debauchery and licentiousness entail as their curse upon their innocent offspring.[60]

Foster then takes readers inside one of the houses, into "an apartment separated by tattered blankets, suspended from the low rafters, and inhabited by several families." He continues:

> Here a mother lies dead-drunk in her squalid bed upon the floor, and her two children are fighting over her body for the bottle which she may not have drained quite to its dregs. There two women, their eyes inflamed and their faces distorted with passion, are swearing furiously at each other, and threatening a war of blows. Yonder, on a cot without a mattress or pillow, lies a paralytic old woman, looking as if living and malignant eyes had been given to a decaying wax-figure.[61]

Foster was "arguably the best and most characteristic of the New York flaneurs of the 1840s," according to literary scholar Dana Brand.[62] Particularly with his *Gas-Light* sketches Foster was producing what historian Blumin has called "the new literary genre of nonfictional urban sensationalism" that was "rooted in the urban sketches and *romans-feuilletons*" of the early nineteenth-century French and British writers.[63] Certainly, Foster and Whitman, and other writers as well, were influenced by Charles Dickens's *Sketches by Boz,* which were published in newspapers in the 1830s in England and collected for book publication in 1836, and in which Dickens set down "the small events in the everyday life of common persons . . . directing his powers of observations and description upon scenes and characters within the daily scope of any loiterer in London."[64] Whitman noted Dickens's collection in his newspaper commentaries and referred to Dickens as "Boz" when Dickens made his visit to America; when Foster visits "The Five Points" in one of his *Slices* sketches, he says that "mere words can convey but a faint idea of the Five Points" and adds that what might be conveyed "has been so well done already by Dickens and Willis."[65] Regardless of literary or journalistic influences, Whitman and Foster are representative of the cultural shift to depict the actual. That is, by roaming the city and writing about what they saw, Foster and Whitman were "*explaining* the new metropolis to a society that was in so many ways affected by its development," as Blumin puts it.[66] In the process, a "street-wise expert" like Foster was also explaining and depicting "the realities that lie beneath the deceptive appearances of the city and its people."[67] In doing so, both writers provide examples of journalism's and American culture's increasing fascination with the actual of American life and city life. They were giving "meaningful representation" to urban life, as Thomas Bender has put it, though Foster went much further than Whitman in documenting the social changes of city life.[68] Despite Whitman's later role as a cultural mediator and influential iconic poet, it is Foster's work, which documented the urban underbelly, that more specifically anticipates the growing number of written and visual portrayals that exposed urban poverty and vice, as well as the emerging chasm of class in America. Fishkin's assessment of Whitman's journalistic achievement applies to Foster more so than to Whitman. That is, Foster came much closer than Whitman in mapping the surface of city life and charting its depths.

FOUR

THE STORYTELLERS

In the second half of the nineteenth century, and especially after the Civil War, a parade of writers across the American continent were depicting the actual in a variety of ways, telling increasingly realistic stories as fiction, nonfiction, and often a mixture of the two in a growing number of newspapers and magazines, providing different avenues to experiencing various aspects of contemporary American life. Sketches and reports of many forms showed and dramatized behavior, values, and issues with American characters and types from across social and economic classes. The work and careers of two very different writers who were contemporaries, Rebbeca Harding Davis and Mark Twain, illustrate the diverse approaches to documenting and explaining the meaning of life being lived in America in the second half of the nineteenth century, particularly the first part.

The writing careers of Davis and Twain emerged and developed about the same time, except Davis's was primarily formed in magazine writing while Twain's was shaped in newspaper journalism. By the time the two died in 1910, both had worked for newspapers and written for magazines, Twain had become a literary celebrity, and Davis's son, Richard Harding Davis, had become better known than his mother. Davis, however, was one of the first writers to show a gritty realism in the lives of some of society's poor and marginalized as well as their human qualities and potential, while Twain employed parody, satire, and humor to poke holes in many commonly held beliefs and stereotypes. Although Twain was the more extraordinary writer of the two, they were both remarkably productive. They are representative because they were both writers who bowed to the popular demands of the market, but who also documented the American scene in whatever outlet or form available and appropriate: newspapers, magazines, books, and in Twain's case, public lectures.

REBECCA HARDING DAVIS

In April 1861, the *Atlantic Monthly* published a story that began this way:

> A cloudy day: do you know what that is in a town of iron-works?
> The sky sank down before dawn, muddy, flat immovable. The air is
> thick, clammy with the breath of crowded human beings. It stifles
> me. I open the window, and, looking out, can scarcely see through
> the rain the grocer's shop opposite, where a crowd of drunken
> Irishmen are puffing Lynchburg tobacco in their pipes. I can de-
> tect the scent through all the foul smells ranging loose in the air.[1]

So opened Rebecca Harding Davis's "Life in the Iron Mills," her vivid fictional tale about the struggles of an immigrant iron-worker and his cousin in a gritty river town, the same kind of town as Wheeling, Virginia—later West Virginia—on the Ohio

River where Davis had grown up and was living when she wrote the story. The repetition of negative words and images from specific selective detail in the opening paragraph continues in the next paragraph, which focuses on the pervasiveness of smoke that "rolls" from the iron mills "and settles down in black, slimy pools on the muddy streets. Smoke on the wharves, smoke on the dingy boats, on the yellow river,—clinging in a coating of greasy soot to the house-front, the two faded poplars, the faces of the passers-by." The narrator says that when she looks from her window she sees "the slow stream of human life creeping past, night and morning, to the great mills. Masses of men, with dull, besotted faces bent to the ground, sharpened here and there by pain or cunning; skin and muscle and flesh begrimed with smoke and ashes; stooping all night over boiling caldrons of metal, laired by day in dens of drunkenness and infamy; breathing from infancy to death an air saturated with fog and grease and soot, vileness for soul and body."[2] Although a work of fiction, Davis's tale was clearly a Wheeling story—and a story of an increasingly industrialized America—solidly based on Davis's knowledge of Wheeling, its mills, and her observation of its workers.[3] As Tillie Olson has written, "it was in front of the Harding house that the long trains of mules dragged their masses of pig iron and the slow stream of human life crept past, night and morning, year after year, to work their fourteen-hour days six days a week," and Davis had observed this year after year, from childhood up until she described the scene in her book at age thirty.[4]

While realistic fiction would eventually become a standard staple of magazines, sentimentality dominated magazine fiction when Davis wrote "Life in the Iron Mills." Yet right from its beginnings in 1857 the *Atlantic* was willing to publish stories that "went counter to the generally honeyed stickiness," as Mott put it.[5] For instance, the *Atlantic* had published fiction by Rose Terry Cooke since its first issue. Cooke's fiction wouldn't stand the test of time as Davis's "Life in the Iron Mills" would, but even her early, more Gothic work eschewed romantic or idealized themes. For instance, Cooke's short story "The Ring Fetter," published in the *Atlantic* in 1859, has a rather exotic atmosphere and overblown characters, including a husband whose cruelty toward his wife is exaggerated, yet the story overall is a critique of marriage and a questioning of the nearly unlimited power of husbands over their wives and thus is a step toward realism with its theme if not its characters.[6] Cooke's fiction in various magazines would become increasingly realistic, mirroring the general shift in magazines toward more vital fiction with contemporary topics and themes. Davis, however, is a representative and pioneering figure in that while her mostly dark story of mill workers may have indeed "exploded with a force that shook America's Eastern intellectual community to its foundation," its ending, although neither "happy" nor sentimental in the conventional sense, nevertheless left room for hope, seemingly designed to provide uplift and affirm "the symbolism and idealism of romance as well as the Christianity and moral efficacy of sentimental fiction."[7] The tale's two main characters are a mill "puddler" named Hugh and his cousin, a cotton mill picker named Deborah, who picks the pocket of a wealthy visitor to the mill so that Hugh can get out and, perhaps, become an artist. But Hugh is caught returning the money and sentenced to nineteen years in prison and Deborah to three years. In despair, Hugh slits his wrists in his jail cell while Deborah, aided by a kindly Quaker, is redeemed after serving her sentence and lives "long years of sunshine, and fresh air, and slow, patient Christ-love." A story that began in gloom and dreariness ends in the hope of a new dawn: "While the room is yet steeped in heavy shadow, a cool, gray light suddenly touches its head like a blessing hand, and its groping arm points through the broken cloud to the far East, where, in the flickering, nebulous crimson, God has set the promise of the Dawn."[8]

Even more strongly and clearly than Cooke and other writers, Davis mediated "idealistic and realistic impulses."[9] Ultimately, however, by depicting working-class life and the demeaning conditions of industrial labor, by allowing her readers to see and feel the hopeless suffering of these immigrant men and women, Davis and the *Atlantic* introduced a fresh perspective and a new type of narrative by trying to make a common, depressing life "real." It was unusual enough that after introducing the bleakness of her mill town and its workers with their "dull lives . . . massed, vile, slimy lives," she was compelled to urge her readers to stay with the tale, even if it was not what they were used to or wanted:

> Stop a moment. I am going to be honest. This is what I want you to do. I want you to hide your disgust, take no heed to your clean clothes, and come right down with me,—here, into the thickest of the fog and mud and foul effluvia. I want you to hear this story. There is a secret down here, in this nightmare fog, that has lain dumb for centuries: I want to make it a real thing to you.[10]

Six months after "Life in the Iron Mills," the *Atlantic* began serializing Davis's novel-length work, "A Story of To-day," published in 1862 as the novel *Margaret Howth: A Story of To-day*. Although the *Atlantic* and its editor, James Fields, encouraged fiction with more current and realistic themes and settings, it was Fields who found Davis's first version of "A Story of To-day" too dark and he rejected it. Davis called that first version "The Deaf and the Dumb," with the title apparently referring to the comfortable and affluent who are unable or unwilling to see and articulate pain, poverty, and misery. Fields wanted Davis to change the title of her second version to "Margaret Howth," which she refused to do, wanting to emphasize with the word "today" the currency of the novel. But she did provide the happy ending missing in the first version. While Davis undoubtedly sacrificed some of the natural integrity of her story (we don't know because the original manuscript of "The Deaf and the Dumb" does not exist), "A Story of To-day" nevertheless is realistic, being a story that is neither exaggerated nor out of time and place. As with "Life in the Iron Mills," she addresses the reader in order to explain her intent, beginning with: "Let me tell you a story of To-Day,—very homely and narrow in its scope and aim."[11] She goes to some length to declare that, during this time of war, she will present "characters besides that of Patriot," characters who will be "whom you see every day, and call 'dregs,' sometimes." In her story of "To-Day," she writes, "there shall be no bloody glare,—only those homelier, subtler lights which we have overlooked."[12] Davis tells her readers she knows what they want: either the "war-trumpet" or pleasing "glimpses of life" that are "idylls delicately tinted." "You want something, in fact, to lift you out of this crowded, tobacco-stained commonplace, to kindle and chafe and glow in you," she observes. Instead, Davis says she wants her readers "to dig into this commonplace, this vulgar American life, and see what is in it." In fact, she adds, "Sometimes I think it has a new and awful significance that we do not see," which is why she wants us "to go down into this common, every-day drudgery, and consider if there might not be in it also great warfare."[13] Thus her tale is, after all, a "war" story but one without armies and cannons, and instead is one that involves the daily struggle for "bread and butter." It is a great warfare "with a history as old as the world, and not without its pathos." Furthermore, it has its casualties: "It has its slain. Men and women, lean-jawed, crippled in the slow, silent battle, are in your alleys, sit beside you at your table; its martyrs sleep under every green hill-side."[14]

Obviously, Davis still is motivated to justify her "common" and real themes and characters. In focusing on plain, everyday life, she abandoned the genteel tradition, but in doing so she briefly defines a very basic type of realistic writing with its focus on the actual. In these early works, Davis is in fact defining a theory of the commonplace.[15] In a later chapter of her "To-day" story, she says she is aware of the "dingy common colors on the palette with which I have been painting" and she adds:

> I wish I had some brilliant dyes. I wish, with all my heart, I could take you back to that "Once upon a time" in which the souls of our grandmothers delighted,—the time which Dr. Johnson sat up all night to read about in "Evilina,"—the time when all the celestial virtues, all the earthly graces were revealed in a condensed state to man through the blue eyes and sumptuous linens of some Belinda Portman or Lord Mortimer. . . . The heroine glides into life full-charged with rank, virtues, a name three-syllabled, and a white dress that never needs washing, ready to sail through dangers dire into a triumphant haven of matrimony;—all the aristocrats have high foreheads and cold blue eyes; all the peasants are old women, miraculously grateful, in neat check aprons, or sullen-browed insurgents planning revolts in caves.[16]

The narrator confesses that she once tried writing of "women rare and radiant in Italian bowers," but a friend would say, "Try and tell us about the butcher next door, my dear."[17]

Despite their concessions to the genteel and idealized, both "Life in the Iron Mills" and "A Story of To-day" are dramatizations of social problems emerging in the newly industrialized and capitalistic America. Davis did tell readers about the butcher, as well as the mill worker, in the process dealing with significant issues of class and gender, and eventually race as well. The issues of class and the effects of poverty Davis depicted were quite similar to those captured by George Foster in his New York City sketches but Davis brings readers inside those issues while Foster invited readers to look and see what he saw as an observer.

Davis dramatized Northern racism in her Civil War novel *Waiting for the Verdict,* which was serialized in *Galaxy* magazine in 1867 and published as a book the following year. Although the time period is the Civil War, the book confronts the postwar problem of what to do with the freed slaves, thereby once again writing a story that confronts an issue of "to-day."[18] It was reissued almost a hundred years later as part of a series called "American Novels of Muckraking, Propaganda, and Social Protest." A brief biography introducing that 1968 edition describes Davis as the "first American author to introduce the labor question into fiction" and interestingly calls "Life in the Iron Mills" her "muckraking article" and *Margaret Howth* "a study of slum life" and "an accurate depiction of the industrial hell which existed in America a hundred years ago."[19] According to the biography's author, Davis continues being a "pioneer and crusader" in *Waiting for the Verdict* by writing about miscegenation, calling it a topic "that still strikes terror into the hearts of the 'respectable.'" This "work of social protest and propaganda for the Negro" is rather complex in plot and character development, and while miscegenation is crucial, and though slavery and racism are its larger topics, it ultimately deals with questions of interracial relations and racial integration and promotes the power of education and community in dealing with America's racial wounds. Because Davis was writing about real, physical, daily drudgery and hunger as well as the resulting spiritual hunger and emptiness, her solutions in many of her dramatizations of social issues were sometimes essentially spiritual rather than the economic or political reform that was needed. But what is particularly significant is that this type of focus occurred in prominent magazines.

Davis was quite prolific as a writer over the next forty years and although she quickly learned to write for the marketplace, it would be a mistake to claim, as some critics have, that she rarely ventured into the "common" as she did in her first two stories. In her short stories, in pieces that mixed fiction and nonfiction into a type of long-form narrative, and in an extensive list of essays and commentaries on a range of issues, often involving class and gender, Davis was often "actualizing her theory of the commonplace," as a prominent Davis scholar has put it.[20] Furthermore, her insistence on focusing and elaborating on the commonplace, on that area of "great warfare," was made possible, as already suggested, by the emerging mass media of the day, magazines and newspapers. Although Davis did not work as a full-time editor or writer for a publication, her writing was not confined to the more highly literary *Atlantic*. Right up to her death in 1910, she published fiction and essays in a number of magazines in addition to the *Atlantic,* including extensive contributions to *Peterson's,* a women's magazine, and regular contributions to *Youth's Companion* and *St. Nicholas,* both youth publications, as well as to *Scribner's, Harper's Monthly, Lippincott's,* and from 1902 through 1906 extensively to the *Saturday Evening Post. Peterson's* published all the popular women's writers and, according to Mott, most of it was "treacle" except for the writing of Davis and Caroline M. Kirkland.[21] She also was a contributing editor for the *New York Tribune* beginning in 1869, writing editorials or commentary as exposés. In 1889 she resigned rather than halt a series of editorials that blamed Northern manufacturers for "hoarding" chemicals that were needed in the South to fight disease. Davis then became a regular contributor to the *New York Independent,* a weekly. Her essays in the *Independent* and the *Saturday Evening Post* were well received and "made her reputation as an essayist."[22] Certainly, this side of Davis's journalism allowed her to specifically address a range of social issues and to provide "lucid insights into American society's evolution," the same insights and perspectives about social problems that she dramatized in her realistic fiction.[23] However, there were other writings for magazines that seemed to bridge fiction and nonfiction but which were also solidly grounded in reality and the "commonplace," as she regularly put it.

For instance, Davis wrote eight sketches for *Scribner's* from 1874 to 1875 that have been described as fictional character sketches. The majority of these eight sketches are fiction, but several appear to be mostly based on observation and bear a certain resemblance to the flanerie accounts discussed in chapter 3. "The Pepper-Pot Woman," for example, consists of a detailed description of an older woman who in the winter sells pepper pot, or stew, on the streets of Philadelphia where Davis lived. We learn that Sarah, the pepper-pot woman, each morning "comes down the kitchen stairs before dawn, washes in the sink, slips into her greasy petticoats and sacque, ties her pad over her bald head, and is ready for the street." Then, in the third paragraph, Davis takes us into the street with Sarah:

> She fills her pails with the hot stew from the back of the stove, and goes out into the still gas-lit streets to supply the eating-stands.

Their keepers are setting out their half-eaten hams, musty pies and heaps of rolls.

"Hello, aunty!" they call as she comes up, yawning as they score down so many quarts against themselves in their leather pass-books. They keep the score, and pay her when they choose. Everybody knows how stupid she is about counting, but she never was cheated more than once or twice in her life. She laughed about it, and then said: "It was nateral," and that was the end of it.[24]

Again, Foster might have written this or something very similar in one of his "slices" for the *Tribune,* or someone very much like the pepper-pot woman might have been selling her stew in Whitman's marketplace. Furthermore, the likes of the pepper-pot woman and her kind would appear regularly, especially in newspaper and magazine columns and sketches in the 1890s.

In the 1880s, Davis wrote of her travels in the South for *Harper's Monthly* with one three-part series about a trip through part of Appalachia and a five-part series about traveling by rail through the Deep South, with a focus on the Gulf states.[25] One Davis scholar, Rose, has called these two series "fictionalized travelogues," "travel narratives," "episodic fictions," and "serialized travelogue"; another scholar, Harris, has called the series "documentary realism" and "quasi-fictionalized."[26] So, they aren't short stories, yet they are about real places and are significantly factual and accurate. Both series involve storytelling with realistic, believable travelers who interact with the people they encounter, people who speak in regional dialect and slang and who dress and behave according to local custom. Neither place nor character are romanticized or idealized. Even while Rose says both series are fiction, she also says, "Primarily, they record a group of tourists' exposure to the local characters, families, geography, sites, lore, and legends of the areas they visit."[27] Thus, they are fiction that accurately records, or to use Harris's terms, they are documentary realism. Rose emphasizes that in writing these accounts Davis was "dispelling falsehood with truth," that she produced "the realistic revision of myth" about the South, its people, and its ways. Through detailed description and extensive dialogue, readers take the journey with the travelers as Davis "leads her readers vicariously."[28] Of the two "travelogues," the Deep South series, called "Here and There in the South," is especially well written, with strong, clear, beautiful prose, and, although not as biting as the travel writing of Twain, Davis's "Here and There in the South" contains touches of irony and satire. Harris contends that with this series Davis regained her "literary artistry" and "artistic energy" and that more than any work she did in the 1880s it deserved to be published in book form. Not only does she note the "keen" tone and the sharp wit, but she says it displays Davis's "astute eye for social forces and personal tragedies" and that her "realism is at its most acute since the early 1870s."[29]

These articles bear some resemblance to what has come to be called literary journalism, or nonfiction writing about real people, places, and events that involve a range of literary techniques and have a distinct interpretative quality in that they are infused with facts and accurate detail but those facts and details make meaning through their presentation and organization around themes and well-defined characters. But it is as though Davis, because of the time period, stopped short of using "real" people and instead creates composites from the people she did observe, otherwise everything else exists in reality. As Rose says, the "characters serve as the vehicles for Davis's cultural mediation," which is to say that there were still considerable, major differences remaining between the North and the South as a result of the Civil War, including strongly negative stereotypes about the South and southerners.[30] Davis and her husband, a Philadelphia newspaper editor, had actually made several trips to the Deep South in search of material that would document the "New South" for Northern readers. The journey from Washington, D.C., to New Orleans, with stays in Atlanta, Montgomery, Mobile, Biloxi, and New Orleans, allowed Davis to document the various responses of the travelers to a host of local characters and to activities and behavior that contradicted standard Northern ideas about the South. Yet significant differences remain and Davis refuses to leave readers with misconceptions. While change is under way and many stereotypes no longer hold up, Davis's main character, a retired Northern clergyman who has been fully open to the idea of a New South, still believes in the end that he is in a "spellbound country, where some mystery of centuries ago slept." As he heads home, leaving behind "melancholy lagoons, the low driving clouds, the forests with their vistas of beckoning spectral mists, all silent as the shores of death, he felt he was going back to a real world, to shops, markets, passions, and life."[31]

Although stylistically very different, Davis and Twain did share something significant: they both were intent on dispelling myth and falsehood with truth. They just went about it in very different ways.

MARK TWAIN

Twain started working for newspapers when he was only twelve and eventually worked as a printer in several cities and as a reporter or correspondent for papers in Iowa, Nevada, and California. He also wrote for the *New York Herald,* the *New York Tribune,* and the *Buffalo Express* after he became part owner of that paper. His work appeared in other newspapers and, like Davis, he wrote articles for the *Atlantic Monthly, Galaxy,* and *Harper's Monthly.* While Twain did some relatively "straight" reporting, always with a strong point of view, which was common in newspaper journalism in the United States at this time, he was developing the humor and satire that would become his writer's trademarks and the defining characteristics of his emerging literary voice. Some scholars consider Twain's sketches, hoaxes, and "descriptive reporting" from his newspaper days to be early examples of literary journalism and regard him as the first significant practitioner of the form.[32] Many of Twain's newspaper sketches (and certainly his hoaxes) written for the *Territorial Enterprise* were fiction, although newspaper sketches generally were nonfiction, impressionistic, subjective, and often about seemingly unimportant or inconsequential events. They were nevertheless significant because they were "about real life" and therefore were documenting behavior in society and culture.[33] But in addition to showing readers the emergent American culture, Twain also *explained* that culture through satire and comedy that allowed him to regularly point to the shortcomings and foibles of public officials, citizens, and other reporters. That work was especially prominent during his time at the San Francisco *Call,* and in the articles he sent to newspapers while traveling.[34] Although what Twain wrote about was somewhat restricted—the *Call* had expectations about what should be covered regarding crime and government—he took advantage of a certain amount of freedom at the paper and in fact took more freedom than the paper gave, to write about that Western and San Francisco, California, culture from his distinct perspective, using various narrative approaches and structures. In other words, Twain's writing increasingly had an interpretative quality, just as

Rebecca Harding Davis's always did, although unlike Twain, she rarely employed comedy and exaggeration. For instance, when he visits a "New Chinese Temple" using passes provided by "our cultivated barbaric friend, Ah Wae," he uses the opportunity to poke fun at a competing reporter but also to satirically play to common stereotypes and prejudices about Chinese culture, freely exaggerating for effect. Here is his description in the article's first paragraph of what it was like entering the temple:

> After suffocating in the smoke of burning punk and josh lights, and the infernal odors of opium and all kinds of edibles cooked in unchristian manner, until we were becoming imbued with Buddhism and beginning to lose our nationality, and imbibe, unasked, Chinese instincts, we finally found Ah Wae, who roused us from our lethargy and saved us to our religion and our country by merely breathing the old, touching words, so simple and yet so impressive, and withal so familiar to those whose blessed privilege it has been to be reared in the midst of a lofty and humanizing civilization: "How do, gentlemen—take a drink?"[35]

Twain goes on to describe temple priests: "The priests march backward and forward, reciting prayers or something in a droning, sing-song way, varied by discordant screeches somewhat like the cawing of crows, and they kneel down, and get up and spin around, and march again, and still the infernal racket of gongs, drums and fiddles, goes on with its hideous accompaniment, and still the spectator grows more and more smothered and dizzy in the closed atmosphere of punk-smoke and opium-fumes." But, he concludes, the new temple is "ablaze with gilded ornamentation, and those who are fond of that sort of thing would do well" to visit the temple.

Even when Twain was writing about a rather routine, daily occurrence such as a runaway horse and cart, he tried to make it more interesting for both himself and the reader—at the same time padding the piece so he could fill space—through humor and satire. He once reported that a horse and cart "were carelessly left unhitched and unwatched" on a San Francisco street and the horse ran away, the cart overturned, and the horse became tangled in its harness. Twain says it is "strange" that some of the many small children who were at play on the horse's romp weren't injured, but not only were they not harmed, "they visited the wreck in countless swarms, after the disaster, and examined it with unspeakable satisfaction." Twain then says, as though it is fact, that "the driver is a man of extraordinary intellect and mature judgment—he set his cart on its legs again as well as he could, and then whipped his horse until it was easy to see that the poor brute began to comprehend that something was up, though it is questionable whether he has yet ciphered out what that something was, or not." He concludes that the driver not having been in the wagon would account "for the misfortune of his not being hurt in the least."[36]

Twain found the demands of his job at the *Call* tedious and he left after only four months at the urging of his editor, who felt the paper was missing too much local news. Despite his disappointment and frustration with the amount and type of reporting required of him at the *Call,* Twain nevertheless was able to further establish his voice and style. The two previous examples are rather typical of much of Twain's *Call* reporting, identified and gathered by Branch, who correctly says that a Twain article can be recognized by its "irrepressible imagination" and because it "often flares up and crackles with the fire of his personal style . . . is potentially explosive."[37] Obviously, Twain wrote with a strong point of view and often in a distinct voice. A writer who worked with Twain at the *Territorial Enterprise* described Twain as someone who "sketched the 'news'" and did so in a style "clear, buoyant" and "original"; that same buoyancy and originality are evident in much of his *Call* reports and sketches.[38] Twain even wrote an "Original Novelette" of about four hundred words for the *Call* that begins this way: "The only drawback there is to the following original novelette, is, that it contains nothing but truth, and must, therefore, be void of interest for readers of sensational fiction."[39] His six-chapter novelette, with the first chapter only one sentence and the last consisting of five sentences, is a "burlesque," and very simply tells a short tale of a philandering husband and wife and could be described as a human-interest sketch. In addition to developing his voice and style, journalism provided Twain with the opportunity to observe and experience a range of people and types—"all grades and classes of people," as Twain put it in a talk—allowing him to increase his knowledge and understanding of human nature and the human condition, which he acknowledged several years later when he said, "Reporting is the best school in the world to get a knowledge of human beings, human nature, and human ways. . . . Just think of the wide range of acquaintanceship, his experience of life and society."[40]

When Twain left the *Call*, he continued to write articles for publications, especially the literary weekly the *Californian*, edited by Bret Harte. He also spent about three months with friends in the gold mining camp where he first heard the story that became "The Celebrated Jumping Frog of Calaveras County," first published as "Jim Smiley and His Jumping Frog" in the New York *Saturday Press* in November 1865. When Twain returned from yarn spinning with his friends in the hills, he wrote for the *Californian* and sent letters or articles to the *Territorial Enterprise*. In 1866, he traveled to the Sandwich Islands (Hawaii) for the *Sacramento Union* and provided the paper with twenty-five reports or "letters," as such articles were commonly called, in effect launching one of the most significant and successful phases of his career, that of travel writer.[41] This trip and its writing would eventually lead to his most popular book, *The Innocents Abroad,* and to his remarkable literary influence and success.

Not as fully satirical as much of his other writing, including *Innocents,* the Sandwich Islands articles are still unmistakably Twain's. Loaded with facts and information designed to instruct the reader, as was typical of travel narratives, they also resonate with Twain's critical perspective, often presented through humor and the use of a crude fictional sidekick, Brown, who allows the more restrained narrator, Twain, to seem kinder, more polite, and more sophisticated. Concrete and vivid descriptions coupled with local slang and dialect give readers a strong sense of place. As one student of Twain's travel writing has said, travel writing "permitted him to use his special literary gifts" that were displayed in "short bursts of pointed observations, anecdotes, episodes, and tales."[42] In these accounts, Twain was often a flaneur, strolling along streets and through markets, shops, and public buildings, and sharing his observations. But he resists the romanticizing that was common to much travel writing by eagerly including unsavory details, often exaggerated, that lend the account authenticity and authority. Here, for instance, is his description of sellers of poi in one section of a Honolulu market:

> Moving among the stirring crowds, you come to the poi merchants, squatting in the shade on their hams, in true native fashion, and surrounded by purchasers. (The Sandwich Islanders always squat on their hams, and who knows but they may be the old

original "ham sandwiches"? The thought is pregnant with inter-est.) The poi looks like common flour paste, and is kept in large bowls formed of a species of gourd, and capable of holding from one to three or four gallons. Poi is the chief article of food among the natives . . . looks like a thick, or, if you please, a corpulent sweet potato, in shape, but is of a light purple color when boiled. When boiled it answers as a passable substitute for bread. The buck Kanakas bake it under ground, then mash it up well with a heavy lava pestle, mix water with it until it becomes a paste, set it aside and let it ferment, and then it is poi—and a villainous mixture it is, almost tasteless before it ferments and too sour for a luxury af-terward. But nothing in the world is more nutritious. When solely used, however, it produces acrid humors, a fact which sufficiently accounts for the blithe and humorous character of the Kanakas. I think there must be as much of a knack in handling poi as there is in eating with chopsticks. The forefinger is thrust into the mess and stirred quickly round several times and drawn as quickly out, thickly coated, just as if it were poultice; the head is thrown back, the finger inserted in the mouth and the poultice stripped off and swallowed—the eye closing gently, meanwhile, in a languid sort of ecstasy. Many a different finger goes into the same bowl. . . . One tall gentleman, with nothing in the world on but a soiled and greasy shirt, thrust in his finger and tested the poi, shook his head, scratched it with the useful finger, made another test, prospected among his hair, caught something and ate it; tested the poi again, wiped the grimy perspiration from his brow with the universal hand, tested again, blew his nose—"Let's move on, Brown," said I, and we moved.[43]

The exaggeration does not detract from the actuality of the piece but allows Twain to memorably depict a somewhat exotic reality with humor, undoubtedly bringing moans of revulsion from some readers.

Twain parodies conventional travel writing at several points, including in a passage that is a gushing single sentence of about five hundred words. Much of it consists of Twain contrasting what he sees as he wanders through Honolulu with similar sites in San Francisco. For example, he says that instead of the "mud-colored brown stone fronts of San Francisco," he saw "neat white cottages surrounded by ample yards . . . thickly clad with green grass, and shaded by tall trees, through whose dense foliage the sun could scarcely penetrate; in place of the customary infernal geranium languishing in dusty and general debility on tin-roofed rear additions or in bedroom windows, I saw luxurious banks and thickets of flowers, fresh as a meadow after a rain, and glowing with the richest dyes." And, "in place of those vile, tiresome, stupid, everlasting goldfish, wiggling around in glass globes . . . in prison houses," he "saw cats—Tom cats, Mary Ann cats, long-tailed cats, bobtail cats, blind cats, one-eyed cats, white cats, yellow cats, striped cats, spotted cats, tame cats, wild cats, singed cats, individual cats, groups of cats, platoons of cats, companies of cats, regiments of cats, armies of cats, multitudes of cats, millions of cats, and all of them sleek, fat, lazy, and sound asleep." He continues through a wide range of what he has observed, including "dusky native women sweeping by, free as the wind" and "a summer calm as tranquil as dawn in the Garden of Eden," until he begins describing the "dead blue water of the deep sea, flecked with 'white caps'" when he is interrupted by Brown, who qualifies Twain's exuberance. He mentions how uncomfortably hot it is and urges Twain to say more about the "'santipedes,' and cockroaches, and fleas, and lizards, and red ants, and scorpions, and spiders, and mosquitoes and missionaries—oh, blame my cats if I'd live here two months, not if I was

High-You-Muck-a-Muck and King of Wawhoo, and had a harem full of hyenas!" When Twain tells Brown that these are just "trifles," Brown responds: "Trifles be—blowed! You get nipped by one of them scorpions once, and see how you like it!"[44] Once again, Twain the reporter as narrator introduces a strong dose of reality through his imaginary friend.

Although Twain was using Brown as a voice of his more negative opinions of the islands, Twain the narrator also was regularly forthright in the letters. When he takes an interisland schooner to another island, he notes the "dim lamp" in his cramped quarters and the "nauseous odors of bilge water," as well as the rat that gallops over him. Then he notices on his pillow "cockroaches as large as peach leaves—fellows with long, quivering antennae and fiery, malignant eyes" that "were grating their teeth like tobacco worms" and had a reputation for "eating off sleeping sailors' toenails down to the quick and I would not get in the bunk anymore." He says he is not telling this "to be spicy" but to "give a truthful sketch."[45]

Perhaps the account from the islands that stood out above all others was his scoop of what had happened when the clipper ship *Hornet* burned at sea. The subhead in the *Union* said, "Detailed Account of the Sufferings of Officers and Crew, AS given by the Third Officer and Members of the Crew," and that's just what Twain gave his readers: a "detailed account" of how the fire started and how the captain and crew abandoned ship into three longboats.[46] Only one longboat made it to land, coming ashore on the island of Hawaii after forty-three days at sea, its fifteen men starving and sick. When the men were hospitalized, Twain was laid up in Honolulu with painful saddle blisters from exploring the island of Hawaii on horseback. The newly appointed minister to China, Anson Burlingame, arranged for Twain to be carried to the recovering shipwrecked men on their cots and Burlingame asked them questions as Twain took down their stories, principally that of the third mate's. Twain said he wrote his account of the burning and sinking ship and the ordeal of the men quickly so that he could get it on the next boat to San Francisco.[47]

In the article, Twain describes the hunger and thirst of the men, their attempts to catch fish and birds, their despair, the pains of extreme hunger that caused the men to eat portions of canvas, the shavings of a turtle shell, and pieces of boots and clothing. Although they didn't speak openly of it, Twain said the men individually thought that a man who had been sick before the fire and was near death would be eaten when he died. The man survived. While readers were fascinated with the details of the survival, Twain's tale was not simply a factual accounting of surviving a shipwreck. It also was a tale of courage and endurance, and of kindness and generosity among the men, with the captain emerging as a genuine leader and hero who had earned the devotion and affection of his men. Twain also took journals of the captain and of two brothers who were passengers on the *Hornet* and provided context and commentary by framing the journal entries with an introduction and a conclusion, thereby creating a more detailed and unified narrative that was published in *Harper's Monthly* in December 1866 as "Forty-Three Days in an Open Boat" with a subhead, "Compiled from Personal Diaries."[48] In his introduction, Twain wrote that "The plain, matter-of-fact journal" of one of the survivors, a passenger, "was as interesting to me as a novel, notwithstanding I knew all the circumstances of the desperate voyage in the open boat before I read it." In giving readers a plain tale of a recent real event in the voice of the participants, Twain perhaps pushed as close to actuality as possible, and this lost-at-sea report, which required no exaggeration to document and bring to life the sensational experience of the survivors, is a stark contrast to the remainder of the Sandwich Island articles with their humor, exaggeration, and satire. One is marked by keen storytelling skills characterized by revealing detail that captures a felt sense of human peril and suffering; the other relies on scene-setting, vivid descriptions, strong point of view, and the divergent observations of two traveling companions, Twain the narrator/reporter and Brown, his rather crude but straightforward pal. Yet both types of depiction are strong, original expressions of the realistic sensibility.

When Twain returned from the Sandwich Islands, the popularity of his series for the *Union* allowed him to go on the lecture circuit, beginning another aspect of his public communication that would be important to him for the remainder of his life. Eager to leave California and ready to do more travel writing, he secured an agreement with the San Francisco's *Alta California* newspaper to write a weekly article or letter and left the city and California in December 1866. By June 1867, he was sailing with a party of Americans to tour Europe and the Middle East, paid for the by the *Alta,* which in the coming months would publish the "Special Travelling Correspondent's" accounts that would make up a significant portion of *The Innocents Abroad; or The New Pilgrim's Progress.* Often overlooked or dismissed, however, are articles he sent to the *Alta* from the time of his arrival in New York (around January 12, 1867) until his departure for Europe on June 8. He gave accounts of his walks around New York as well as visits to the theater, opera, and lectures through mid-March, when he visited his family in St. Louis and sent letters from there. He was sending letters from New York again by mid-April, although at first they dealt primarily with his visits to Keokuk and Hannibal, where he had lectured after seeing his family in St. Louis. While in New York, Twain had no specific job to go to so he spent much of his time strolling the city daily, a genuine flaneur, and his reports and sketches of walking and observing the city place him within the American flaneur tradition. Because of that, and because these articles are seldom discussed and not as well known as much of Twain's other writing, they merit further consideration here.

As he told readers in his first piece from New York, "I room in East Sixteenth street, and I walk," and he walks "from there to anywhere else" because the omnibuses are too slow.[49] Twain had worked as a printer in New York in 1853 and at first his letters consisted of comparing then and now, including giving a detailed accounting of how much more expensive New York had become. To a certain extent, Twain's accounts of his jaunts about town are similar to those of Foster as flaneur, but most of Twain's articles, while having a strong perspective, are lacking Foster's depth and detail. Some of his observations, however, are quite perceptive. For instance, he notes that the "model artist" shows, which Foster had written about as a way for men to view naked women and which Twain had apparently visited when he was in New York in 1853, have been changed to a "Grand Spectacular Drama" and are "the wickedest show you can think of" but have become acceptable and just another form of entertainment. He goes into extensive detail, noting, for instance, "seventy beauties in Dazzling half-costumes; and displaying all possible compromises between nakedness and decency. . . . Beautiful bare-legged girls hanging in flower baskets; others stretched in groups on great sea shells, others clustered around fluted columns; others in all possible attitudes; girls—nothing but a wilderness of girls—stacked up, pile on pile."[50]

In another dispatch, he comments on the emerging gap between rich and poor, but doesn't depict it in the way that others, including Davis, would do:

They have increased the population of New York and its suburbs a quarter of a million souls. They have built up her waste places with acres of costly buildings. They have made five thousand men wealthy, and for a good round million of her citizens they have made it a matter of the closest kind of scratching to get along in the several spheres of life to which they belong. The brown-stone fronter and rag-picker of the Five Points have about an even thing of it; the times are hard for one as for the other; both struggle desperately to hold their places, and both grumble and grieve to much the same tune. What advantage there is, though, is all in favor of the rag-picker—he can only starve or freeze, but the other can lose caste, which is worse.[51]

Parts of two other articles are especially interesting in that they more specifically and concretely capture a slice of urban life. In one letter, he describes what it was like to spend a night in jail after he and a friend tried to break up a fight but were taken to the Station House and placed in a cell until police court early the next morning. As he sits on a wooden bench in a "lock-up" partitioned from the courtroom, he describes the "rather haggard and sleepy" crowd of which he is a part, including "first-rate young fellows, and well dressed . . . one a clerk, one a college student, and one an Indiana merchant," an "old, seedy, scarred, bloated and bleeding bummer," "a negro man . . . with his head badly battered and bleeding profusely," a "bloated old hag . . . with a wholesome black eye, a drunken leer in the sound one, and nothing in the world on but a dingy calico dress, a shocking shawl, and a pair of slippers that had seen better days," who turns out to be from the notorious Five Points section of the city, and two "flash girls of sixteen and seventeen" who had been arrested for prostitution.[52] He also shared with his California readers his visit to the Blind

Asylum, which Whitman also visited and documented. It is one of his more focused New York articles, most of it devoted to the blind people he encounters, and much of the rest of the letter deals with the city's "boot-blacks." At one point, Twain goes into a "Boot-Black Brigade Chapel," where a preacher is, according to Twain, "under the extraordinary impression that he can save their souls." When the preacher tells the story of Lazarus being brought to life after being dead three days, Twain says that among the boot-blacks "there was a pretty general telegraphing of incredulity from eye to eye . . . and one boy with a shock head and rags all over to match nudged his neighbor, and said in a coarse whisper, 'I don't go that, Bill do you?—'cause he'd stink, wouldn't he?' When the preacher tells the story of the loaves and fishes, one of the boot-blacks says: 'Say, Jimmy, do you suck that?' The other boy replied: 'Wee, I do'no. It mought a ben, mebbe, if they warn't many of 'em hungry. I see the time, though, when I could a et them twelve laves myself, I could, less'n they was busters.'"[53] That Twain spends more time with the likes of the boot-blacks indicates their appeal, which he specifically identifies in language that would be appreciated by his California audience: "They are a wild, lawless, independent lot, those bootblacks and street boys, and would make good desperado stuff to stock a new mining camp with."[54] Huck Finn also would have recognized the boot-blacks and street boys as his brothers, and Foster would recognize the tone, detail, and slang that characterize several of Twain's sketches.

When Twain returned from his excursion across the Atlantic and decided to do a book version of the trip, he did not merely prepare the *Alta* letters for book publication; rather he revised, edited, and added some material from his notebooks, generally improving the clarity of the letters by eliminating California references so it would appeal to a wider audience and varied tastes, and by providing coherence by filling in gaps and providing transitions. Significantly, for instance, the Azores letter is the *Alta*'s first, while in the book, the Azores come at the end of chapter 5 and consist of all of chapter 6, thereby creating a more legitimate beginning of the story of the tour by introducing characters as the ship departs and sails the Atlantic. Twain used his notebooks as well as the notes and publications of others to create new material for his book version. Essentially, however, the journalism was not jettisoned but instead was further shaped, built upon, and developed. He created a more unified narrative and more coherent characters, but he still made extensive use of the *Alta* reports, frequently repeating passages and entire paragraphs verbatim. Some chapters in *Innocents* consist almost entirely of one or more *Alta* letters, but Twain did not repeat a single *Alta* report word-for-word. Often, his changes merely improved diction or style.

The general consensus is that Twain toned down some of the letters' cruder or harsher passages, and for the most part that is true but there are significant exceptions. For instance, in the Azores section the negative depictions of the Azores' Portuguese people, as with so many of the people the tourists encounter on their tour, are presented negatively in both the letters and the book, and the book's language is even a bit harsher than that of the letters. For instance, in the letters, Twain describes the Portuguese boatmen as a "swarm . . . dark-skinned, piratical," and people on the wharf as beggars who are "bare-footed and ragged and dirty vagabonds." In the *Innocents Abroad,* some of the exact language is used but he adds "swarthy, noisy, lying . . . with brass rings in their ears, and fraud in their hearts," and they are "ragged, and barefoot, uncombed and unclean, and by instinct, education, and profession, beggars" as well as "vermin."[55] Distance and reflection do not change his assessment of the "eminently Portuguese community." In both the letters and the book, the Portuguese remain "slow, poor, shiftless, sleepy and lazy."[56] Some changes, however, made the book prose less specific and insipid, but less offensive. For instance, describing priests in Genoa in an *Alta* article, he says: "They are all fat and greasy. They would try out well. The generality of them would yield oil like a whale." In the book, he simply says, "They are all fat and serene."[57]

Twain's negativity is a result of his somewhat complex role as narrator. Twain is a writer depicting Europe as any American might see it on such a trip. At times he is somewhat superior, other times naïve, but always relying on his own observations rather than the fancy guidebook descriptions of the places he visits, puncturing holes in myth, legend, and unearned reputation and uncritical renown through vivid description, satire, humor, and exaggeration. He has no patience with the countless Europeans and Middle Easterners who make a living off of misleading, using, and taking advantage of heedless American tourists. In the book's preface, Twain says that the "purpose" of *The Innocents Abroad* is "to suggest to the reader how *he* would be likely to see Europe and the East if he looked at them with his own eyes instead of the eyes of those who travelled in those countries before him," and he says that he has "seen with impartial eyes, and I am sure I have written at least honestly, whether wisely or not."[58]

Some Twain scholars have tended to see *Innocents* primarily as a satirical critique of a culture and world that was "largely a sham, the nature of which had been meretriciously falsified by the travelers who had preceded him (Twain) as well as by the guides on the spot," as one has put it.[59] But scholars also have focused on the book's satirical depiction of and critique of the nature of touring and American tourists. But in the end, regardless of what one considers its primary focus, Twain satirizes both the people and sites on the tour, which never match expectations, nor the claims of previous travelers or the many published accounts, and he satirizes the tourists in his party, especially those only too willing to mouth the opinions and praises of those guidebooks and previous visitors regardless of the actuality they encounter. In Milan, Twain and his compatriots go to see Leonardo da Vinci's "The Last Supper" and he notes how people come "from all parts of the world" to "glorify this masterpiece," and when they stand before the painting "with bated breath and parted lips," they speak "in the catchy ejaculations of rapture." He then lists ten of those "catchy" phrases, such as "O, wonderful" and "Such grace of attitude!" "A vision! A vision!" But for Twain, the painting is a "mournful wreck" that is "battered and scarred in every direction, and stained and discolored by time;" its "colors are dimmed with age; the countenances are scaled and marred, and nearly all expression is gone from them . . . there is no life in the eyes." Twain wonders, "How can they see what is not visible?" A bit later, he concludes:

> You would think that those men had an astonishing talent for seeing things that had already passed away. It was what I thought when I stood before the Last Supper and heard men apostrophizing wonders, and beauties and perfections which had faded out of the picture and gone, a hundred years before they were born. We can imagine the beauty that was once in an aged face; we can imagine the forest if we see the stumps; but we can not absolutely *see* these things when they are not there.[60]

What is particularly significant in this passage and in *The Innocents* generally is not just Twain's questioning of myth, legend, and the ideal, but his persistent advocacy of and belief in the personal observation of things—and life—as they are rather than as they should be, making Twain not just a practitioner of the real and actual but a critical voice as well.

Twain's satirical focus as a journalist on what he had observed and experienced in Nevada, California, the Sandwich Islands, New York, and touring abroad clearly places him in company with several twentieth-century literary journalists, such as James Agee in "Havana Cruise," A. J. Liebling in *The Earl of Louisiana,* or Lillian Ross in "The Yellow Bus." His work is also akin to some of Tom Wolfe's shorter pieces—such as "The Girl of the Year," "The Woman Who Has Everything," or his Las Vegas article—and especially the works of Hunter S. Thompson. Like the aforementioned twentieth-century writers, Twain the reportorial writer and storyteller produced journalism and nonfiction that was pictorial; his "characters were realistic, his voice impudent and unregenerate, but his spirit humane."[61] Twain's journalistic articles from the Sandwich Islands, Europe, and to a far lesser extent from New York, all have an interpretative quality that could justify their being labeled as literary journalism. It is easy to agree with Nelson's assessment that "Twain's travel accounts offer such a panorama of unforgettable characters, zestful narrative, yarn-spinning and humorous exaggeration, unbridled optimism, striking observation, wry comment, and richness of imagery and metaphor that they stand as hallmarks of participatory journalism even today."[62] Certainly, that case could be made convincingly for *The Innocents Abroad.* But it also has been made for Twain's next book, *Roughing It,* considered by Nelson to be Twain's "finest literary reportage."[63]

Roughing It is an account of Twain's Western experiences from 1861 to 1865, though it wasn't started until 1870 and not published until 1872, as Twain and his publisher tried to capitalize on Twain's soaring popularity after the remarkable success of *The Innocents*

Abroad. While *Roughing It* recreates the reality of the Western experience at a particular time with Twain's typical humor, satire, and exaggeration, and comes alive through dialogue and dialect, detailed scenes and incidents, and a range of characters and types that together define a region, it is not based on Twain's more recent observation and experience. It is largely constructed from Twain's memory of places, people, and events, on newspaper clippings from the period, and on a scrapbook that his brother had kept of their travels. In order to fill out the book, Twain tacked on sixteen chapters in the last third of the book based on his excursion and stay in the Sandwich Islands. As with much of Twain's nonfiction, it mixes fact and fancy, but is solidly grounded in the actual—real people and places—that are built upon and made meaningful through interpretation. While it could be considered a form of literary journalism very broadly defined, it clearly is more than a "travel book" or a memoir. As one Twain scholar has declared, *Roughing It* is also "a fictionalized autobiography, an extended tall story, a sketch book of people and places, and at least in the first half, a picaresque novel."[64] Twain himself called it "a personal narrative," as well as "a record of several years of variegated vagabondizing" that contains "quite a good deal of information."[65]

Although a recognizable Twain style existed by 1870, Twain's first piece for the *Atlantic Monthly* reveals his willingness to experiment with point of view and narrative structure and is a rare instance for this stage of his career in that he wasn't satirical or humorous, but somewhat sentimental. It is a small example of Twain and Davis intersecting in tone and theme. Titled "A True Story, Repeated Word for Word as I Heard It," it involves two characters: the white narrator, seemingly Twain, and the black cook, Aunt Rachel, actually Mary Ann Cord, the cook at a farm near Elmira, New York, where Twain and his family lived in 1871. Aunt Rachel had once been a slave but she is good-natured and full of laughter. She and the narrator are sitting on the porch on a summer evening and the man asks her how she has managed to have no troubles in her sixty years. She says, "Misto C____, is you in 'arnest?" The man is surprised and says he's never heard her even sigh, and she starts to tell her story: "Has I had any trouble? Misto C____, I's gwyne to tell you, den I leave it to you," and most of the remainder of the story is Aunt Rachel telling in her slang and dialect of how she had been a slave, how her owner was forced to sell all her slaves in auction, putting Aunt Rachel, her husband, and her children in chains and splitting them up for sale, including her youngest, Henry. Thirteen years later, while cooking for union soldiers, she's inadvertently reunited with Henry, and Twain ends the tale with Aunt Rachel saying, "Oh, no, Misto C____, I hain't had no trouble. An' no joy!"[66] It would be Twain's first solid attempt to sympathetically and authentically depict blacks. It rings true because Aunt Rachel convincingly displays human qualities recognizable to any reader, particularly the strong emotional ties of a mother and child and the longing for family and children. A year after it was published, William Dean Howells, editor of the *Atlantic,* referred to the "rugged truth of the sketch" and called it a "dramatic report of reality which we have seen equaled in no other American writer." "A True Story," Howells claimed, was "a study of character as true as life itself, strong, tender, and most movingly pathetic in its perfect fidelity to the tragic fact."[67] Howells's enthusiasm should not mask the significance of his assessment and his use of Twain to support and advocate for writing drawn from real life. If his claim that such realism has never been equaled seems hyperbolic today, his description of it as a "dramatic report of reality" does not. The brief sketch consists of writing based on an actual, ordinary person whose story illustrates an aspect of an extraordinary issue that in its transcription-like telling calls into question popular views, including the stereotype of the happy, carefree slave or "negro."

Davis's story of a trip through the South was illustrated by William Hamilton Gibson, the popular nature artist, who did the landscapes and buildings, and W. H. Drake, whose vivid, realistic sketches of newly freed slaves are poignant and strikingly in contrast to many of Gibson's detailed but idyllic landscapes. For some time, it had become standard in many publications to provide drawings of scenes from stories but it increasingly became common to illustrate fiction and nonfiction with sketches of real, current places and people, whether a street scene of Mobile, a mountain cabin, or a group of blacks by the roadside, as in "Here and There In the South." Had Twain's sketch of Aunt Rachel appeared in any number of other publication besides *Atlantic,* such as *Harper's Monthly* or *Scribner's,* for example, it is highly likely that the piece would have had at least one illustration since by the 1870s most magazines were starting to illustrate both fiction and nonfiction and by the 1880s most publications were not just depicting people and places in words, but were also allowing readers to "see" those people and places in wood-engraved illustrations, further privileging the sense of the real and actual through timely and often graphic visual depictions. This shift to employing more and more visual depictions to capture the actual was led by the illustrated weeklies.

FIVE

PICTURING THE PRESENT

In July 1868, readers of *Harper's Weekly* saw a version of Rebecca
Harding Davis's "slow stream of human life," as she described her
mill workers moving to and from the mill, in a dramatic full-page
illustration by Winslow Homer, "New England Factory Life—
'Bell-Time.'" Although not the iron mill workers of Davis's story,
Homer's illustration depicted a mass of factory workers at "bell-
time"—the end of the working day—leaving the mill. Men and
women of various ages, and children as well, plodding home, a
walk they would have taken six days a week after working at the
mill ten to thirteen hours each day. Some faces look blank, perhaps expressing an inner emptiness, while others look haggard,
tired, and grim; the drawn face of a bent old woman and the sad,
forlorn face of a much younger woman walking next to her stand
out from the others. All carry their food "buckets." An item on
a separate page titled "New England Factory Life" tells readers
that the scene captured by Homer is of workers "wending their
way home" from the Washington Mills, which employed 2,500
"operatives" in Lawrence, Massachusetts.[1]

A major impetus toward the visual came from the illustrated

weeklies such as *Frank Leslie's Illustrated Newspaper,* later called *Leslie's Illustrated Weekly,* and *Harper's Weekly: A Journal of Civilization.* Whether in prose or pictures, these periodicals were documenting changes in society. The documentation, however, was selective and either validated a type of existing reality or constructed from observed actuality new or modified versions of reality. Of course, as with prose sketches, articles, and stories, the illustrations of actual people, events, and activities presented the artists' and wood engravers' versions of those people, events, and activities.

Leslie's was first published in December 1855 and *Harper's Weekly* first came out in January 1857. Frank Leslie had managed the engraving department at the *Illustrated London News* before coming to America, and his New York publication was clearly modeled after it, as was *Harper's Weekly,* although its creation also was influenced by *Leslie's,* despite significant differences between the two. Right from the start, *Leslie's* focused on current news events, essentially establishing visual images as a "significant reporting tool."[2] *Harper's Weekly,* however, tended to emphasize political news, issues, and events, or essentially the topics that weren't significantly covered in *Harper's Monthly.* Its illustrations until the start of the Civil War largely consisted of public men as well as landscapes, scenery, ships, and specific activities, such as a man training his horse or a couple strolling an avenue. Although heavily illustrated, such publications were still filled with text. For example, while *Harper's Weekly* always had a large sketch on the cover page of the publication and at least two full pages of illustrations with captions inside, most issues of the sixteen-page weekly had at least four to six pages of solid text and no illustrations, with the last two to three pages consisting of advertising that contained a few small, standard illustrations to go with an ad, which meant that half the publication's pages had no illustrations. The second, third, and sometimes the fourth page contained columns of commentary, as well as news and information on "Domestic Intelligence," "Foreign News," or columns on topics titled "Literary" and "Humors of the Day," among others, including George William Curtis's column, "The Lounger," a commentary on arts and manners. Fiction and poetry were common on other pages. While *Leslie's* also had pages solid with text and no illustrations, consisting of commentaries, editorials, and brief reports, it more regularly joined sketches and text to report recent news events. It sometimes seemed to be a visual supplement to the daily penny papers, while at other times seemed first cousin to the *National Police Gazette.*[3]

Harper's Weekly, Leslie's, and others like them were unique to their time and played a significant role in ushering in new expectations for experiencing events, people, and life being lived through popular publications. *Harper's Weekly's* editors promised in the first edition to "present an accurate and complete picture of the age in which we live," while Frank Leslie claimed in his publication's first issue that by "seizing promptly and illustrating the passing events of the day" his publication would provide "actuality" that would only further enhance "the record of events."[4] A year later, Leslie said an illustrated publication "of a high order" had become "a necessity to the reading public" and that *Leslie's* was giving the public a "history recorded not only in language, but made attractive by truthful illustrations" that would provide the best possible picture of "American events, American life, and American associations."[5] While the focus on timely news distinguished *Leslie's* from *Harper's, Leslie's* also made efforts to constantly remind readers of the authenticity and accuracy of its images. Besides commenting on the role and efforts of its artists, *Leslie's* also first placed the artist at the scene by having the artist include himself in some sketches. Before the Civil War, this happened most prominently in *Leslie's* crusade against the "swill milk" industry, when the publication's chief artist, Albert Berghaus, appeared in several illustrations sketching the scene depicted, thereby validating the authenticity of the scene.[6] When it was clear that the illustrated weekly would thrive, *Leslie's* declared in 1856 that it would continue to "reflect, like a faithful mirror . . . the living, active world, in miniature."[7]

Leslie's tended to be more sensational, whether the sensation involved fictional tales or tales of actual events. For instance, one week in 1857 the cover of *Leslie's* screamed the title of a fictional serialization: "The Night Shriek or, the Stolen Will, A Tale of New Orleans by Mrs. J. D. Baldwin of that City." That and the beginning of the story took up the top half of the page while the bottom half contained a sketch of a scene from the story.[8] Several inside pages were dominated by a real news story, a murder headlined, "Mysterious Murder, Eminent Citizen Assassinated." Illustrations of the murder coverage included the victim's body in its coffin, with the coffin in the sitting room of the victim's home, where the murder occurred. There were also detailed diagrams of the rooms of the home, of police guarding the premises, and another of the victim in his coffin, but this one was a close-up featuring the chest and head. In a commentary, *Leslie's* bragged about its full coverage of the crime, and noted what readers could see: "the murdered man lies upon the floor, he is seen placed in his coffin, even his heart, as it presented itself with the fatal wounds, is visible for examination." *Leslie's* had, the editorial declared, satisfied "the eager public desire to examine, to see for themselves." Overall, it bragged, the publication had provided "the most perfect combination of word and picture detail of a fearful event that was ever issued by the press."[9]

Illustrations had accompanied fictional accounts in publications and generalized sketches of buildings or landscapes had been common for some time, but the illustrated publications clearly brought focus to things as they are rather than as they might be or should be or as they appear solely in a work of the imagination, even when that present was shaped by the imagination, popular sentiment, or common beliefs and values. Focusing on the present did not mean that the illustrations were fully accurate reproductions or that, for instance, Homer's picture of mill workers at the end of the day was an *exact* replication of what bell time looked like when Homer was there, or that Leslie's depiction of a train collision that occurred on a February night in 1871 in New Hamburg, a Hudson River community north of New York City, had the exact angle of a burning train plunging into the river, or that the passengers who survived ran from the train *exactly* as shown. But it does mean that in both cases these were real places, real people, and real events, which distinctly contrasts with most published visual illustrations from the previous generation and prior to the 1850s in the United States. The tired mill workers, from children to old men and women, did indeed get off work en masse at 6 P.M. at the Washington Mills in Lawrence, Massachusetts, and a twenty-five-car freight train consisting mostly of filled oil tank cars going south toward New York City did indeed collide with a passenger train going north from the city, causing a burning sleeper car to plunge into the water when the bridge collapsed. Just as the illustration shows, passengers escaped from two other cars.[10] The very process that involved the artist at the site, the wood engraver reproducing an artist's sketch that was often done on the run, sometimes with notes from the artist to the engraver to add more horses, more trees, and so forth, and the editor deciding on placement and captions, would naturally guarantee that the illustration was probably not an entirely accurate representation, but a close approximation. At times, the illustration came from reconstructing incidents and events after the fact. After coverage of an Atlantic shipwreck, for instance, *Leslie's* stated that "Most of these scenes so pictured are real: others are pictorial reprints of authentic statements and descriptions, whereby our artists have caught and transfixed the reports of the telegraph."[11]

The Hudson Valley train wreck is just one example of why one historian of *Leslie's* claims that first *Leslie's* and then the other illustrated periodicals "called into being a new profession, that of the pictorial journalist, or artist-reporter."[12] Frederic Hudson, writing in 1873, also referred to these publications as "news pictorially reported and described." In the first paragraph of his chapter on "The Illustrated Papers" he provides a contemporary perspective on the role and impact of the illustrated publications:

> Illustrated papers have become a feature. Every newspaper stand is covered with them. Every railroad train is filled with them. They are "object-teaching" to the multitude. They make the battlefields, the coronations, the corruptions of politicians, the balls, the racecourse, the yacht race, the military and naval heroes, Napoleon and William, Bismarck and Von Beust, Farragut and Porter, Grant and Sherman, familiar to every one. They are, in brief, the art gallery of the world. Single admission, ten cents.[13]

The timely visual coverage of the illustrated publications was a new form of cultural communication that created an even greater sense of immediacy and a distinct kind of accessibility to current events, to people and to activities *beyond* the reader's neighborhood or workplace, yet at the same time they often documented goings-on or conditions *in* a reader's neighborhood or workplace. The range of illustrated items, in fact, was far greater than noted by Hudson, who doesn't mention, for instance, depictions of crowded railway stations, lunchrooms, markets, jails, the poor and the laboring class, marches, rallies, and riots, to name just a few. Even a cursory look through the illustrated publications from the late 1850s through the 1880s reveals extensive evidence for one art historian's claim that popular illustrated publications such as *Scribner's Monthly, Harper's Weekly,* and *Leslie's* "were filled with scenes portraying everything from blast furnaces and bridge building to train wrecks and natural disasters" and such illustrations were often praised by critics for their "vitality, originality, and *national* character."[14] The "bridge building" included depictions of the construction of what would become an icon, the Brooklyn Bridge, which took thirteen years to complete, from 1870 to 1883. When finished, it was the longest suspension bridge in the world and considered to be a technological wonder. *Harper's Weekly* and *Leslie's* visually documented the bridge's construction over that thirteen-year period, even depicting the mass panic on the bridge on Memorial Day, a week after the opening, when many in a crowd of bridge sightseers thought the bridge was collapsing.[15] Alan Trachtenberg has noted that in the nineteenth century photographs came to be viewed as "a way of bringing the distant near and making the strange familiar."[16] The same could be said for the sketches, or wood engravings, of the weeklies and magazines.

The range of illustrated coverage of the illustrated magazines is hinted at in a collection of illustrations, *New York in the Nineteenth Century,* which contains 321 illustrations that ran primarily in *Harper's Weekly* but also in *Leslie's* and the short-lived *Illustrated News.* These "views of New York life," as they are described in the introduction, are grouped under categories rather than chronologically or by publication: Memorable Events, Daily Life, Sports and Pastimes, Popular Entertainments and Cultural Life, Politics, City

Services, Business and Commerce, the Waterfront and the Harbor, Transportation. Even within those categories the range of content varied significantly. For instance, under Sports and Pastimes occur depictions of horse racing, polo, gambling, dog shows, horse shows, lacrosse, baseball, swimming in a "public bath," college football, boat races, ice skating, tennis, steamer excursions, beach gatherings and picnics, parades, opera, clamming, amusement park rides, dancing, and so on. Daily Life depictions include May Day celebrations, scenes at the train station, auctions, diners at lunch, a beer hall in the Bowery, inside the Lawyers Club, newsboys passing time, activity at a pawnshop, homeless men sleeping on the basement floor of a police station, encampments of the poor, homeless children warming themselves at a steam grating, rag-pickers plodding through the city, tenement life in a heat wave, opium smokers in a Chinese clubhouse, summer on Broadway, a funeral parade. All of that and more naturally gave readers a stronger connection to the present and to actuality but also to significantly emerging class distinctions.[17] An illustration of an event that occurred recently or depictions of buildings, streets, and places actual and current, existing scenes of poverty and of wealth, all called attention to the real and immediate at the expense of the ideal, the imaginary, or the historical. In fact, these publications generally believed that they were documenting history as it happened and therefore contributing to the historical record.

That quality of immediacy became particularly striking during the Civil War when circulation of both *Leslie's* and *Harper's Weekly* climbed significantly as they filled each issue with news of the war by visually depicting battles, camp life, combat, and home front activities and incidents. Visual images of American life were readily available before and during the war from a number of picture publishers, the largest being Currier and Ives. These pictures were sold for as little as five cents in bookshops and from street hawkers. Most of them sentimentalized life and romanticized war, with many of the scenes from the Revolutionary War, created by artists who had never participated in battle as either an observer or a soldier.[18] At the start of the Civil War many of the images in *Harper's Weekly* and *Leslie's* seemed to be stock war depictions, with little to distinguish them and with a tendency to prefer "stereotyped heroics," as one historian has put it.[19] Even though *Leslie's* was used to depicting dramatic events as they unfolded in a style based on "hair-raising thrills and sensational crusades" and was therefore more likely to portray war's violence than *Harper's,* it nevertheless tended to depict war as the classical, academically trained painters had done, with battlefields as a vista or armies gallantly clashing.[20] Furthermore, these images couldn't always be counted upon to depict what actually happened. When Union forces were routed at Bull Run, for instance, readers of both *Harper's Weekly* and *Leslie's* saw scenes of heroism and courage, with Alfred Waud of *Harper's* showing the soldiers' retreat as an orderly withdrawal rather than ragged and panic-stricken as it really was, which was how Arthur Lundley sketched it for *Leslie's.* As the war progressed and as the artists/illustrators saw more of the soldiers and the battle sites, the images were, for the most part, more clearly grounded in actuality rather than in artists' renditions of historical battles and wars in which they had little to no experience. At the conclusion of the war, in a commentary titled "Our Artists During the War," *Harper's Weekly* raved over the role and impact of its illustrators, declaring that the nation owed a "national debt" to the war's illustrators, claiming that "thousands and thousands of the faces and events which the war has made illustrious are tacked and pinned and pasted upon the humblest walls" in homes all across the country. They provided, *Harper's* said, a "pictorial history of the war which they have written with their pencils in the field . . . a history quivering with life, faithful, terrible, romantic, the value of which will grow with every year." What the artists specifically captured was "the fierce shock, the heaving tumult, the smoky sway of battle from side to side, the line, the assault, the victory—they were a part of all, and their faithful fingers, depicting the scene, have us a part also." Similarly, Leslie said his artists were "avant couriers of history," and that *Leslie's* illustrations provided "a complete Pictorial History of the War."[21]

Although the *Harper's* commentary mentioned a number of the illustrators by name, it did not note Homer. Other war artists, such as Alfred Waud or Theodore R. Davis, were better known and more productive over the entire length of the war. Yet of all the Civil War illustrators, Homer became the best known and most highly regarded as an artist.[22] His sketching for publication, however, started several years before the war, with *Ballou's Pictorial Drawing Room Companion* in Boston, and he continued to illustrate for popular publications after the war, primarily *Harper's Weekly* and *Every Saturday,* but also fiction in *Galaxy.*[23] Most of his war sketches for *Harper's Weekly,* particularly those done in the first couple years of the war, were very similar in tone and type to other war sketches appearing in the publication, and suffered from the same limitations. For instance, Homer's "The Surgeon at the Rear during an Engagement," which ran in the *Weekly* in June 1862, shows wounded soldiers receiving prompt attention from a surgeon and his team, an ambulance wagon quickly bringing the wounded from the front to receive individual treatment. The scene, of course, has all the trappings of authenticity, but one critic insists that the illustration is "a gross distortion of fact intended to reassure that . . . the Union soldier was receiving care worthy of his sacrifice."[24] While the sketch definitely dealt with recent

events and presented realistic figures—wounded soldiers and a
surgeon and his assistants—it very much stretched reality because
casualties were very high and the wounded were not attended to
so easily and quickly, with many lying unattended on the battlefields for hours and even days. Some were simply abandoned. But
by running the sketch, *Harper's Weekly* called attention to the crucial role of the field surgeon. In a column headed "The Army of
the Potomac," *Harper's* said that the surgeon sketch was intended
to introduce readers "to the most painful scene on the battlefield,"
and explained that in tying arteries, closing wounds, setting broken
limbs, and performing amputations "within sight and sound of
the cannon," the surgeon was "often one who requires the most
nerve and the most courage." The commentary also alluded to the
authenticity of Homer's illustrations when it noted that Homer
had "spent some time with the army of the Potomac, and drew
his figures from life."[25] Each issue of *Harper's Weekly* contained
some discussion of several of the war sketches so that words and
pictures were made to work together to present a distinct version
of the war and its participants. Also, as the war progressed, the
illustrated weeklies became more willing to visually depict the
results of battle, running sketches that showed soldiers searching
for the dead and wounded or burying the dead.

Many of Homer's illustrations were distinctive, particularly
when they focused on individual scenes or specific instances rather
than busy battle scenes and formations. A sampling of tone and
content in Homer's work can be seen in a June 1862 issue of
Harper's Weekly that contains a two-page spread of six of Homer's
illustrations called "News from the War." Included is an "authen-
ticating" drawing of Alfred Waud sitting on a barrel while he
sketches three soldiers standing at attention while other soldiers
look on, with the caption "Our Special Artist." But two of the

most compelling sketches involve the war's personal pain. One is of a woman clearly grieving over the death of a loved one. She is sitting at a table in her home, slumped over with her head down, a letter hanging from her fingertips. Although somewhat familiar, if not a cliché, the image nevertheless highlights a consequence of war. Another sketch shows two returning soldiers standing on a street corner in Richmond. One soldier has an amputated leg and stands on crutches; the other has an arm in a sling, with a hand either fully bandaged or missing. They watch a stylish young woman walk by who looks straight ahead, seemingly ignoring them. A well-dressed couple has already passed, and a black woman, carrying a basket of vegetables on her head glances their way. A touch of both realism and irony emerges behind and above the two soldiers where a sign says "Cavalry" and depicts a man on horseback with a drawn sword.[26]

Homer's experiences as an illustrator, and his sketches from the war front, formed the basis of his early artistic works as he began to build a reputation as a painter of the common and everyday. Relatively early in the war *Harper's Weekly* ran a Homer illustration called "The Army of the Potomac—A Sharp-Shooter on Picket Duty." The illustration was actually based on one of Homer's first oil paintings, although it wasn't completed when he did the sketch. The painting came from his experience with the Army of the Potomac's Peninsula Campaign in southeastern Virginia. The completed oil painting is simply called *Sharpshooter* and, along with *The Bright Side* (1865), *Prisoners from the Front* (1866), *Halt of the Wagon Train* (1866), and *The Veteran in a New Field* (1865), is among a number of highly regarded renderings that emerged from Homer's work as a war illustrator for *Harper's Weekly*. *Sharpshooter* is the only one of these paintings that deals directly with the war's killing or fighting.[27]

A version of *Halt of the Wagon Train* also appeared in *Harper's Weekly,* but the publication illustration was done before the painting. The *Harper's Weekly* sketches for each of these contain more detail and more information than the paintings. For instance, the *Halt of the Wagon Train* rendering for publication captures a moment of active rest and repose of an army supply wagon and is crowded with men around a campfire in the foreground, with one man standing and waving a long fork in the air as though he is calling the others to supper; whips, horse collars, cups, and crates litter the ground near the men. Mules are to the side behind the men, and more mules are nearer a fading line of covered wagons that are in the background. At least three additional groups of men appear in different parts of the scene. The sketch is busy with detail. The painting, however, is stripped of so much detail. One man has replaced thirteen in the foreground and he's calmly leaning against a pole and smoking a pipe. An indistinct group of five men, similar to a group that had been in the center of the illustration, are lounging in the middle of the painting, seemingly fully relaxed; the covered wagons, fewer in number, still form a fading line across the painting but they also are at the center and very close to the men. Half the number of men appear in the painting compared to the illustration. The illustration would seem to depict a typical wagon train stop and attempts to show the range of men doing different things during this "halt," including sleeping, getting warm, eating or preparing food, swapping tales, smoking, arguing, and so forth. There is much to look at and to catch a reader's attention. Homer is essentially reporting what he has seen, capturing a moment in the wagon train's journey, giving readers of *Harper's Weekly* the sense that they know what it's like at a supply wagon train camp. The painting, on the other hand, clearly shows a moment, but it is a more focused moment and its elements are unified to convey relaxation and lassitude.

A difference in purpose and theme is less evident in comparing the sharpshooter sketch and the sharpshooter painting. In the *Harper's* sketch, a canteen hangs on a branch near the shooter, who is in a tree, getting the attention of the reader almost immediately. The canteen tells readers that the shooter, this bird of prey, will wait patiently in his perch for his human target. The painting, however, has no canteen. The illustration also has a bit more clarity than the painting, as the shooter stands out from the surrounding tree branches whereas the shooter in the painting is part of the lush green of the branches. The shooting eye of the marksman, a "steely, glinting eye," can be seen in the illustration but not in the painting.[28] Yet both the periodical illustration and the oil painting convey an almost inhuman patience and a coldly calculating concentration, although the black-and-white illustration comes off harsher than the color painting. *Harper's Weekly* readers could see, at tree level, one of the infamous sharpshooters they had been hearing so much about; viewers of the painting wouldn't see the canteen, but would see an even more intense focus on the shooter and a sense of a "brutal elegance" in an image that remains an iconic symbol of the Civil War.[29] Comparing the two, illustration to painting, they clearly have a different purpose. The painting, after the fact and with time to shape and modify, allowed Homer to energize "the canvas by encapsulating imminent violence," as the curator of a Homer exhibit has put it.[30] Homer's intent was at least partially conveyed in a comment about sharpshooters in a letter he wrote in 1896: "I was not a soldier—but a camp follower & artist, the above impression (a sketch in the letter of a soldier in the gun-sight of a sharpshooter) struck me as being as near murder as anything I ever could think of in connection with the army & I always had a horror of that branch of the service."[31]

When an exhibition of Homer's Civil War paintings and sketches occurred in San Francisco in 1988, curator Marc Simpson said the drawings contained "a truthfulness derived from close observation" and that they testify to "Homer's keen powers of observation."[32] Simpson also said the paintings show "the commonplace activities and situations that Homer so faithfully described."[33] He notes a claim made in a 1944 Whitney Museum of Art exhibition book that "no other artist left so authentic a record of how the Civil War soldier looked and acted."[34] That contention echoed a comment from a Homer contemporary, art critic and author George W. Sheldon, who wrote regarding Homer as a painter, about twenty years after the war: "He paints what he has seen; he tells what he has felt; he records what he knows."[35] Thus, Homer as journalistic illustrator and as artistic painter found the source for both in the same material and embodied the impulse to depict the real and actual across forms of cultural expression in each form.

As already suggested, periodicals depicted a range of people and activities in pictures and prose, particularly in the years after the war; depictions of the urban poor and the working class, particularly factory workers, became more common although neither dominant nor ubiquitous. Mill workers' lives, such as those portrayed by Rebecca Harding Davis, had a place and a presence in various narratives and illustrations. By the 1870s, the sad scenes of prisoners at the Tombs described by George Foster in his urban sketches came to life in several drawings in *Harper's Weekly* while *Leslie's* readers could get a look at Five Points living conditions.[36] But it wasn't as though the illustrated weeklies or *The Atlantic Monthly* and other magazines were full of realistic fiction or timely pictures made from drawings and woodcuts that accurately captured city life or the lives of workers and immigrants. Nevertheless, while it may be an exaggeration to claim that the pictorial papers "unearthed the hidden horrors of poverty," the pictures of, say, homeless children warming themselves over a sidewalk grate did lend greater immediacy by more vividly and viscerally presenting what had been described in words for decades, thereby making the combination of the two—words and pictures—more striking, whether that combination created fear or sympathy. Even when there were depictions of the poor, however, they were often negative, particularly in *Leslie's*. The Five Points scene just mentioned, for instance, appeared on the cover with this cutline: "New York City.—Among the poor—A summer evening scene at the Five Points."[37]

It was not uncommon for illustrations to depict types, regardless of class, and that was the case in this sketch. The scene has an infant, two children, and three adults idling the day away amid trash and next to a pile of rubble; a fourth adult is a street vendor, who is talking with a barefoot boy, who may be too poor to buy the vendor's ice cream. The boy and the vendor were standard types for such street scenes, but so was the downcast mother holding an infant, the slumped over man (perhaps sleeping off a drunk), and the baby sitting on the ground sucking its thumb and being ignored. Most striking, however, is an unkempt man almost at the center of sketch, leaning against the building, smoking a pipe and staring right back at the viewer/reader. His stare is threatening and defiant and he appears dangerous, reinforcing a long-standing perspective of a Five Points tough, which would make him a gang member, a Tammany enforcer, or both.[38] The illustration's caption instructs the reader to "see Page 363," where there is a description of Five Points and the illustration. The written account, full

of inflated prose, reflects a common stereotype in its description
of Five Points as not simply a slum but also an evil place. The
brief piece says that the very words, *Five Points,* "seem, as they are
written, to redden with the blood-stains of unavenged crime," to
the point that just tracing the words yields "murder in every syl-
lable, and Want, Misery and Pestilence take startling form." Even
the air around this "world of wretchedness," around this "Slough
of Despond should be heavy with restless spirits of suicides, of the
assassin's unprepared victims, of infants stifled ere they could feel
the breath of heaven, of broken-hearted mothers, of despairing
Magdalens." Only the police and the Sisters of Charity dare to
even enter this "City of Sin," according to *Leslie's,* which acknowledges that some improvements are apparent, such as a church to
finally lure "the besotted denizens of the Points from their reeking
cellars, from their filth-streaming rookeries," with the Jesuits dar-
ing to establish a church in "the camp of the Prince of Darkness."
While change is slow, the church, that "piloting lamp of Christ,"
will eventually be followed by industry and commerce, the "hand-
maidens of civilization." But for now, if missionaries had written
"entertaining sketches of 'Child Life at the Five Points,'" they
would be of "sad lives" with "short chapters." They would document lives that go "From Nowhere to a Gutter, from Gutter to a
Cell, from Cell to Court, and thence to the Tomb of the Living
or the Scaffold."[39] The written description dances around the root
problem of such poverty, suggesting that hope might come with a
combination of religious and commercial development. Especially
in *Leslie's*—although in other publications as well—the message of
such a depiction was clear: unfortunately, some of those living in
such awful conditions were part of the undeserving poor, facing
poverty and misery because of their own personal degradation and
immorality and therefore unworthy of either aid or sympathy.[40]

Eventually, photography would provide striking images of important news as well as compelling illustrations of poverty and need, but that wouldn't happen until the late 1890s as technology made it possible to reproduce photos in newspapers and magazines and photos replaced sketches and drawings as the principal form of visual communication. Nevertheless, photos played a role in illustrating the Civil War, as wood engravers at the illustrated weeklies used photographs to create images for publication.[41] Photographs from the war also were published in books after the war although they weren't very popular with a war-weary public that wanted to leave it behind.[42] But the stereograph and stereoscope as well as photo exhibitions also caught the attention of the public and of commentators who generally saw photography as the most accurate way to capture reality.

The response to photography beginning with the daguerreotype after the mid-nineteenth century, but especially after the Civil War, reflected the overall cultural demand for realistic depictions of American life and a remarkable faith among many that photographs could duplicate reality and preserve it. As early as 1839, when photos—or daguerreotypes—were first introduced, they were described as a mirror image and therefore real and truthful, and Edgar Allan Poe was quick to declare the daguerreotype "undoubtedly . . . the most important, and perhaps the most extraordinary triumph of modern science."[43] What made it so "important" and "extraordinary"? According to Poe, it produced images that disclosed "a more absolute truth, a more perfect identity of aspect with the thing represented" than a drawing could produce, and was, in fact, "infinitely more accurate in its representation." Poe compared the daguerreotype's picture to that in a "positively perfect mirror," which comes "as near the reality as any other means."[44] Across the culture, in a range of publications intended for various audiences, discussion of photography came to be characterized by a handful of representative words used by Poe: "reality," "mirror," "representation," "truth." The prevailing sensibility was that with the camera, "nature paints herself."[45]

About twenty years after Poe's declarations, Oliver Wendell Holmes, prominent essayist, poet, and physician, wrote three important and influential articles for the *Atlantic Monthly* in 1859, 1861, and 1863 in which he considered the impact and implications of photography and the stereoscope. In his first article, he called the daguerreotype "the mirror with a memory" because a photograph could document how people and places looked over time. What the photograph had done was fix "the most fleeting of our illusions, that which the apostle and the philosopher and the poet have alike used as the type of instability and unreality," wrote Holmes, adding, "the photograph has completed the triumph, by making a sheet of paper reflect images like a mirror and hold them as a picture."[46] Because so many seemed to consider photography's depictions absolutely true, a mirror of nature and life, even infallible, a belief "held with the irrational conviction of myth" despite any evidence to the contrary, as Trachtenberg has written, it clearly satisfied a strong cultural need.[47] This was clearly expressed by a Rev. H. J. Morton in an 1864 essay on "Photography as a Moral Agent" that appeared in an issue of *Philadelphia Photographer*:

> What we want in a witness are capacity and opportunity for accurate observation, and entire honesty. Now the camera of the Photographer has exactly these qualifications . . . it adds perfect freedom from all partiality and hypocrisy. It sees everything, and it represents just what it sees. It has an eye that cannot be deceived, and a fidelity that cannot be corrupted. . . . Hence the camera seeing with perfect accuracy and microscopic minuteness, and

representing with absolute fidelity, is a witness on whose testimony the most certain conclusions may be confidently founded.[48]

Morton also said that photography could be used to "perfect knowledge," but perhaps a bit more realistically he also said it "brings the world face to face with its great men, its orators, its poets, its statesmen, its heroes." Mathew Brady, a pathbreaking photographer because of his Civil War photographs, made his reputation before the war by essentially establishing the notion of the photographer as national historian through photographic portraiture, showing his portraits of famous Americans and typical citizens alike at popular galleries in New York and Washington. Years later, he would tell a newspaper reporter that right from the start he thought of himself as "under obligation to my country to preserve the faces of its historic men and mothers."[49] According to Holmes, photographic portraits were particularly revealing of the real character of a person. "There is no use in their putting on airs," he writes, "the make-believe gentleman and lady cannot look like the genuine article" in a photographic portrait. In fact, "the picture tells no lie" but shows "the social grade" of the person in the photo and also can reveal "mediocrity," the "ill-tempered," "anxiety," and those who are "infirm of purpose and vacuous of thought."[50] For Whitman, a visit to a daguerreotype gallery that attracted "crowds continually coming and going" to its floor-to-ceiling pictures was another form of strolling through the urban crowd, not because of the crowds of viewers but because of "*the* pictures . . . before all else." Writing in the *Brooklyn Eagle* about such a visit, he declared: "You will see more of *life* there—more variety, more human nature, more artistic beauty . . . than in any spot we know of." The "great legion of human faces," declared Whitman, are "speechless and motionless, but yet *realities.*"

Not only do viewers "identify the semblance with the reality," according to Whitman, but the eyes in a photographic portrait "sometimes goes beyond what comes from the real orbs themselves."[51] The images were better to Whitman than the people crowding the streets and markets of the city because he could gaze, stare, and look without being self-conscious. In his 1859 article, Holmes said that looking at a good photo through a stereoscope "is a surprise such as no painting ever produced." Here, according to Holmes, is what the photo does that the painting does not:

> The mind feels its way into the very depths of the picture. The scraggy branches of a tree in the foreground run out at us as if they would scratch our eyes out. The elbow of a figure stands forth so as to make us almost uncomfortable. There is such a frightful amount of detail, that we have the same sense of infinite complexity which Nature gives us. A painter shows us masses; the stereoscopic figure spares nothing,—all must be there, every stick, straw, scratch, as faithfully as the dome of St. Peter's, or the summit of Mont Blanc, or the ever-moving stillness of Niagara.[52]

Thus, Whitman saw the masses in one fell swoop when he visited galleries with hundreds of photos, while Holmes saw in photographs detail and character revealed, but both believed they saw actuality. Both believed they saw the real thing.

Even without reproduction of photos in newspapers and magazines, display of Civil War battlefield photos still had an impact. When Brady exhibited photos from the Battle of Antietam at his New York gallery in 1862, the *New York Times* noted that Brady's photos had "done something to bring home to us the terrible reality and earnestness of war." It was, said the *Times,* as though

Brady had "brought bodies and laid them in our dooryards and along the streets."[53] Holmes, who was on the Antietam battle-field four days after the battle and went to the Brady exhibition, wrote that it wasn't for him "to bear witness to the fidelity of views which the truthful sunbeam has delineated in all their dread reality," but then he makes just such a claim for the accuracy of Brady's photos: "The 'ditch' is figured, still encumbered with the dead, and strewed, as we saw it and the neighboring fields, with fragments and tatters. The 'colonel's gray horse' is given in an-other picture just as we saw him lying." Because of that accuracy, Holmes said Brady's photos captured the reality of the war: "Let him who wishes to know what war is look at this series of illustra-tions. These wrecks of manhood thrown together in careless heaps or ranged in ghastly rows for burial were alive but yesterday."[54] But Holmes then calls into question every romantic depiction of war and the value of the current sacrifice with rather stunning claims about these photographs from the Antietam battlefield:

> Many people would not look through this series. Many, having seen it and dreamed of its horrors, would lock it up in some secret drawer, that it might not thrill or revolt those whose soul sickens at such sights. It was so nearly like visiting the battlefield to look over these views, that all the emotions excited by the actual sight of the stained and sordid scene, strewed with rags and wrecks, came back to us, and we buried them in the recesses of our cabinet as we would have buried the mutilated remains of the dead they too vividly represented. Yet war and battles should have truth for their delineator. It is well enough for some Baron Gros or Horace Vernet to please an imperial master with fanciful portraits of what they are supposed to be. The honest sunshine
>
> > "Is Nature's sternest painter, yet the best";

And that gives us, even without the crimson coloring which flows over the recent picture, some conception of what a repulsive, brutal, sickening, hideous thing it is, this dashing together of two frantic mobs to which we give the name of armies.[55]

Of course, there were readers and commentators who recognized that photographs were versions of reality and not necessarily "Reality" or absolute truth. But generally there was agreement with Holmes's contention that the photograph was superior to art and illustrations as a depiction of record and that view continues to be held. Yet sometimes, in fact, the illustration from an engraving was more honest and compelling than an individual photo. For example, a *Harper's Weekly* illustration of the Gettysburg battlefield, "The Harvest of Death—Gettysburg, July 4, 1865," contains content from three separate photos, two by Gardner and one by Timothy H. O'Sullivan, that are integrated in a compelling way that captures the aftermath of the battle far better than the content of the individual photos. The illustration is therefore both more informative and more meaningful.[56]

Holmes for the most part is simply saying, "It's true and accurate," but in his comment about portraits he acknowledges, as the *Times* comment does, the impact and therefore the meaning of photos—not simply their potential emotional impact, but their power to make meaning and tell a story. Another important Civil War photographer, Alexander Gardner, who worked the battlefields with Brady for a while before breaking away, made that emotional and meaningful connection between photo and viewer even stronger by writing descriptive photo captions, some rather lengthy, in *Gardner's Photographic Sketch Book of the Civil War.* Gardner would often make "factual" statements about the photos that were erroneous, and he also did not acknowledge when bodies or objects in the photos had been arranged just for the photo. Gardner's caption with one photo, "Field Where General Reynolds Fell," taken by Timothy O'Sullivan, identifies the dead soldiers as Confederates but the same bodies are in another photo in the book, "A Harvest of Death," also taken by O'Sullivan, and there Gardner says the bodies are Union. Furthermore, General Reynolds apparently didn't fall anywhere near the spot captured in the photograph. After a long introductory paragraph, the second paragraph of the caption for "Field Where General Reynolds Fell" says that the photo shows "only a single spot on the long line of the killed," and then Gardner writes:

> Some of the dead presented an aspect which showed that they had suffered severely just previous to dissolution, but these were few in number compared with those who wore a calm and resigned expression, as though they had passed away in the act of prayer. Others had a smile on their faces, and looked as if they were in the act of speaking. Some lay stretched on their backs, as if friendly hands had prepared them for burial. Some were still resting on one knee, their hands grasping muskets. In some instances the cartridge remained between the teeth, or the musket was held in one hand, and the other was uplifted as though to ward a blow, or appealing to heaven. The faces of all were pale, as though cut in marble, and as the wind swept across the battle-field it waved the hair, and gave the bodies such an appearance of life that a spectator could hardly help thinking they were about to rise to continue the fight.[57]

A visual image of war communicates on its own, affecting different viewers in a variety of ways. But as previously noted, increasingly words and images would work together to depict a distinct reality or version of events. By misrepresenting the content of the photo

images, Gardner "transformed the photographs from mere histori-
cal documents into visual parables," according to William Stapp.
Stapp further explains what this means as it applies to the "Field
Where General Reynolds Fell" photo:

> Even though Gardner's poetic description of the dead in "Field
> Where General Reynolds Fell" completely contradicted that hor-
> rid image of the clump of bloated, sun-blackened, three-day-old
> corpses in Timothy O'Sullivan's photograph, it nonetheless im-
> mutably fixed the meaning of this image for his contemporary
> audience, whose assumption that the photograph was inherently
> truthful resulted in an absolute and uncritical suspension of dis-
> belief. The photographic image was so obviously derived directly
> from reality that the purported identification of that reality went
> unquestioned, just as the American public's emotional need to
> believe the sentiments Gardner expressed in the *Sketch Book* guar-
> anteed their acceptance. In this context, the photograph readily
> became the vehicle for moral truth. If expression of this truth
> required mistitling an image, misinterpreting it, or even interfering
> physically with what was being photographed to achieve a more
> effective image, it was entirely justifiable.

Gardner had, as Stapp maintains, "proved that the camera could
both document events and be the instrument of assigning meaning to them."[58]

A particularly appropriate example of just how words and images—in this case drawings rather than photographs—came to
work together in publication to create a perspective that relies
on the actual and immediate while at the same time building
and strengthening stereotypes and myth or creating meaning or
fables not necessarily evident in the images alone occurred in

Harper's Monthly in 1880. *Harper's* published an in-depth, very up-beat article on Pittsburgh, which the author presents as the City of Smoke or Smoky City but finally as the City of Iron, noting, however, that if it were not the Iron City, it could be known as Coal City or Glass City. But overall Pittsburgh, with its smoke and grit that blankets the city and its workers, is romanticized as a fascinating industrial giant:

> She is the Smoky City only because of her forest of chimneys, whose tongues of flame speak of fires within that are boiling or melting the metal that gives the name to the age in which we live. Your true Pittsburgher glories in his city's name, in her wealth, and, generally speaking, in her dirt. Her densest smoke is incense in his nostrils, and his face brightens when, in approaching the grimy burg of his nativity, he sights her nimbus of carbon from afar, or, after night-fall, her crown of fire, and the stranger soon learns to understand this feeling. The great Iron City's mills and her wonderful furnaces are inspiring to the dullest.[59]

The article is full of detailed descriptions of steelmaking, pipe making and glassblowing, and facts and figures about all the natural resources needed and where they come from, as well as the importance and nature of the city's three rivers. In other words, it's loaded with facts and information. But what is most interesting and original about the article are the powerful and compelling illustrations done by Walter Shirlaw, a highly regarded illustrator and artist who was best known for his painting *Toning the Bell*. Twenty-one illustrations are used and seven of the article's twenty pages are dominated by a single dramatic picture. While a couple of sketches from a height and distance are light in shading and depict mostly clear skies, most of the pictures are dark and smoky, while the interiors of the mills and workers seem dark and foreboding and just a bit mysterious. Without the article's language, the images are fascinating, showing mill workers who are big and strong but with facial features that are indistinct; they work amid extreme heat and the patchy light from the furnaces and molten metal. None are individualized. The scenes border on the supernatural, which is only reinforced and enhanced by the article's prose. Readers are told that the "pernicious fumes" and "the nocturnal appearance of a range of coke ovens in full blast so nearly embodies the orthodox idea of Satanic scenery that unregenerate Pittsburghers have comparatively few surprises in store after this life."[60] Later he says that "Dante, in conceiving his 'Inferno,' must have had in mind just such a scene as is witnessed nightly in the crucible department of a Pittsburgh steel-works." One mill has installed electric light that, according to the writer, "gives the glare of the furnaces a gory hue." There are references to "livid light," "lambent flames," and "deepest shadows," which come from the "the brawny forms of negro puddlers" who "glow in the light of liquid metal they stir." Here's how the men working in the crucible are described:

> In the men assigned this labor human endurance seems certainly to have reached its limit. The steel-melter, grasping such a pair of tongs as might have been used upon St. Dunstan, steps directly over the fiery pit below, seizes a crucible, and, with apparent ease, draws it, cherry red, to the surface. Man and glowing jar seem part and parcel, and equally impervious to the fearful heat. Salamander muscles come into graceful play as the melter beheads the sealed crucible, which he tilts slowly until its contents are decanted, amid vivid coruscations, into the mould. In raiment the melter from his

waist down is an Esquimau, from his waist up a Hottentot, a Zulu, or anything innocent of clothing.[61]

The words and images work together to create an underworld where the workers are savages or less than human. They are, in effect an exotic "other," in contrast to the distinctly human puddlers depicted by Rebecca Harding Davis eighteen years before this article, or Homer's mill workers trudging home at the end of the day. Absolutely nothing is written or visually depicted about the lives or families of the ironworkers, which further makes them "part and parcel" of the mill, cogs in the industrial process. Ironically, the same year "Pittsburgh" was published, the artist Thomas Anshutz painted "The Ironworkers' Noontime," which captures—and humanizes—workers of various sizes and ages outside a mill in Wheeling, where Davis grew up and wrote about the mill workers she saw daily.[62]

In addition to descriptive detail and facts, the "Pittsburgh" article briefly employed the kind of local slang that was strongly identified with depictions of the real and actual. In seeing a historic landmark, a blockhouse where the original Fort Duquesne stood, the writer comments to a woman living there, "a quaint old building this," and the woman responds: "If it's acquainted wid this house ye are, I wud be axin' yez for why I am payin' the sum of foive dollars the month's rint for the same, an' bud the two rooms of it, an' the lady kapin' shtore on the flure below, an' payin' only the thriflin' sum of four dollars, an' she wid a fine big room" (51). This woman might have been found in Twain's writing. But rather than use the local dialect and slang to illuminate the place and its people, even in a humorous fashion, unfortunately the author of the "Pittsburgh" article inserts it as humor that pokes fun at the ignorant poor woman who doesn't know what "quaint" means. We learn no more about her or her situation. While the Pittsburgh article was selective in constructing a version of the city as a marvelously smoky industrial jewel, its combination of words and images tended to mythologize Pittsburgh and industrialization while objectifying and dehumanizing workers, in effect still mixing the romantic and the real, using the actual to give a specific meaning to a place called Pittsburgh.

Regardless of the ultimate meaning-making of the various visual and narrative sketches, photographs, articles, and short stories, and the normal daily journalistic coverage, the call to focus on the real and actual had increasingly strong advocates and they continued to use newspapers and magazines to make their case. Two of them were extremely influential in shaping the agenda of two important magazines, while the third became the leading advocate of local color.

SIX

CARVING OUT THE REAL

In the 1870s, when readers of newspapers, magazines, and books were reading the likes of Rebecca Harding Davis, Mark Twain, and others, Cincinnati readers could learn about the lives of those on the margins of urban society, including the victims and perpetrators of horribly violent crimes, by reading articles by Lafcadio Hearn in the local newspaper. Hearn was only nineteen when he arrived in Cincinnati from England in 1869 and in 1872 he began a five-year stint writing and reporting for first the Cincinnati *Enquirer* and then the Cincinnati *Commercial* before leaving for New Orleans, where he worked for another five years for two of that city's newspapers.

By their very nature, newspapers at this time covered a gamut of current events and breaking news that brought continued attention to the concerns and behavior of contemporary society, but there also was further development in what came to be called "human interest" articles. These were sometimes trivial, but also sometimes poignant and revealing of the human condition and a clear extension of the more casual renderings, short and long, that had appeared in the penny papers for years. Hearn's reports connected him to more than one emerging form of journalistic depiction of the actual. His extremely graphic reports, for instance, place him within the center of the more sensationalistic journalistic tradition, while other samples of his journalism show him to be a chronicler of the urban poor, especially blacks who lived in places called Bucktown, Rat Row, or Sausage Row, where the prostitutes lived. Those newspaper accounts, as well as his writing from the French West Indies for *Harper's Monthly,* also make Hearn one of the early American literary journalists. In many respects, he was as much an American flaneur as Foster or Twain. Finally, in some instances of both the sensational and the more literary journalistic, Hearn was very close to being an early investigative reporter or what would come to be called muckraking at the end of the century.

While it's possible that Hearn could have read Twain's *Innocents Abroad* since it was widely read in America, England, and Europe, he certainly was familiar with Dickens's *Sketches of Boz* as well as Henry Mayhew's *London Labour and the London Poor* and thus had models for his own reporting. His fascination with the macabre, however, led him to delve where neither Dickens nor Boz ventured and where the *Tribune*'s George Foster only touched around the edges. His articles were about murders, hangings, dissections, abortion houses, the "Stink Factory" where dead animals were processed, suicides, opium dens, autopsies, building hauntings, and grave robbing, to name a few. As Jon Christopher Hughes has written, Hearn's "best stories described the misfits, the outcasts, those on and over the fringe of society. He was comfortable in the dirty, often ugly underbelly of Cincinnati" and he "pursued ghastly crimes, questionable professional practices, and injustices with lust." Hearn found his stories by "tirelessly searching the crowded streets of the city," talking with a range of sources, in-

cluding coroners and the police, but also "murderers, petty criminals, thugs on 'Rat Row' . . . saloon keepers . . . entertainers, artists" and the prostitutes living and working in the "ranches" on
Sausage Row.[1] Yet he also wrote sympathetic sketches of the poor
and marginalized, having lived among them while writing about
them.[2] But whether he wrote sensationally detailed descriptions
of crimes and activities such as body embalming, autopsy dissections, or a close look at a neighborhood and its down-and-out
residents, Hearn's articles are characterized by concrete, extensive
detail, dialogue and dialect, and scene-setting, all coming from
observation, interviews, and conversation with those who might
know someone or something. In one article, Hearn takes his readers into a neighborhood of poor people, some good and getting
by, others thieves and prostitutes, and he hooks up with a couple
of policemen who are looking for a female thief. He describes a
"mongrel building, half brick, half frame" that is a "notorious . . .
hive of thieves," a prostitute "ranch" where the police look for
their thief, and Hearn tells of the time when one of the police officers was nearly murdered in this house when he was "pounced
upon . . . by a belligerent crowd of harlots and ruffians" and
women "slashed at him in the dark with razors."[3] When they exit
the house, Hearn and the patrolmen are in an alley that once was
very dangerous but now many of the thieves and prostitutes who
used the alley are in the "Workhouse." Hearn writes:

> There were two women in white dresses sitting on door-steps
> a little further on down the alley—one a bright quadroon, with
> curly hair, twisted into ringlets, and a plump, childish face; the
> other a tall white girl, with black hair and eyes and a surprisingly
> well cut profile. Both are notorious; the former as a Sausage Row
> belle; the latter as the mistress of a black loafer, whom she supports

by selling herself. Her sister, once quite a pretty woman, leads a similar existence when not in the Workhouse. The patrolmen point them out, and pass into a doorway on the south side of the alley, leading to the upper story of the dwelling tenanted by John Ham, barkeeper. Mrs. Ham, an obese negress, with immensely thick shoulders, comes forward to meet the patrolmen.

"Who's upstairs, Mrs. Ham?

"Dey's no one only Molly, fo' God."

"Where's Long Nell?"

"In de Wuk-hus."

"And Little Dolly?"

"Wuk-hus."

"And crooked-back Jack?"

"Wuk-hus."

"Ah, they've cleaned out these ranches since I used to run this beat before. Come up, gentlemen." Through a dark hall-way, over a creaking floor to a back room, and the patrolman's club plays the devil's tattoo upon the rickety planks. The door unlocked and "Molly" makes her appearance.

Molly is the colored belle of this district. What her real name is neither her companions nor the police officers know. So far she has never been in the Workhouse. She seemed to be about eighteen years old, of lithe and slender figure; complexion a Gypsy brown; hair long and dark with a slight wave; brows perfectly arched and delicately penciled; dreamy, brown eyes, nose well cut; mouth admirably molded; features generally pleasing. But Molly is said to be a "decoy" and a thief, and her apparent innocence a sham. The room is searched and found empty.

"Where did you get these?" exclaimed Tighe, picking up from the table a handsome pair of jet bracelets with heavy silver setting.

"They were made a present to me."

"That's too thin! Who gave them to you?"

"A man uptown."

"What man?"

(No answer.)

The officer lays down the trinkets with a frown; tells Molly that he has a good mind to lock her up "on suspicion"; and departs, looking unutterable things. "Did she steal them?" we ask.

"Oh, no," is the reply; "I only want to scare her a little for I happen to know who gave them to her. It is a curious fact that business men and people of respectability get decoyed down here occasionally by girls like that, and get infatuated enough to bring them presents. She wouldn't tell, though, even if I locked her up."[4]

Hearn perhaps best demonstrated his combination of reporting and storytelling skills in his coverage of what came to be known as the "tanyard murder." Hearn wrote at least eight articles on the revenge murder in a tannery in which the victim was beaten with a club, stabbed with a pitchfork, and the body was stuffed into a furnace and burned. Many of his articles on the murder were printed in newspapers around the country. One of the three men charged with the murder, and apparently the instigator, had ruthlessly beaten his pregnant daughter before going to kill the man who had taken advantage of her. Near the end of the trial, the wife of one of the killers tried to kill her baby and Hearn very specifically describes what she did and what she said as she threw the baby against a trunk and then a wall. Readers of Hearn's articles also learned that this woman's husband was a bigamist and criminal who had served time in jail. Details and revelations piled up day-to-day and the coverage, which included illustrations, easily captured the public interest. Hearn's contacts, along with public records and testimony, allowed Hearn and the *Enquirer* to present the array of facts but also a range of views of the people involved. Hearn's combination of reporting and storytelling skills allowed him to not only tell what had happened and how it had been done, but also why it had happened, so that the articles strung together yield a story of revenge through murder, but also a story of a cruel, intimidating father's torment of a wayward daughter and his bullying of his timid son. Hearn describes the father and instigator, Andreas Egner, by using a splattering of concrete description mixed with rather predictable, imprecise images of evil, which nevertheless take readers inside the courtroom, even if Hearn only confirms their suspicions about Egner:

> The whole manner of Andreas Egner is marked by a most repulsive feline cunning. He moves only with the stealth action of a cat on the watch. His lean, sharp, leathery features are expressive of little but cautious cunning. Otherwise it could not even be called characteristic but for the vulture nose and the pitilessly firm mouth—a long but lipless mouth, that looks like the seam of a saber-slash across his face than any thing else. As his conduct to his daughter shows, he is quite as great a coward as he is a villain; and does not meet any eye directed upon him. He never looked up but in a rapid, surreptitious glance; and there glances were generally accompanied by a dark, satanic smile. (In the newspaper, "FELINE CUNNING" and "DARK, SATANIC SMILE" are pulled out and run in caps above the text that uses those phrases.)[5]

Hearn's first, lengthy report on the crime takes on the form of a story with a narrative flow provided by pullout captions above sections of the text. For example, here are the captions, most of them appearing in full caps and all but a couple a part of the narrative, in the first part of the article: Fear of a Dreadful Secret, The Dramatis Personae, In Her Bedroom, The Elder Egner Swore, Last Time He Was Seen Alive, Gurgling Noise of the Strangling Man, About Seven O'Clock Yesterday Morning, Six-Pronged Pitchfork. The story is full of gruesome details about the remains of the burned victim and the manner of the murder. Hearn mixes past and present tense for effect, with the present tense contributing to the narrative flow and the sense of a story being told. Here is Hearn switching from past to present in mid-paragraph:

> Judging by all the evidence the murderers were familiar with the premises and its canine guardians; for, were they not, they could not have gained access to them without encountering the dogs, and being probably torn into fragments by them. They in all probability entered through the gate leading from Egner's to the tanyard, and ensconced themselves in the harness-room, which they knew their victim must pass on his way to this lodging. When he entered, as was his wont, by the small gate opening on Gamble alley, they were peering in through the open door of the harness room awaiting their opportunity. A few more steps in darkness and silence, and the watchman's throat is suddenly seized with a grasp of iron. Then commences
>
> THE TERRIBLE STRUGGLE FOR LIFE
>
> The night is pitch dark, fit gloom for the dark deed it veils. The victim is a young and powerful man, muscled like Hercules; but he has been wholly taken by surprise, he is unarmed, and he finds by the strength of the grasp on his throat that his antagonist is more than a match for him in mere brute force. (This paragraph goes on to describe how many people were in earshot when the victim was stabbed with a pitchfork.)[6]

Perhaps more culturally important—and perhaps more culturally interesting—than Hearn's newspaper writings on murders, animal blood–drinkers, abortionists, and so forth are Hearn's stories of life on the levee. The introduction to a collection of these newspaper pieces correctly calls them "human documents" that Hearn assembled because of his "omnivorous interest in the world about him" and his "desire to record what he saw and felt."[7] This collection, *Children of the Levee,* brings together twelve articles that Hearn did about the black steamboat hands who lived and worked on the levee. The collection's editor notes in the preface that Hearn got the material for the levee stories when he "accompanied policemen on the beat, peered into levee haunts, witnessed the revels of roustabouts, and listened to their endless superstitions." Cincinnati, with about 250,000 residents, was the largest inland city in the United States, according to the 1870 Census, and a center of railroad and riverboat trade. Although the city was largely German and its wealthiest citizens were of German descent, a good number of the city's 6,000 African Americans who weren't working as domestics or as farmhands lived along the riverfront and worked as stevedores, dockworkers, porters, riverboat deckhands, and firemen, although some operated boardinghouses and taverns, while others were involved in gambling, prostitution, and theft.[8] Hearn tried to capture the speech rhythms and intonations in the dialect he heard and he treated the blacks he wrote about with respect and often sympathy. Taken together, his articles contain a record of speech, customs, and folkways of a Cincinnati subculture.

Included in the collection is "Pariah People," discussed before, but two sketches that are particularly strong examples of short works of literary journalism are "Dolly: An Idyl of the Levee" and "Banjo Jim's Story," both published in the *Cincinnati Com-*

mercial in 1876. "Dolly" is the most complete of the sketches and reads like a short story with a distinct beginning, middle, and end. It tells of a levee resident, Dolly, who is romanticized by Hearn and depicted as a woman of beauty and nobility who ultimately dies from a broken heart when she learns that "her man," a riverboat worker, has married someone else. Here is the beginning:

> "The Lord only," once observed Officer Patsy Brazil, "knows what Dolly's real name is."
>
> Dolly was a brown, broad-shouldered girl of the levee, with the lithe strength of a pantheress in her compactly-knit figure, and owning one of those peculiar faces which at once attract and puzzle by their very uniqueness—a face that possessed a strange comeliness when viewed at certain angles, especially half-profile, and that would have seemed very soft and youthful but for the shadow of its heavy black brows, perpetually knitted Medusa-wise, as though by everlasting pain, above a pair of great, dark, keen, steady eyes. It was a face, perhaps rather Egyptian than aught else; fresh with a youthful roundness, and sweetened by a sensitive, passionate, pouting mouth.[9]

As the piece continues, Hearn adds detail to develop her character through depictions of scenes and incidents, much of the material coming from police officer Patsy Brazil, complete with realistic dialogue and dialect and concrete description that ground the story in actuality and authenticity, despite its romantic aspects, which come from Hearn's distinct point of view that perhaps is marked by his own infatuation with Dolly.

Each of Hearn's levee sketches has a different opening that distinguishes them and that's true of "Banjo Jim's Story," which begins with a descriptive overview of the levee that creates a strong sense of place:

> Melancholy, indeed, is the river-view when a rainy day dawns in dull gray light upon the levee—the view of a rapid yellow river under an ashen sky; of distant hills looming dimly through the pallid mist; of steamboat smoke hanging sluggishly over the sickly-hued current; and, drearier yet, the ancient fronts of weather-stained buildings on the Row, gloomy masses of discolored brick and stone with gaping joints and shattered windows. Yet of rainy nights the voice of wild merriment echoes loudest along the levee,—the shouts of lithe dancers and the throbbing of bass viols and thrumming of banjos and the shrieking of fiddles seem to redouble in volume.
>
> On breezy, bright nights, when the stars glow overhead, and the ruffled breast of the river reflects the sky-purple or the rich silver of a full moon, the dusky folks seek mirth for mirth's sake. But in nights of foul weather and fog, some say the merriment of the Row is attributable to the same strange cause which prompts solitary men in desolate houses or desert places by night to seek relief from loneliness by waking echoes in the gloom with shout or song.
>
> Ghostly at all times, especially to those who live in old dwellings, are rainy nights; full of creeping sounds and awesome echoes and unaccountable knockings and mysterious noises, as of footfalls upon ancient floors, that groan when walked upon. Now, the old Row is faced with old houses, and they say that of rainy nights the dead hide in the shadowy old doorways and haunt the dark nooks of the deserted dancing halls, which have been closed up since the great flood. And the habitants of the levee fear the dead with an unutterable fear.

"Look-a-hyar, ole gal," cried Banjo Jim to Mary Pearl, when the poor woman was dying in her dance-house on the Row,—"if you's a-gwine to die, don't you be a comin' back hyar after you's done dead, cos' I'se a-gwine ober the ribber—*I* is." And when Mary died, Jim went over the river with several of the levee girls. For the dead may not pass over the water, according to the faith of the roustabout.[10]

As the tale of Banjo Jim unfolds, the piece becomes rich with aspects of the lives and beliefs of the people of the levee.

Hearn left Cincinnati and moved to New Orleans and continued to write for newspapers, even becoming associate editor of the small and struggling New Orleans *Item* before joining the larger *Times-Democrat* in 1881. By 1887 he was in New York and soon traveling to the French West Indies. He wrote a number of sketches of life on the islands, two of which were published in *Harper's Weekly* in 1889. *Harper's Weekly* had also published two of his New Orleans sketches about voodoo and superstitions in the city in 1885 and 1886.[11] If Hearn had gone to New York instead of New Orleans, he might have fit fine working for Charles Dana's New York *Sun,* although he would have had to simplify his writing style but stick to his range of topics.

In the years after the Civil War, particularly in the century's last two decades, a range of voices persistently elucidated and refined the concept of depicting the actual, the common, the everyday, the quotidian, in effect explaining and defining what Davis, Hearn, Twain, and a host of other journalists and writers were trying to do. Although Hamlin Garland would declare in 1894 that for fiction writers "the present is the vital theme," newspapers, as already demonstrated, had been depicting and reporting the present in various ways for some time. While the early penny paper editors, such as Day and Bennett, made it clear in their words and in their coverage that they would to a large degree focus on the current and what interested readers, after the war Dana bought the *Sun*, the largest circulation newspaper from the late 1860s to the early 1880s, became its editor, and further clarified what it should mean to report the present through news and human-interest writing. But even Dana's ideas were formed long before he started the *Sun*.

In 1850, while Dana was managing editor of the *Tribune*, he wrote in "The Newspaper Press" that a distinctive American journalism style was developing that allowed the journalist to be "a writer who seizes upon the events of the day and holds them up, now in this aspect, now in that, flinging on them the most condensed and lively light."[12] When he took over the *Sun*, he declared, in one of his most often cited statements, that the paper would be about clarity and getting to the point of the news and that it would "endeavor to present its daily photograph of the whole world's doings in the most luminous and lively manner."[13] Forty years later, he told an audience that a newspaper had to be "founded upon human nature" and it "must correspond to the wants of the people." That meant reporting the news, which is "everything that occurs, everything which is of human interest." That could mean crime and sensationalism, but it also could mean feature stories about people going about their daily lives, or "human interest." Dana declared in the same lecture that "whatever the Divine Providence permitted to occur I was not too proud to report."[14] While Dana preached accuracy, he also said that the accurate, detailed report should be "enlivened with imagination, or with feeling, or with humor" so that the article becomes "a literary product."[15] Ultimately, Dana said, the best journalism is "vivid and animating."[16] To a large extent, that meant plain, simple, and short, and that might have doomed Hearn with Dana,

since in Cincinnati and New Orleans Hearn strung together ad-
verbs and adjectives and was once known as "Old Semicolon."
Regular features such as "Jottings about Town" and "Life in the
Metropolis—Dashes Here and There by the Sun's Reporters"
alerted *Sun* readers to a variety of events, incidents, and information that connected readers to the immediate but rarely imbued
these brief items with meaning. Significantly, as Janet Steele has
explained, the *Sun's* "rapid-fire paragraphs" on a range of disconnected topics depicted the city as fragmented: "Violent death,
happy coincidence, and personal tragedy coexisted in the pages of
the *Sun* as 'jottings,' 'dashes,' and 'sunbeams,' much as they did on
the streets of the city. The only meaning that the *Sun* bestowed
on such seemingly random events was that they were all of equal
importance in the life of the metropolis."[17] The catch-all reporting was becoming regularized in newspapers in other urban areas
as well, and by the last two decades of the century newspaper journalism was regularly presenting readers with insight and pictures
of the many sides of urban society and culture, showing its various
parts. Meanwhile, magazine fiction increasingly tended to consist
of stories that focused on supposed connections rather than differences, but at the same time magazines were consistently giving
voice to the desirability and necessity of writing that depicted the
real rather than the ideal.

MAGAZINES: ALDEN, HOWELLS, AND GARLAND

From January through August 1894, *Harper's Magazine*—then
called *Harper's New Monthly Magazine*—began serializing the
novel *Trilby* by George Du Maurier. The decision to run this
gothic novel with a Paris setting and written by a French-born

Englishman was made by the magazine's editor, Henry Mills Alden, which is a bit ironic. After all, although he was not well known to the public, he was remarkably influential, held in high esteem by a wide range of writers, journalists, and editors, and known as a staunch advocate for a distinctive American literature grounded in realism. Publishing *Trilby* would seem to contradict much of what he stood for. But Alden also believed his job as editor meant finding material that would entertain his readers and he was astute at recognizing writing that would appeal to those readers. *Trilby* became so popular that *Harper's* circulation jumped by 100,000 and, along with the book's publication in September, Trilby dolls, shoes, hats, and luncheons became the rage. Nine acting companies toured the country dramatizing the story.

This early "blockbuster" illustrates not just journalistic influence but also the ongoing realism-romance tension. It shows that despite an ascendant public expectation for the real and actual, the public also found appealing predictable characters, in this case the innocent young artist's model, Trilby, deftly manipulated, hypnotized, and used by the evil Zvengali. In the end, both Trilby and Zvengali meet untimely deaths although others who were part of their lives give the story a partially happy ending. But the serialization of *Trilby* did not necessarily indicate backpedaling on Alden's part when it came to depicting the actual. At the same time that *Trilby* ran, the magazine was loaded with non-fiction by Richard Harding Davis, Edward Eggleston, Howells, and Frederic Remington—illustrating his own writing—plus descriptive articles on cities such as Charleston and Philadelphia, a series on "Great American Industries," and a look at "The New England Negro" framed by the story of a ninety-year-old Connecticut woman descended from slaves. Also in the *Trilby* issues were fiction by Howells; Richard Harding Davis; Constance Fenimore Woolson, a realist writer held in particularly high regard by Henry James; Brander Matthews's "Vignettes of Manhattan"; and Charles Dudley Warner, who had written *The Gilded Age* with Mark Twain.

Thus, Alden could both encourage and support the current and real in fiction and nonfiction, but he also could sense when something more romantic, sentimental, or ideal might appeal to his readers. That Alden quality was evident in his selection of two very different pieces from Hearn. In 1888, he published Hearn's novella, "Chita: A Memory of Last Island," and in 1890 a work of nonfiction, "A Winter Journey to Japan." "Chita" would have appealed to Alden because of its rather complex narrative structure and shifting point of view. The tale takes place on an island in the Gulf south of New Orleans and the first part reads like a nonfiction travel sketch but ultimately it is dark in a Gothic fashion. Rather than revealing depictions of human behavior and contemporary values, the story is overwritten and thick with mood and atmosphere. Consider, for example, this passage and notice how wind and voice are granted significance and life by making them proper words: "Then the Wind grew weird. It ceased being a breath; it became a Voice moaning across the world—hooting—uttering nightmare sounds—*Whoo!—whoo!—whoo!*—and with each stupendous owl-cry the ooing of the waters seemed to deepen, more and more abysmally, through all the hours of darkness."[18] In "A Winter Journey to Japan," which is really about Hearn traveling by train across Canada to Vancouver where he boards a ship to Japan, Hearn's writing is cleaner and somewhat leaner, in direct contrast to the prose of "Chita," and even a bit stripped down from his newspaper days. After an extended scene- and journey-setting beginning, Hearn presents a day-by-day account that is often impressionistic through repetition of and juxtaposing words and color:

> Morning. Heavily snowing out of a heavy gray sky. White drifts line the way. Beyond them, on either side, is a waste of low growths,—young black spruce and dwarf birch—straight as lances; the silvery bark of the birch, strongly relieved against the somber spruce, gives their leafless shapes the aspect of poles stuck in the snow.
>
> So bordered the line rises and sinks, by long slow stages, through white valleys, and between white hills.[19]

Alden was from a working-class background, and when he was only seven, he started working in a cotton mill in Hoosick Falls, New York. At age fourteen he paid his way through a private school, Ball Seminary, by doing janitorial work at the school. The school's principal, impressed with Alden's intellect, made certain he got accepted at Williams, where Alden paid for his education by teaching at nearby schools and doing a range of summer jobs. But he also was an intensely dedicated student who earned the name "Metaphysics" from his classmates. That combination of serious study and common labor gave Alden an appreciation for the common and everyday as well as high standards for good writing, whether poetry, fiction, essays, or journalism. He never sought the spotlight, however, so his name wasn't even known among regular *Harper's* readers even though he edited *Harper's Monthly* for fifty years, from 1869 to 1919. His good friend, William Dean Howells, declared upon Alden's death that Alden had been "the greatest editor of his time" and "an editor perfect in his time and place," an assessment that was echoed in notices of his death in many newspapers and magazines.[20]

Alden was fit for his time specifically because of his belief in the necessity for a distinctively American realism in literature, but also because his personal background combined with his early experience as a writer and journalist. When he was twenty-five, he started contributing editorials to several New York City newspapers while teaching at a boys' school, and the *Atlantic* published a few articles he wrote on ancient Greek culture. But it was after he was commissioned to put together a descriptive book on the Central Railroad of New Jersey that he caught the eye of Harper and Brothers, which published the book, and in 1863 he joined the publishing house's editorial department. After a short time in which he assessed article submissions to *Harper's New Monthly Magazine,* he became managing editor of *Harper's Weekly,* which at that time focused on covering the war. Thus, Alden was quickly thrust into the immediacy of depicting the most important event of his time. Not only did he select articles for publication but he also wrote the captions for the illustrations and came to appreciate "the art of pictorial illustration," as he put it, claiming years later that the timely illustrations, particularly of battle scenes, were "memorable for their accuracy and graphic delineation."[21] At the same time, Alden and Alfred H. Guernsey, editor of *Harper's Monthly,* were collaborating in assembling and writing *Harper's Pictorial History of the Great Rebellion,* volume one being published by Harper and Brothers in 1866 and volume two in 1868. In the preface to volume one, Alden and Guernsey declared that their purpose had been "to narrate events just as they occurred; to speak of living men as impartially as though they were dead." Essentially claiming their objectivity, they further stated that the book was based on "authentic documents" and that they "made no statement which we have not believed to be true, and also substantiated by unquestioned evidence," while any conclusions, they contended, were based on "facts." In the preface to the second volume, they say they that the book being an illustrated history did not influence their writing and they explain that they wrote it "as we should have done if the interest of our readers depended upon the unadorned recital of facts." They then note many of the official reports and documents they used.

Alden's experience with the *Weekly* effectively laid the groundwork for his preference for writing that clearly connected to American life and society and he indicated that preference in both his selection of articles and fiction as editor of *Harper's Monthly* and in his commentaries in the magazine's regular feature, the "Editor's Study." When Alden wrote about the magazine on its fiftieth anniversary in 1900 he pointed out that in the publication's first couple of decades there was "no special timeliness in an acutely journalistic sense" in the magazine and very little of substance by American writers. But when he became editor he advocated for change that consisted of more contributions by American writers and "better illustrations."[22] He also said at that time that the magazine's "literary triumphs" had been principally gained "through faithful realism and a vivid appreciation of local color and character." Alden explained that from the mid-1870s onward whatever could be told "in the form of a story" took that form rather than "that of a conventional magazine article." Fiction or nonfiction became, according to Alden, human documents, and fiction that was not based on "emotional experience or the facts of life, individual or social" was a "waste of the divine faculty."[23] The "drama of the present," including human conflict of every sort should be the goal.

Alden gave voice to his beliefs regularly in the "Editor's Study" and many of those pieces can be found in *Magazine Writing and the New Literature,* published in 1908. The book, both scholarly and historical in tone as Alden analyzed changes that were occurring mostly in fiction, compared current writing efforts to writing from the past. Most of the essays reinforce the notion that writing, especially fiction, should be about life being lived and very specifically stated that. In the book's introduction, Alden said the book's essays were more about "life" than literature and that the "New Literature," that is, a more realistic fiction, was about seeing life and interpreting it: "we behold the reality and take it, in all its inexplicableness."[24] In one of the essays he declares, "We willingly follow where the path inevitably leads—to see life as it is," while in another he says that "realism enlarges instead of narrowing the writer's field of creative work. Life is the theme—not what we think about it, but what it discloses to our developed sensibility."[25] Thus, Alden's and *Harper's* realistic writing seeks the truth, "which discloses the real values of our earthly existence and experience in their living terms, and which give to common things and associations their full meaning," compared to the romance, which was associated with what was "alien and remote."[26] In his "Editor's Study" essays he keeps coming back to these ideas, reinforcing them month after month, year after year. He again refers to writers who give "living reality fit embodiment" and this sensibility is contained in a sampling of additional phrases he uses to explain his ideas.[27] For instance, the writer "must see plainly, without colored glasses or magnifying lenses . . . without notional distortion"; such writing contains "our plain, common life"; this "new realism" in its "real meanings" and "true representation" gives readers a "familiar earthly setting and is shot through with the pains and delights naturally incident to human earthly existence"; rather than the "mock-heroic and mock-sublime" this new writing gives us "a large body of plain people who are simply human and whose lives are real."[28] Much of Alden's

philosophy had been enunciated by Rebecca Harding Davis, using much the same language as Alden, in her books and articles from the 1860s and 1870s, when Alden the young editor was getting established.

In addition to defining and explaining contemporary literature that dealt with the present and, often, the common and every-day, Alden argued convincingly that such writing blossomed in America primarily because of its magazines but also because of its newspapers. In the second half of the nineteenth century there occurred, according to Alden, "the intimate blending of a maga-zine with the thought and life of a whole people," thereby making the magazine "a Real Encyclopaedia of the living world."[29] Not just an "encyclopaedia" but an encyclopedia of the "real." Conse-quently, the purpose of the magazine had become "the imagina-tive interpretation of life and Nature" that not only expressed a cultural sensibility but also stimulated it and influenced it.[30] Even the newspaper had played a role in cultural meaning-making, claimed Alden, because the newspaper "is not merely a chronicle; it charges the day's doings with their meaning and tendency, in-vesting incident and circumstance with the guise of fancy and humor."[31]

In 1882, Alden offered William Dean Howells $6,000 for a story, but said it had to be "a story of American life & character" that did not have a "plot based on exceptional or unusual manifes-tations of human character," which, Alden suggested, was true of Howells's novel *The Undiscovered Country.*[32] Howells had recently resigned as editor of the *Atlantic,* having joined the magazine as assistant editor in 1866, assuming the editor's position in 1871. As editor, Howells had encouraged writing about contemporary American life and as the century progressed, Howells emerged as perhaps the leading voice of an American literary realism, yet here was a behind-the-scenes editor prodding Howells to move more clearly in that direction in his own writing. Although Howells worked as a printer in his youth and reported for several newspapers in Ohio, where he grew up, he turned down opportunities to pursue a reporting career, including a police reporter position in Cincinnati, preferring to create romantic poetry and fiction. He later indicated a bit of regret that he had not stuck with journalism, wondering if perhaps he had made a mistake: "I think that if I had been wiser than I was then I would have remained in the employ offered me, and learned in the school of reality the many lessons of human nature which it could have taught me." He gave up, he wrote in 1916, the opportunity to learn in "that university of the streets and police stations, with its faculty of patrolmen and ward politicians and saloon keepers."[33] He didn't stick with it, he explained in 1895, because his goal at that point was "to live for literature . . . and for nothing else," and as a young man he didn't see literature "as an expression of life" as he would later.[34] In other words, when he was young, neither he nor the culture believed literature was necessarily about life actually being lived. Reflecting on his youth, he made a particularly interesting observation about his journalism and poetry that further highlights Howells's gradual shift from seeing life only in books to valuing the actual experienced and "the gait and speech of life:"

> Journalism was not my ideal, but it was my passion, and I was passionately a journalist well after I began author. I tried to make my newspaper work literary, to give it form and distinction, and it seems to me that I did not always try in vain, but I had also the instinct of actuality, of trying to make my poetry speak for its time and place. For the most part, I really made it speak for the times and places I had read of.[35]

He changed that view and his reliance on books rather than life for material gradually over time, working it out in his fiction, especially his first novel, *Their Wedding Journey,* but before that with his nonfiction travel writing, *Venetian Life,* published in 1866, after Howells had served four years as American consul to the city, and *Italian Journeys,* published in 1867. While in Venice, Howells's accounts of life in Venice had appeared as travel letters or sketches in an Ohio newspaper and in the *Boston Advertiser.* Three years before Twain's *Innocents Abroad* was published with its satire of tourists and tourist sites, Howells indicated that his purpose in *Venetian Life* would be to remove the "illusion" of Venice as well as its "sentimental errors" and present Venice as he saw it, thus adopting a theme that would be very similar to that of Twain's classic travel book, although Twain was just as interested in satirizing American tourists' attitudes and behavior.[36] One scholar has called *Venetian Life* "a highly successful fusion of Howells's literary and journalistic talents" and the same might be said of *Italian Journeys.*[37]

Italian Journeys consists of a series of sketches of Howells's travels around Italy before he returned to the United States after relinquishing his consul position. Many of the book's sketches first appeared in the *Boston Advertiser,* the *Nation,* and the *Atlantic.* In both books, but especially in the Italian sketches, Howells plays the flaneur, strolling the boulevards and lanes, gazing upon the spectacle and sharing what he sees through detailed descriptions and bits of dialogue and conversation, occasionally spiced with a bit of sarcasm if not satire. Unlike his early journalistic days in Ohio, in Italy Howells was more willing, even eager, to write about the observed life rather than escape into romantic depictions, a philosophical shift that played out in his fiction.

While Howells's first novel, *Their Wedding Journey,* is mediocre at best, it nevertheless reveals Howells continuing to articulate what he had come to value in both nonfiction and fiction. Right at the outset of the novel he declares that his concern is with "ordinary traits of American life" the "little well-known" and "accessible places," and to do anything different would require "a skillful romancer," as he confronts issues that Rebecca Harding Davis had dealt with in her own writing years before.[38] Life is not just "pretty periods," as one character puts it and as Howells once thought it—that same character later says that it's time for America and its readers to "get over this absurd reluctance from facts" and time to "make the ideal embrace and include the real, till we consent to face the music in our simple common names, and put Smith into a lyric and Jones into a tragedy."[39] Repeatedly in *Their Wedding Journey* Howells alludes to the "ordinary" and praises it.

Following the success of two novels, *A Modern Instance* and *The Rise of Silas Lapham,* Alden asked Howells to write "The Editor's Study" for each issue of *Harper's,* allowing Howells to further define his views of fiction and realism, elaborating on the ideas he had toyed with in his early nonfiction and his early fiction. Alden later would list Howells as the "leader" as both critic and fiction writer of the realism of the late nineteenth century, a view that was echoed by another strong proponent of the real and regional, Hamlin Garland. One finds language in those "Editor's Study" essays about literature, fiction, and realism very similar to that of Alden. (Howells made a point of modifying and publishing "Editor's Study" pieces from 1886 to 1891 in a book, *Criticism and Fiction.*) For instance, he said that "realism is nothing more and nothing less than the truthful treatment of material," and, sounding much like Whitman, he says "let fiction cease to lie about life; let it portray men and women as they are, actuated by the motives and the passions in the measure we all know . . . let it show the different interests in their true proportions . . . let it speak the dialect, the language, that most Americans know."[40] At the same time, while Howells was calling for accurate stories about life being lived, he was somewhat more of an elitist than Alden and did not have Alden's appreciation of newspaper journalism nor Alden's willingness to give readers popular fiction. At one point, he says that if an American ever wrote a story of guilty love as good as either *Anna Karenina* or *Madame Bovary* an American magazine wouldn't even publish it. Perhaps a more pertinent question is whether either more popular American magazines or the higher-end literary publications in the last two decades of the nineteenth century would publish anything like Rebecca Harding Davis's *Life in the Iron Mills.*

To a certain extent, Howells was primarily interested in a rather narrowly defined realism that was a "high" literary form and hence he advocated a specific type of literary art that yielded a coherent reality and eliminated social differences.[41] Nevertheless, Howells supported the work of writers such as Stephen Crane, including Crane's controversial *Maggie: A Girl of the Streets,* which Crane was unable to get published in a magazine and which he published himself in 1893 when no publisher would touch it. After Crane's success with *The Red Badge of Courage* and three years after Crane wrote and self-published *Maggie,* Crane revised some of the book's language and it was officially published. Howells praised that 1896 *Maggie* in a review for the *New York World* newspaper under the headline "New York Low Life in Fiction." Howells was impressed at how Crane's story was "really and fully" a "study" and with Crane's use of dialect.[42] The reviewer in the *New York Tribune,* however, said it was "ill-advised" for Crane to have his story published, and he criticized Crane for putting "on paper the grossness and brutality which are commonly encountered only through actual contact with the most besotted classes."

The problem, according to the reviewer, was that Crane saw "only dullness and dirt" and his themes were "entirely sordid, disgusting and vicious."[43] The *Tribune* reviewer wanted charm and humor to balance out the roughness and so did *The Nation*'s reviewer, who found *Maggie* to be "depressing" and called Crane "a rather promising writer of the animalistic school," explaining that what he calls animalistic others call "wonderful realism." This "species of realism . . . deals with man considered as an animal, capable of hunger, thirst, lust, cruelty, vanity, fear, sloth, predacity, greed, and other passions and appetites that make him kin to the brutes, but which neglects, so far as possible, any higher qualities which distinguish him from his four-footed relatives, such as humor, thought, reason, aspiration, affection, morality, and religion."[44]

That was a standard response to so-called low-life depictions. That is, realism was fine as long as it gave a more complete picture of all aspects of life being lived. In other words, some critics and readers wanted their realism, their actuality, tempered with a bit of idealism and romanticism. Even Hamlin Garland responded in this fashion, although he praised the 1893 *Maggie,* calling the book "a work of astonishing good style," "the voice of the slums," and "the most truthful and unhackneyed study of the slums I have yet read, fragmented though it is." But Crane's story lacked "rounded completeness," according to Garland. While Crane had "met and grappled with the actualities of the street in almost unequalled grace and strength," he needed to write in the same way about "the families living on the next street, who live lives of heroic purity and hopeless hardship."[45] That criticism was significant because Garland's was another influential voice in the call for a more realistic literature, or what he called "veritism."

By "veritism" Garland meant a type of realism that blended the verisimilitude of detail with individual perception, or as the writer sees things. Thus the veritist combined realism and impressionism. In an essay in *Forum* magazine in 1894, he described this literary impressionism as "the truthful statement of an individual impression corrected by reference to the fact."[46] The actual detail came from local color, which Garland said came from the writer who "spontaneously reflects the life which goes on around him." In a novel, that would mean "such quality of texture and back-ground that it could not have been written in any other place or by any one else than a native." Ultimately, said Garland, "life is the model, truth is the master."[47] Unlike Alden and Howells, Garland never worked as a journalist but his fiction and essays on literature and art regularly appeared in newspapers, including syndication by both McClure's Syndicate and Bacheller Syndicate, and an extensive amount of his writing appeared in a variety of magazines, including *McClure's, Harper's Weekly, Harper's Monthly, Century, Saturday Evening Post, Arena,* and many others. *McClure's* ran his biography of Grant, *Ulysses S. Grant: His Life and Character,* from April 1897 through May 1898, before it was published as a book. Best known for his stories of hardworking Midwestern farmers, some of his earlier fiction, such as the stories in *Main-Travelled Roads,* provide extensive evidence of just the type of full view, both the sun and the rain, that he was urging in Crane's writing. "Up the Cooly," a story of an educated son's return to his western Wisconsin roots, is full of lush description of the hills and valley that the son left so long ago, but he returns to a depressing farm life "with all its sordidness, dullness, triviality, and its endless drudgeries" and a brother and mother seemingly as worn down as the house in which they live. Near the end, the brother says: "I mean life ain't worth very much to me. I'm too old to take a new start. I'm a dead failure. I've come to the conclusion that

CARVING OUT THE REAL

life's a failure for ninety-nine per cent of us. You can't help me now. It's too late."[48]

When Crane gave Garland a copy of *Maggie,* he recommended that Crane send a copy of the book to another realist writer, Brander Matthews, whose sketches that make up *Vignettes of Manhattan* were running in *Harper's Monthly* at the same time as *Trilby.* Crane did send the book to Matthews, who was an influential literary critic and Columbia University professor of drama, and asked Matthews to tell him what he thought of the book. There is no record that Matthews responded to Crane, but after he received Crane's book he did provide some "heroic purity" by writing a "vignette" about his own Maggie, "Before the Break of Day," which ran in *Harper's Monthly* in July 1894. Matthews's Maggie, as Lawrence J. Oliver has pointed out, becomes a modest emblem of the American dream. She loves her factory job because of the money she earns—factory work for Crane's Maggie is a "dreary place of endless grinding"— and she escapes the clutches of a brutal man and falls in love with a good, loving bartender. They manage to buy a saloon and the story ends with Maggie displaying remarkable courage in protecting the couple's meager life savings from the man who treated her so badly. He shoots her but it is only a flesh wound and all that is missing from the story's last paragraph is "They lived happily ever after." As Oliver says, Matthews was ignoring his own contention that a novelist should "set up no false ideals" and should "erect no impossible standards of strength or courage or virtue."[49] He also was ignoring much of what Howells was calling for. Although Matthews's vignettes and his pieces collected in *Outlines in Local Color* appear to be snapshots of urban reality, with detailed scene setting and local neighborhood dialects, the perspective has a specific frame. They clearly are grounded in the real and actual and based on Matthews's own observations, but their purpose was to show that there could be something pure and noble in life on the margins, that New Yorkers shared a commonality regardless of background and circumstances.

The disagreement over Crane's tale as well as the variations on what encompasses "actuality" and what should define realism shows the degree to which magazines and newspapers were vehicles for this ongoing discourse. Probably because the ending to Davis's *Life in the Iron Mills* had just enough sunshine as well as a certain amount of Garland's "heroic purity," it could have been published in one of the major popular magazines. But it was the very existence of mass-circulation journalism that stimulated and enabled both the practice and theory of depicting the actual, in nonfiction and fiction, journalistically and artistically, and allowed for the fact-fiction, and real-romantic discourse to continue. The ongoing discussion of how and what should be depicted was not just occurring in the more prominent magazines. The *Arena,* for example, did not have anywhere near the circulation of the magazines such as *Harper's* or *Century,* or the influential literary pedigree of the *Atlantic,* but it had an influential readership and it tended to be bolder than those magazines in its article and story selection.

First published in 1889, the *Arena* was primarily a magazine that advocated for social reform, giving voice to socialistic ideas and often printing articles that other magazine wouldn't touch. The English writer W. T. Stead, for instance, said the *Arena* was "never dull" because it was willing to publish a "mad article"; the magazine was, said Stead, "strained almost to the breaking point with overcharged earnestness."[50] It published exposés that included touching articles that moved people to action, but it also was a strong supporter of Garland's local color fiction and published his Midwestern farm stories in the *Arena* before publishing them as the book *Main-Travelled Roads.* The *Arena*'s founder, B. O. Flower, complained about the lack of "veritism" in the American theater, saying it was artificial, masking life rather than mirroring it, and he extended that criticism to literature generally, claiming that all "pictures and voicings have lacked the true ring of life's verities in anything like a full or vital way" and "only that which is true, or, if ideal, is in perfect alignment with the eternal verities as found in life, can produce a lasting impression on the deeper emotions of humanity." The strength and distinguishing characteristic of the "modern school of veritists or realists" was in their "fidelity to life as it is," according to Flower, who clearly was expressing exactly what was being expressed about the same time by Alden, Howells, Garland, and so many others.[51] In the same essay, Flower notes the response of a reader of one of Garland's stories in the *Arena*:

> This gentleman said: "I read this sketch more than a week ago, and have been miserable ever since. I knew such things existed, but I never *felt what it meant before.*" That is exactly what true work does. It compels the reader to feel as well as to accept in an intellectual way. Now when our veritists appreciate that there is something needful beyond a statement of bald facts, we shall have the real with all its vivid power, reinforced and vitalized by realistic or truthful idealism. . . .
>
> The trouble with the past has been that either the idealism given was false, or was so divorced from its proper relation to the real as to act as an anaesthetic on the people, and from this pseudo-idealism, religion, literature, and the drama suffered.[52]

Dana, Garland, Alden, and Flower all expressed very similar concepts through essays, talks, articles, and story selections, explaining and defining a significant cultural paradigm. While Flower and

Arena published Garland's fiction, they also published some of Crane's New York City sketches that captured, as Hearn's Cincinnati pieces had twenty years before, the lives of the poor and marginalized. Crane's writing for newspapers and magazines became a part of a rich collection of written and visual depictions, stories, and sketches that documented life in the 1890s and early twentieth century, and included striking first-person participatory journalism that reached deeper into urban actuality than Foster could have imagined.

———————◇———————

SEVEN

EXPERIMENTS IN REALITY

By the time Stephen Crane's 1896 version of *Maggie* was published, he was well known as the author of *The Red Badge of Courage,* a realistic war novel written by a twenty-two-year-old without a single minute of combat experience. Nevertheless, some reviewers and critics claimed that *Red Badge* obviously had been written by a veteran of the Civil War. Similarly, when *Maggie* was published, reviewers well aware of Crane being a journalist and novelist assumed that *Maggie* was based on Crane's journalistic observations and consequently his depiction was as realistic as a photograph.[1] Although Crane had worked summers as a correspondent covering Asbury Park on the New Jersey shore for his brother's news service (the New Jersey Coast News Bureau), when Crane wrote *Maggie* and published it himself in 1893, he really hadn't yet lived and worked in New York City and had written only one sketch, in 1892, that dealt with city life.

His coverage of people and events at the shore, always written with a strong point of view and clear voice, regularly appeared in the *New York Tribune,* but none of these articles were strongly related to the topics and themes of *Maggie.* In fact, there was little that was fresh and original in *Maggie,* and in reviewing the book, Frank Norris declared that most of Crane's characters were "old acquaintances in the world of fiction." While the dialect and local color were of the Bowery, Norris said, otherwise the people depicted could have come from Zola.[2] Although the quality and authenticity of *Maggie* have continued to be argued and a case can be made that it is an example of romantic slum literature rather than an authentic realistic portrayal, *Maggie* nevertheless was part of the realism-romance discourse by virtue of its topic and its treatment by critics. Crane was certainly influenced by the surge in fiction, nonfiction, religious tracts, magazine illustrations, and so forth, that dealt with poverty, slums, and the rapidly expanding underclass that had become part of the Gilded Age cultural context, much of it defined, discussed, and depicted in newspapers and magazines, as well as in books. But perhaps more importantly, he also was familiar with Jacob Riis, whose classic work of nonfiction, *How the Other Half Lives: Studies Among the Tenements of New York,* was published in 1890 and whose lecture, with photographs of the New York City slums, Crane attended in Asbury Park in the summer of 1892.

With Americans pouring into New York—and into other cities as well—and with ships loaded with immigrants landing daily at Ellis Island, the city was becoming a tightly packed mixture of colorful and strange customs and people, many of whom were merely trying to survive. In the search to capture life being lived, nothing seemed more real to many writers than the city's lower depths. Fiction writers, journalists, painters, and photographers all seemed to agree with writer and reporter Hutchins Hapgood's statement: "When a man seeks his stuff for writing from low life he is at least sure of one thing, namely, that what he sees is genuine."[3] From this intense desire to record and depict the urban masses came paintings of tenement alleys and rooftops by Robert Henri and John Sloan; photographs of sweatshops, tenements, and immigrants by Jacob Riis and later by Lewis Hine; and stories of urban helplessness and broken dreams by Crane, Dreiser, and Sinclair (to name just three), but also by a number of journalists and nonfiction writers, Riis and Hapgood among them. To a certain extent, as already suggested, a belief existed that from New York's low life could be produced high art, not in the traditional sense, but according to the emerging standards of realistic expression.

Newspapers were especially attempting to tell their readers about this part of the urban milieu, motivated not by a desire to produce art, as was true of many magazines, but by a desire to present a daily picture of the city and nation as demanded by the marketplace of readers. It was not unusual for New York papers to send reporters out "slumming" to the Bowery or Mulberry Bend to produce articles that had a distinctive tone that contrasted with the other street scene articles in which the writer would try to capture Broadway or some other major thoroughfare on a summer evening or a Sunday afternoon. In these articles, there is a sense of joyful participation on the part of the writer as the more fortunate and affluent are portrayed. But often in the slumming articles the reporters are more reluctant participants who risk exposure to low-life dirt and degradation so the reader, who obviously has not been there, can experience this part of the city as well as Broadway or Fifth Avenue. A *Sun* article headlined "Sentiment in the Bowery" was typical. The opening paragraph notes that the "low resorts" on the East Side are dying out and claims that those remaining are simply "relics" of another era. The second paragraph establishes the perspective:

> It was the reporter's duty, a few nights ago, to enter one of these resorts on the Bowery. The place itself can be described in a few words: It was a long narrow room with a low stage at one end, and perhaps thirty round tables ranged in three rows along the floor. On the walls were gayly colored posters announcing the annual entertainment and ball of half a dozen societies whose names are not to be found in any directory. The place was brightly illuminated by two powerful electric arc lights, under which it was quite difficult to detect the rouge on the faces of the women.[4]

So, it wasn't pleasure, the reporter wants his readers to believe, but duty that led him to this establishment that caters to painted women that are of questionable repute. Using descriptive detail and bits and pieces of dialogue and conversation, the reporter reveals what he observed that night: faded, fallen women who spent the entire evening pestering crude, coarse men into buying them expensive drinks, and who took turns singing sad, sentimental songs about happier days in better places, until about 1:00 A.M., when "the waiter with the lustiest voice cried: 'Everybody out!'" and the men left disappointed.

In contrast to the *Sun* article is one by H. J. O'Higgins for the *Commercial Advertiser* when Lincoln Steffens edited the paper and was trying to implement his "idea of a literary journalism."[5] O'Higgins wrote as a travel writer but his travels were into New York City neighborhoods and his pieces ran under the standing head, "Trips in Manhattan." His "The Italian Quarter And Its Resorts" doesn't rely on stale images, clichés, or stereotypes. Here is the opening, which establishes a harsh, cold scene:

> The winds that swept down Fifth avenue seemed to have scoured this narrow street of the Italian quarter with a sand-blast. The

cobblestone shone like clean steel. The sidewalk flags were blown bare of the house refuse that usually collects on them. The rusty tenements had been stripped of their summer decorations of bed and body clothing, and although you could guess that the people who lived in them were not appreciably cleaner for the cold, they had all been driven indoors from the deserted pavements, and the moon and the street lamps lit a respectable street.

When O'Higgins goes inside, instead of the dirty, often hostile, atmosphere of the typical Bowery club depicted in many newspaper sketches, he finds warm, friendly establishments. He sees "ordinary Italians whom you see on the streets—some of them fruit vendors, some corporation laborers, some tradesmen and some workmen in blue jeans. You saw no drunkenness. They merely talked and smoked ceaselessly there, under the gas jets, in an atmosphere of strong tobacco, musty sawdust and old beer." He uses an argument between Italians and a Frenchman over a pool game to dispel "'guidebook' stories of the murderous Italians."[6]

The descriptive detail and dialogue in both the *Sun* and the O'Higgins articles lend them immediacy and authenticity and allow the reader to observe along with the reporter. But the result in the *Sun* article is somewhat superficial and merely reinforces a popular stereotype and a very common version of urban low-life reality, while the O'Higgins piece uses contrast and description to present a fresh perspective that humanizes the Italian quarter. Because the *Sun* article reinforces negative stereotypes, readers aren't so much observers of actuality, but instead are voyeurs. That same newspaper voyeurism could be played out when slumming expeditions by society dandies and their ladies were written up, as was the case when a group in opera dress visited the Mulberry Street police house and jail, which had "become one of the things to do" nights.[7] Of course, there were other compelling and authentic accounts of life in Bowery and other similar neighborhoods, often written by journalists who were appalled by what they observed. Riis was one of those.

How the Other Half Lives represents a mix of two strains of journalistic realism and the ascendancy of the expression of the actual. On the one hand, it exposed the conditions of the tenements, pushed for reform, and was an early example of the muckraking that served as a call to action and was so significant at the turn of the twentieth century. But it also was a continuation of descriptive narrative that started to bloom in the 1840s, a literary journalism that went beyond the facts toward cultural interpretation. The book grew out of Riis's own struggles and the abject poverty he experienced as an immigrant and out of his job as a police reporter for the *Tribune* from 1877 to 1890, specifically when working out of an office in Mulberry Bend, "the foul core of New York's slums," as Riis described it in *How the Other Half Lives*.[8] Mulberry Street and streets surrounding Mulberry were lined with the tenements that Riis wrote about and nearby were Little Italy, the Bowery, and the notorious Five Points section, which was pretty much cleared by 1895.

Riis, however, wasn't the first to write about the awful conditions in New York's tenements. Publications started calling attention to the situation in the 1870s. For instance, *Harper's Weekly,* anticipating Riis, ran three articles, each with a full page of illustrations, in March and April 1879 under the heading, "Tenement Life in New York." The first article opens with the phrase that Riis first used in talks he gave on tenement life and would become the title of his book: "It is a time-worn adage that one half of the world does not know how the other half lives, and it might almost be added, neither does it care." The relatively brief articles mostly describe what is shown in the illustrations, which appear on a separate page, but regardless of what is shown or written, the writer says, "No brush could paint and no pencil describe with all the vividness of the truth itself the utter wretchedness and misery, the vice and crime, that may be found within a stone's-throw of our City Hall, and even within an arm's-length of our churches."[9] The "Tenement Life in New York" pieces, however, are only one of several columns of information, news, and commentary in *Harper's Weekly* and not stand-alone articles, while the illustrations were not given the cover, and they compete for attention with other illustrations, including those depicting the British fighting a war in Afghanistan. More significantly, while the description of the slums is detailed and specific, and the *Harper's* writers avoid stereotypes that too often described the tenement dwellers as subhuman, except for brief comments from a resident, one never gets a close look at the people or their lives. On the other hand, when Riis wrote about the tenements of Mulberry Street, he wasn't simply coming in for a look and leaving; he was immersed in the area because of his police reporting job with the *Tribune.*

As a police reporter, Riis saw almost daily the crowded, filthy living conditions of the tenements, with their inadequate sanitation, crime, disease, and child neglect and exploitation.[10] While he covered the typical range of news events—"all the news that means trouble to some one: murders, fires, suicides, robberies, and all that sort," as he put it in his autobiography—he also tended to acknowledge the humanity of the people he covered rather than depict them as somehow subhuman. What Riis experienced as a reporter was "all a great human drama," he said when his reporting days were over, and even the seemingly smaller goings-on were "acts that mean grief, suffering, revenge upon somebody, loss or gain." It is the reporter's task, he wrote, "to portray it that we can all see its meaning, or at all events catch the human drift of it."[11] To capture the meaning of the human drama, his newspaper articles in the 1880s were generally descriptive. For instance, the incredibly crowded tenements became ovens in the extreme heat of summer, causing great misery but even more disease and death than usual. Riis wrote:

> On very hot nights a sort of human shower regularly falls in the tenement districts of sleepers who roll off the roofs, where they have sought refuge from the stifling atmosphere of their rooms. . . . The sultriness of those human beehives, with their sweltering, restless mass of feverish humanity; the sleep without rest; radiating from pavement and stone walls; the thousand stenches from the street, yard and sink; the dying babies, whose helpless wails met with no comforting response; the weary morning walks in the street, praying for a breath of fresh air for the sick child; the comfortless bed on the flags or on the fire-escape—these are sights to be encountered there.[12]

As Daniel Czitrom has pointed out, much of Riis's imagery at this time depicted the tenement dwellers as a large, dehumanized mass, their individualized humanity largely ignored, portraying the anonymity of city life that was also present in the *Harper's Weekly* coverage.[13] Yet implied in his reporting here, and later in the 1880s when he became more of a crusading journalist and reformer, was an acknowledgment that such conditions were not inevitable and due to the natural immorality of certain ethnic groups but to their environment and specifically to their awful living conditions.

A taste of Riis the writer, particularly the human-interest writer, rather than Riis the crusader can be found in *Out of Mulberry*

Street: Stories of Tenement Life in New York City, an 1898 collection of what he describes in the preface as reprints of his newspaper and magazine pieces. Riis explains that he has been asked upon what "basis of experience, of fact" had he built *How the Other Half Lives* and he says that the "stories" in the book "contain the answer," adding that they are "true."[14] The collection provides a good sampling of just how Riis could give his slum residents common, human qualities identifiable to any reader, although some of the book's selections were written well after Riis's police reporting days. For instance, "Heroes Who Fight Fire," the last piece in the collection, was published in *Century* in February 1898, the same year the book was published. Similar to much literary journalism, Riis's *Mulberry* sketches are unified by either plot or theme or both, and have a beginning, middle, and end. Here are samples of the opening of three different articles from the volume:

> Joe drove his old gray mare along the stony road in deep thought. They had been across the ferry to Newtown with a load of Christmas truck. It had been a hard pull uphill for them both, for Joe had found it necessary not a few times to get down and give old 'Liza a lift to help her over the roughest spots; and now, going home, with the twilight coming on and no other job a-waiting, he let her have her own way. It was slow, but steady, and it suited Joe; for his head was full of busy thoughts, and there were few enough of them that were pleasant.

> Something came over Police Headquarters in the middle of the summer night. It was like the sighing of the north wind in the branches of the tall firs and in the reeds along lonely river-banks where the otter dips from the brink for its prey. The doorman,

who yawned in the hall, and to whom reed-grown river-banks have been strangers so long that he has forgotten they ever were, shivered and thought of pneumonia.

The sergeant behind the desk shouted for some one to close the door; it was getting as cold as January.

A woman with face all seared and blotched by something that had burned through the skin sat propped up in the doorway of a bowery restaurant at four o'clock in the morning, senseless, apparently dying. A policeman stood by, looking anxiously up the street and consulting his watch. At intervals he shook her to make sure she was not dead. The drift of the Bowery that was borne that way eddied about, intent upon what was going on. A dumpy little man edged through the crowd and peered into the woman's face.

"Phew!" he said, "it's Nigger Martha! What is getting' into the girls on the Bowery I don't know. Remember my Maggie? She was her chum."[15]

All three pieces are snapshots of Bowery life and its characters and although Riis approaches sentimentality in many of these pieces and doesn't hesitate to show goodness if not nobility among the slum dwellers, in most of the selections the reader is knocked back to reality with a distinctly unsentimental ending.

As Riis continued writing about the slums in the 1880s, he increasingly turned to facts and statistics from reports and studies and proposed laws. He also turned to photography, first doing so on midnight trips in the slums with the sanitary police as a "way of putting before people what I saw there," he said.[16] With the photos, Riis essentially gave slide lectures—known as magic lantern slides—that made the case for cleaning up the slums. Most of his audiences were Christian church–related and he emphasized their Christian duty to join his crusade. "It is the surroundings that make the difference," he told them.[17] After one of his talks, he was asked to write about the topic by the editor of the *Christian Union* and two articles appeared in that publication as "The Tenement House Question" in May 1889, in which he referred to the "Other Half." Then in December 1889 *Scribner's* published Riis's eighteen-page article "How the Other Half Lives: Studies Among the Tenements," with twenty illustrations, one a full-page, drawn from Riis's photographs. The *Scribner's* article significantly widened his audience and resulted in the much-expanded *How the Other Half Lives,* published in the fall of 1890.[18]

Riis and his book document a time and place both textually and visually, the book being an opportune exploration of a serious urban problem. But it also harkens back to Riis's feature writing for the *Tribune* and connects him as well to writing about the city's first tenements by the likes of a George Foster in the 1840s, and to Hearn's portrayals of "the other half" in Cincinnati in the 1870s. The book, however, lacks the strong thematic unity one expects in a book-length work of literary journalism in the late twentieth and early twenty-first centuries. Czitrom describes it as an "eclectic pastiche of history, statistics, journalism, and human-interest sketches" held together by Riis's genius for synthesis.[19] Yet among its discrete twenty-five chapters, *How the Other Half Lives* does contain elements of literary journalism, including scene setting and occasional dialogue or conversation, so that the individual chapters display the coherence one finds in a shorter literary journalistic sketch. For instance, after a couple pages of "telling" consisting of a mix of facts and opinion, "The Sweaters of Jewtown" takes readers into "the sweater's district" and into a Ludlow Street tenement. The piece becomes a journey through a neighborhood of garment workers who work where they live:

Up two flights of dark stairs, three, four, with new smells of cabbage, of onions, of frying fish, on every landing, whirring sewing machines behind closed doors betraying what goes on within, to the door that opens to admit the bundle and the man. . . . Five men and a woman, two young girls, not fifteen, and a boy who says unasked that he is fifteen, and lies in saying it, are at the machines sewing knickerbockers, "knee-pants" in the Ludlow Street dialect. The floor is littered ankle-deep with half-strewn garments.[20]

From there, Riis moves on through the district, from place to place, describing what he sees, asking questions of the garment workers, who say how much they make in this world of cheap labor making cheap clothing, until the journey and day both end and Riis leaves his readers with some striking images and the meaningful juxtaposing of his day with a day in the tenement:

Evening has worn into night as we take up our homeward journey through the streets, now no longer silent. The thousands of lighted windows in the tenements glow like dull red eyes in a huge stone wall. From every door multitudes of tired men and women pour forth for a half-hour's rest in the open air before sleep closes the eyes weary with incessant working. Crowds of half-naked children tumble in the street and on the sidewalk, or doze fretfully on the stone steps. As we stop in front of a tenement to watch one of these groups, a dirty baby in a single brief garment—yet a sweet, human little baby despite its dirt and tatters—tumbles off the lowest step, rolls over once, clutches my leg with unconscious grip, and goes to sleep on the flagstones, its curly head pillowed on my boot.[21]

Riis's day will soon end with the comfort of home, whereas the baby is just beginning a life of ceaseless work and poverty and no "home" in the conventional sense.

The plight of the poor only became worse when the stock market crashed in 1893 and the United States found itself in the worse depression the nation had experienced up to that time. The most brutal year of the depression, historians seem to agree, was 1894, the same year that Stephen Crane experienced daily poverty and homelessness as well as wealth and privilege and captured the nature of each in two *New York Press* articles, "An Experiment in Misery" and "An Experiment in Luxury." It was also the year that Crane supposedly joined the line of bums and unemployed to wait for a cheap meal and bed, applying his imagination and literary skills to his own observable material rather than applying it to the familiar characters and settings that he had read about in the writing of others. The result was "The Men in the Storm," which ran in the *Arena*. Crane, unlike Riis, came from a comfortable middle-class background and wanted to experience the marginalized of the city in order to try to understand their situation in a personal, individualized sense and then write about it. It was, to a large extent, a brief immersion. Whereas Riis and Hearn had come out of poverty and Hearn continued to live among the marginalized after he was a working journalist, Crane hoped to know what it *felt* like to be down-and-out in New York City.

The facts of the economic depression were widely reported in newspapers, which also often spearheaded efforts to provide for those in need. The *Tribune,* for example, operated a "Coal and Food Fund" for the poor and regularly ran articles on the status of the needy and what was being done for them. One January day the *Tribune* ran an article with the headline "The Cry for Help,

What Is Being Done to Answer It," when only two days previously it had printed an article on "A Hunger-Stricken Horde,
Larger Crowds Each Day Seeking for Food." Here is the first
paragraph of "A Hunger-Stricken Horde":

> It was long before the sun had arisen yesterday morning that hun-
> dreds of famished men, worn-out and tired from their long tramp
> through the streets during the weary hours of the night, began
> ranging themselves in lines, patiently waiting to get into the base-
> ment of the Traveler's Club Mission . . . to get some warm food.
> Perhaps not one out of a hundred of the men who are fed there
> every day looks like a professional beggar or a tramp. They are all
> fellows who wear honest faces, and as soon as they have eaten the
> breakfast they start out once more in courageous but apparently
> fruitless attempts to obtain employment. The doors were opened.[22]

Among the information provided later in the article is that "a special meeting of the Business Men's Relief Committee, which was
organized less than two weeks ago to raise money for increasing
the People's Five-Cent restaurants, was held yesterday afternoon."
The *New York Press,* which published much of Crane's writing
about the city, handled the situation with more of a feature approach with the headline "In Poverty's Realm, Distress and Suffering Spreading as Savings Are Exhausted, Cold Snap Hard on
Poor." The article has a general lead, then moves to the cases of
two families, and then notes the groundbreaking idea for construction of a project that is supposed to provide jobs for many
unemployed. Here are the first few paragraphs:

> If the suffering among the thousands of unemployed in New York
> city could be indicated as a thermometer indicates heat or cold the

result would be a surprise to the many who know nothing of the misery that poverty entails. But there is no way to feel the pulse of a large city same as a physician feels the pulse of his patient.

The Press has investigated many individual cases. Here are two families who need relief, and they are only samples of thousands of similar or even worse cases that exist:

William Smith lives with his wife and three children on the ground floor of a tenement house at No. 625 West Forty-eighth street. For five months he has been idle. The family's savings melted away and then the pawnshop was visited. First bric-a-brac and Sunday clothes went. Then the furniture and bedding began to go. Now they have practically nothing left. The rent is long overdue and there has been nothing for the children to eat except occasional donations of bread from sympathetic neighbors. A little help or work for the husband, even at starvation wages, would be appreciated.[23]

In contrast, Crane tried in his articles to do what the *Press* said was impossible: to "feel the pulse of the city." In 1895, he wrote that he had "decided that the nearer a writer gets to life the greater he becomes an artist, and most of my prose writings have been toward . . . that misunderstood and abused word, realism." In another letter, Crane wrote that he had "developed all alone a little creed of art which I thought was a good one. Later I discovered that my creed was identical with the one of Howells and Garland."[24] The twenty-year-old Crane had covered a lecture Hamlin Garland gave on Howells and realism at Asbury Park in the summer of 1891. According to Crane's report, Garland emphasized Howells's insistence that the writer be true "to things as he sees them" and Howells's belief in "the truthful treatment of material."[25]

Although "The Men in the Storm" was published in October, six months after the "Experiment" articles, it is highly likely that Crane stood in the storm with the hungry and homeless in February. Just as the writer of the *Tribune*'s "A Hunger-Stricken Horde" made it clear that the men lining up at the mission had "honest" faces and were not tramps, so does Crane say in "The Men in the Storm" that many of the men waiting in a storm to receive help had "that stamp of countenance which is not frequently seen upon seekers after charity," rather they were "men of undoubted patience, industry and temperance . . . who at these times are apt to wear a sudden and singular meekness . . . and were trying to perceive where they had failed, what they had lacked."[26] As we will see, it was important to distinguish those impoverished and unemployed from the typical tramp. But that is the only element of Crane's article that is similar to other coverage.

Crane relies on repetition of imagery and contrast to depict the scene and capture the plight of the men. He begins his account by setting the greater scene of a city snowstorm: "At about three o'clock of the February afternoon, the blizzard began to swirl great clouds of snow along the streets, sweeping it down from the roofs and up from the pavements until the faces of pedestrians tingled and burned as from a thousand needle-prickings." The opening goes on to describe an almost frantic escape as people seek refuge. Pedestrians are described as "huddled" and "stooping like a race of aged people," as "models of grim philosophy," and as "black figures" struggling against the storm beneath the rather foreboding "dark structure of the elevated railroad." The "dreariness of the pitiless beat and weep of the storm" seems to spare no one. But then Crane switches tone and imagery in the second paragraph and says the hurrying people are off "to places which the imagination made warm with the familiar colors of home";

they had an "expression of hot dinners." In other words, who cares about a nasty storm when a cozy room and a hot meal are waiting? At that point in the narrative, Crane's article would appear to be like the many found in newspapers when a storm hit. For instance, the *Sun* told of how the city had to dig out of the storm, but also ran "Bells A-Jingling All Day Long" that began this way:

> The jingle of sleigh bells and the laughter of fur-clad revelers made pleasant music in Central Park yesterday. Every street and avenue leading to the snow-clad pleasure centre contributed its quota to the throng, until the sleighs glided past with the continuity of a procession.
>
> The afternoon muster set in strongest from Fifth avenue, and bore eloquent testimony to the luxury and leisure of the excursionists.[27]

The contrast between the affluent frolicking in the snow, or those Crane calls the "infinitely cheerful," and the poor standing cold and hungry in breadlines was too obvious for Crane to ignore, writing after the fact, and he drops the contrast into the laps of his readers when he tells them that not everyone is dashing off to warm homes and hot meals, that in front of a West Side poorhouse gather the "homeless" and "wanderers of the street" waiting patiently for the door to open so they could pay five cents for a bed for the night and coffee and bread in the morning. Crane then uses detailed description marked by repetition of imagery and the slang and dialect of the homeless men as they stomp their feet to keep warm and jostle to keep their place in line, to show readers just how isolated and vulnerable these men are. Their situation, homeless in a storm, dehumanizes them, according to Crane's depiction, as he describes them as a "mass" or "a collection of men," "a compressed group of men," "bodies of men," a "collection of heads," "a mob," a "thick stream," "sheep," and "fiends." They are all, tramps and the recently unemployed, "mixed in one mass so thoroughly that one could not have discerned the different elements." As the snow "beat in among the men," Crane says they looked "like a heap of snow-covered merchandise" rather than human beings. The longer they wait, the less human they become, telling "grim" and "uncouth" jokes, taunting a rich man looking down upon them from a window above, and laughing "ferociously like ogres" when he moves from the window. They push and become a mass of brute force crushing against the building, "panting and groaning in fierce exertion." When they finally enter the building, they become "suddenly content and complacent" and human again.[28] Thus, while most newspaper accounts sympathized with the plight of the unemployed, few accounts went beyond the facts to this level of cultural interpretation. Crane's is a tale of isolated men who have lost their individuality. That same level of interpretation occurs in "An Experiment in Misery."

"An Experiment in Misery" has appeared in a number of Crane collections, always without the original *New York Press* beginning and conclusion, as revised by Crane for his first collection. The original opening and ending, however, provide a realistic frame that introduces the young man conducting this "experiment" and reveals his motivation while establishing the authenticity of the sketch. The theme is the same in both the original and revised versions, and, like "The Men in the Storm," it deals with identity and societal and individual perception in attempting to get the "feel" of the facts of poverty and homelessness. The original begins with a simple sentence: "Two men stood regarding a tramp," and then the younger of the two wonders how the tramp "feels" being homeless and with little or no money. His older friend replies: "You can tell nothing of it unless you are in that condition yourself." So, the young man decides to find out what it is like— "Perhaps I could discover his point of view or something near it," he says—and he gets some ragged clothes and tries "to eat as the tramp may eat, and sleep as the wanderers sleep." In addition to "An Experiment in Misery," the headline said "An Evening, a Night and a Morning with Those Cast Out."[29]

In *How the Other Half Lives,* Riis conducted his observations of life in the tenements first while covering crime but then accompanying inspectors, public officials, and crusaders concerned with conditions in the tenements. He gathered facts and impressions, always matching his impressions with data. In donning the clothing of the homeless, Crane was less concerned with the facts of poverty, as Riis had been with the sociological facts of tenement life, and far more concerned with the cultural meaning. Crane's article was distinguished from most accounts on homelessness and poverty by its intense, striking metaphors and imagery and the interplay between perception and reality and its role in society's creation of identity. As Michael Robertson perceptively observes, in "An Experiment in Misery" Crane "wrenches the tramp out of the immediate context of economics, politics, and journalistic hysteria" and focuses instead on "problems of perception and understanding."[30] Crane interprets, and makes a statement about the poor and life in the city through his use of storytelling and literary methods, in contrast to Riis, who interprets directly through facts tied to scenes connected through commentary. Yet both Crane and Riis are part of the same realistic sensibility that came to characterize urban culture.

"An Experiment in Misery" and "An Experiment in Luxury" ran on consecutive Sundays in the *New York Press* and together they demonstrate how a person's identity is fluid and shaped by the clothes he wears and the environment in which he finds himself, not just because he is treated differently based on his appearance and what he represents to society, but also because a person's *behavior* and *thinking* are shaped by the environment. In "An Experiment in Misery," the youth conducting the experiment starts to think like a tramp and "wears the criminal expression that comes with certain convictions," and the young man in "An Experiment in Luxury" starts to think that he is better than others. The *Press* conclusion to "Misery" returns to the original question: is it possible to "feel" what a homeless person feels? The young man rejoins his older friend who asks, "Well, did you discover his point of view?" And the youth replies, "I don't know that I did, but at any rate I think mine own has undergone a considerable alteration."[31]

Crane's two accounts of poverty and wealth ran at a time of near hysteria in the United States over what had come to be known as the "tramp menace," and the same month that Coxey's Army of unemployed was marching to Washington to protest the depression and to call for government intervention to create jobs. Newspaper coverage of tramps was universally negative, as were Riis's tramp depictions in *How the Other Half Lives,* reflecting the common view of tramps. Tramps and "tramping" had become common with the expansion of railroads in the 1870s and an economic depression in 1873. The tramp population largely consisted of vagabonds who hopped the rails, riding from town to town and region to region, begging, looking for handouts, and running scams. Most were not seeking full employment, unlike many of Coxey's Army. Tramps generally were not victims of misfortune or circumstance, but were in "voluntary exile," to use the phrase of a leading social welfare historian.[32] In *How the Other Half Lives,*

Riis runs through the different types of people who live in the Mulberry Bend area and notes that "shunning the light, skulks the unclean beast of dishonest idleness," the tramp. "A Raid on the Stale-Beer Dives" is one of the book's stronger literary journalistic chapters, with its natural plot progression that begins with roll call at the police station where police squads were sent "to make a simultaneous descent on all known tramps' burrows in the block," clearly suggesting that tramps were vermin to be cleared out. A door is kicked in at one dark, rickety place, and inside the bug-infested building, Riis and the police see, "grouped around a beer-keg that was propped on the wreck of a broken chair, a foul and ragged host of men and women, on boxes, benches, and stools. Tomato-cans filled at the keg were passed from hand to hand. In the centre of the group a sallow, wrinkled hag, evidently the ruler of the feast, dealt out the hideous stuff."[33] They move from dive to dive, arresting tramps as they go, thirteen here, seventy-five there, with Riis explaining in detail how the beer dives operate and pointing out that "their customers, alike homeless and hopeless in their utter wretchedness, are the professional tramps and these only."[34] Near the end, Riis tells of how on a different visit to "the Bend" he persuaded "a particularly ragged and disreputable tramp" to pose for a photograph, which became part of the book's collection of photos. It would have made a fitting end to the chapter, but instead he ends the chapter with two long paragraphs answering the question, "Whence these tramps, and why the tramping?" In answering the question, he compares "toughs" with tramps. They both think "the world owes them a living," writes Riis, and that belief leads the tough to become a thief, while the tramp becomes "a coward."[35]

Crane, of course, wasn't the only journalist trying to see what it was like to be down-and-out, and in fact he was part of any

number of journalists of the 1890s who briefly tried to experience life on the streets, including other reporters for the *New
York Press,* which published Crane's "experiments." Before he left
Philadelphia and came to New York to work for the *Sun,* Richard
Harding Davis, one of the best-known and most popular journalists of his time, masqueraded as a burglar, "Buck Meiley," and spent
days and nights drinking and talking with con men, pickpockets,
and thieves before writing about how petty criminals prey on the
public.[36] Perhaps the most famous journalist to go undercover was
Nellie Bly, a reporter for the *World,* a newspaper that regularly had
its reporters tell readers of the Sunday paper what it was like to
be, for instance, a firefighter by becoming a firefighter for a day.
In 1887, Bly faked insanity and was committed to the Women's
Lunatic Asylum for ten days and wrote a first-person account as
a series that exposed neglect and abuse at the asylum. Her articles
were collected for book publication as *Ten Days in a Mad-House.*
Bly's exploit was well known, but it would be highly likely that
Crane was familiar as well with the experiment of Josiah Flynt,
who took up the tramp life for far more than Crane's single night
and single day.

By 1894, Flynt had become the emerging expert on tramp life.
In 1889, before it had become common for journalists to spend
a night or two on the street as a tramp, Flynt spent eight months
riding the rails and living the tramp life, and he later tramped in
England and Europe and published popular articles on the tramp
life throughout the 1890s. Flynt is often called a sociologist and
even the "originator of 'realistic sociology'" and his articles tend
to have the authoritative voice of serious field study; at least one
historian considers Flynt the first muckraker.[37] When Jack London's 1907 book about his own tramping across America in 1893
to 1894, *The Road,* was published, he dedicated it to Flynt, "The

Real Thing, Blowed in the Glass," which was tramp talk for genu-ine or first-rate.[38]

Flynt was only twenty years old when he conducted his ex-periment in 1889, and between 1890 and 1895 he studied at the University of Berlin, but at the same time he started writing ar-ticles about his time on the road, beginning with a piece that ran in the *Contemporary Review* in 1891. After having some of his contentions in that article challenged, he briefly returned to the road to again verify his impressions. That article was followed by three articles in the more widely circulated *Century Magazine* in late 1893 and early 1894, and additional articles were published in the 1890s in *Century*, but also in the *Atlantic Monthly, Harper's Monthly*, and *Harper's Weekly* until all the articles were collected and published in 1901 as *Tramping with Tramps: Studies and Sketches of Vagabond Life.*[39]

In one of his articles, "Club Life Among the Outcasts," pub-lished in *Harper's Monthly* in 1895, he explained in the article's first paragraph why he had played the role of tramp, at the same time emphasizing that his account was entirely based on actual experi-ence: "I wanted to know what their life amounted to and what pleasures it contained. It appeals to me as a field for exploration just as Africa or Siberia appeals to so many other people, and in what follows I can say that there is no fact or opinion which is not founded on personal experience or personal inquiry."[40] Flynt more formally expands on his purpose and clearly sets a more scholarly tone for *Tramping with Tramps* in the book's author's note, where he states that the book "attempts to give a picture of the tramp world, with incidental reference to causes and oc-casional suggestions for remedies." More significantly, he says that laboratory study "to discover parasitic forms of life," with the results published in a book provide "valuable contributions to knowledge." Similarly, his book shares what he has "learned concerning human parasites by an experience that may be called scientific" and his purpose and work are just like that of the lab scientist.[41] In the book, Flynt placed his articles as chapters in three categories: Studies, Travels, and Sketches, with a fourth section consisting of "The Tramp's Jargon" and a glossary. Although Flynt's author's note gives the impression that the book's content might read like a scientific treatise, the chapters remain as they were when published in popular magazines, regardless of the category: highly accessible and readable.[42]

Walter A. Wyckoff was another "investigator," as he referred to himself, who hit the road—not as a tramp, but as an unskilled laborer—for eighteen months, from 1891 to early 1893. Wyckoff was from an affluent family and had graduated from Princeton in 1888. During a conversation with an older man in July of 1891 he realized that he had lived a rather sheltered life and he lacked real-world understanding of labor issues. So he set off walking across America, paying his way by working at whatever unskilled job was available along the way. His account of his work and travels was published first in *Scribner's* and then as two books, *The Workers, An Experiment in Reality: The East* in 1897 and *The Workers, An Experiment in Reality: The West* in 1898. But in 1901 he also entered the literature of tramp writing with *A Day with a Tramp and Other Days,* which was also drawn from notes of his walk across America ten years earlier. (When his books were published, he was a professor of political economics at Princeton.) Only a few pages into his encounter with a tramp, who he describes in his opening paragraph as a twenty-two-year-old Irish American named Farrell who was "a little more than six feet high, and as straight as an arrow," Wyckoff pays homage to Flynt, nicely summarizing Flynt's achievement in documenting a subculture that Americans tended to despise but knew little of substance about it prior to Flynt:

> Everyone knows of the very thorough-going and valuable work that Mr. Josiah Flynt has done in learning the vagrant world, not only of America, but of England, and widely over the Continent as well, and the light that he has let in upon the habits of life and of thought of the fraternity, and its common speech and symbols, and whence its recruits come, and why, and how it occupies a world midway between lawlessness and honest toil, lacking the criminal wit for the one and the will power for the other.[43]

The "Day with a Tramp" of the book's title, however, was only forty pages of a nearly two-hundred-page book, with the book's "Other Days" seeming to consist of material Wyckoff didn't fit into his first two books, including an enlightening look at farm life in the book's longest piece, "With Iowa Farmers." Yet Wyckoff's "experiment in reality," particularly his first two books, on working at all sorts of unskilled jobs across the country, often being treated like a tramp—although somewhat stilted at times stylistically—were successful in informing readers about the struggles and lives of a whole class of society, the unskilled worker.

While Riis was filing his police reports and writing his human-interest articles for the *Tribune,* that newspaper was publishing other sympathetic accounts of the poor. Charles F. Wingate, a well-established journalist by the 1880s who had published *Views and Interviews on Journalism* in 1875, wrote a series of nine articles for the *Tribune* that ran on consecutive Sundays from December 4, 1884, through February 22, 1885, largely covering the same ground that Riis would cover in *How the Other Half Lives.* The articles were about, for example, "Italian Dives and Dens,"

"Life in the Hebrew Quarter," "Slums of the Fourth Ward," and "Overcrowded Tenements," with most of the articles dealing with the conditions of and life in the tenements.[44] Accompanied by a police officer, Wingate did his best to capture in words what he observed but felt that he simply could not "do justice" to the squalor he found there.

About the same time, social reformer and women's advocate Helen Campbell also wrote a series of articles for the Sunday *Tribune* in which she attempted to document the lives of poor women who sewed long hours many days of the year doing piecemeal stitching and garment making. Her articles were collected and published as *Prisoners of Poverty: Women Wage-Workers, Their Trades and Their Lives* in 1887. In the book's preface, she says that the articles "were based on the minutest personal research into the conditions described. Sketchy as the record may seem at points, it is a photograph from life; and the various characters, whether employers or employed, were all registered in case corroboration were needed."[45] Five years earlier, articles she had written for two magazines (*Sunday Afternoon* and *Lippincott's*) on social inequities and the role of Christianity in bringing peace to those who have faced hardships were collected and published as *The Problem of the Poor: A Record of Quiet Work in Unquiet Places.* As with *Prisoners of Poverty,* Campbell notes the book's authenticity in the preface, saying that her "sketches" were a "record of actual experiences in New York City."[46] *Prisoners* contains facts and data about pay, hours worked, and number of items sewn, all joined with individual stories featuring the language and voices of the women workers. *The Problem of the Poor* is less factually grounded than *Prisoners of Poverty* and consists of extended quotations—in the form of extended personal testimony—from a number of poor immigrants.

In 1895, Campbell continued her documentary crusading with *Darkness and Daylight; Lights and Shadows of New York Life,* with supplementary texts by a journalist and the former chief of police detectives, and with an introduction by the pastor of Plymouth Church. The publisher's preface immediately states that the book provides "scrupulously exact descriptions of life and scenes in the great metropolis," characterized by "authenticity, incontrovertible facts, and startling revelations" combined with "the most truthful and realistic" illustrations. The preface then goes into detail about how the illustrations were drawn from photographs taken when the publisher and photographer "explored the city together for months, by day and by night, seeking for living material on the street, up narrow alleys and in tenement houses, in missions and charitable institutions, in low lodging-houses and cellars, in underground resorts and stale-beer dives, in haunts of criminals and training-schools of crime, and in nooks and corners known only to the police and rarely visited by any one else." The camera does not lie, the publisher declares, adding, "In looking on these pages the reader is brought face to face with real life as it is in New York; *not* AS IT WAS, but AS IT IS TO-DAY. . . . Nothing is lacking but the actual *movement* of the persons represented."[47] The book is more than seven hundred pages long, full of information, impressions, a string of characters telling their tales, and missionary zeal—on the title page Campbell is listed as "Mrs. Helen Campbell" and given two titles, City Missionary and Philanthropist.

While it may be that Crane's accounts of city life on the margins were the most purely subjective and least factual, the works of some daily reporters as well as the more heavily fact-based "investigations" built around the assorted vignettes of Riis, Flynt, Wyckoff, and Campbell also went beyond the facts. They give readers interpretations, without the same use of metaphor, imagery, and symbolism, but nevertheless they become symbolic and meaning-making through selection and placement of descriptive detail and facts, as well as a point of view governed by reformist intent and a belief in the social gospel. Just about all journalism and book-length nonfiction dealing with current issues, concerns, people, and places made claims of authenticity, as has been demonstrated, and that authenticity was enhanced by joining text and pictures, without always making the extreme claims of Campbell's publisher. Riis, however, would eventually become recognized as much for his photography as for his prose, and his photographs of slum life were certainly an early example of documentary photography.

Of course, writing and illustrating the actual in the 1890s wasn't just about covering poverty, although that consistently was a common topic across publications. While Riis declared that the late nineteenth century was "an age of facts" and that was just what he was providing in *Children of the Poor,* his 1892 follow-up to *How the Other Half Lives,* it also was a time when feature writing and nonfiction storytelling were common and expected and were particularly prominent in the Sunday newspaper. To give those facts meaning, it also was a time when, as Dreiser later put it, the "Color" in a story was rated just as highly by editors as the "Facts."[48] In much newspaper writing, that "color" was just window dressing for the "facts," a way to make them more interesting, but with Riis, for instance, the "color" made the facts meaningful, while with Crane, the color—what a journalism textbook of the time called "nonessentials"—contained the meaning because it technically wasn't simply "color," but a window into understanding human behavior, values, and the urban environment.[49] In other words, in their many attempts to depict and document aspects of culture and society, newspapers and magazines

presented many versions of reality. That was captured by Lincoln
Steffens in his *Autobiography* when he described how the murder
of a young woman in Little Italy, near Riis's Mulberry Bend, was
covered in several different ways. He said he went to the scene and
carefully inspected it and talked with neighbors who told him how
the murderer had come into a courtyard with an organ-grinder
and while the organ played and the children danced, the murderer
rushed to a window where the woman was watching and cut her
up. According to Steffens, at least three different versions of the
murder appeared. The majority of reporters chose the sensational,
the obvious detail of blood and horror; Riis used the crusading
approach that would raise indignation of the public and lead to
reform and the elimination of Mulberry Bend ("And by the way,
it went," wrote Steffens. "Such was the power of Riis!"). Steffens
was more interested in storytelling, in looking beyond the facts of
the incident, and he wrote it as a Little Italy slice-of-life. Steffens
called his approach "descriptive narrative" and he said descriptive
was not "news" but "only life."[50]

The more sensational and popular newspapers did not shy away
from claiming that they were bringing daily real life to their readers. For instance, William Randolph Hearst's *New York Journal*
ran items daily labeled "News Novelettes from Real Life: Stories
Gathered from the Live Wires of the Day and Written in Dramatic Form." This was clearly an attempt to entertain the reader,
but it also was a way of telling the reader that what was being
presented was more than the facts. Unfortunately, the title was
somewhat misleading and the items generally were sensationalized accounts of incidents of crime and violence, or the "recital
of divorce details and the pictorial expose of the secrets of the
boudoir," as one 1896 newspaper editorial put it.[51] Nevertheless,
the paper's need to declare "Real Life," even if those real-life

stories were exaggerated and limited, demonstrates the pervasiveness of the realistic sensibility at the time.[52] Garland was not alone in his belief that readers could find in newspapers "sketches of life so vivid one wonders why writers so true and imaginative are not recognized and encouraged," and by 1906 a commentator in *Scribner's* claimed the American newspaper was "a huge collection of short stories."[53] Most New York City newspapers printed articles in which reporters avoided formula writing, both in news and feature stories, by using details and manners, narrative, and dialogue. Such writing often was a step away from the emerging form of everyday journalism but a step toward literary journalism. For instance, when five boys ran away from a Catholic boys school in 1894, the *New York Times* chose to run more than a quarter of a column on what happened after the boys ran away, making it a short tale of Mooney, "a natural-born bad boy," and four boys he led astray. After opening the article with the fact of the "escape" and the names of the five boys, the writer then tells the story in the familiar "once upon a time" approach:

> About 10 o'clock Friday over 100 boys were marched into the stocking manufacturing room in the factory building in charge of Brother Peter. Here they worked two hours and went to wash after which they were to play. When the boys marched out, Patrick Mooney and his little gang of four remained behind. Then they managed to get into the passenger elevator and descended to the ground floor.
>
> Quietly they opened the door of the building, and walked toward the skating pond. Several employees of the place saw them, but, knowing that it was playtime, they thought that the boys had been given leave to go skating as a reward for good behavior.

One of the protectory boys named Lewis, who had a dog with him, asked them where they were going.

"We're agoin' skatin', come along wid us," replied the fugitives.

"Where's yer skates?" asked Lewis.

"We don't wan no skates," was the answer.

"I tink youse fellers are runnin' away, and I'll make yez come back," and Lewis set the dog on them.

The boys pelted the dog and Lewis with stones and drove them away. Then they went across the ice and divided into two parties.[54]

The piece goes on to describe how the boys caught a train but were recognized by three school workers who were taking the train home. They apprehended the boys, with the exception of Mooney who jumped from the train and wasn't found. Compared to good fiction or magazine journalism of the time, the article is superficial and simple. Rather than true dialogue, it makes a weak attempt at dialect, providing the slang expressions that rang true, just as they had for George Foster fifty years before, for Bret Harte and Mark Twain thirty years before, and for Lafcadio Hearn twenty years before. It was, however, an attempt to make a real incident read like a story, presenting another sliver of life in the city.

A similar storytelling approach often was used for out-of-town articles, such as when the *New York Tribune* told on its front page of how a New Hampshire woman saved a train:

The Boston bound White Mountain Express on the Boston and Main Railroad was twenty minutes late when it passed through North Wakefield, N.H., about 4:45 P.M. yesterday. A storm of wind and rain was raging, but despite the murky atmosphere the heavy train was rushing onward at high speed in the endeavor to make up the lost time. Hardly had it left North Wakefield station when the engineer saw a woman on the track, frantically waving a white cloth. Evidently there was danger ahead. A push at the throttle shut off the motive power, and a quick twist of the air-brake lever was instantly responded to by a slackening of speed. The train stopped with the cowcatcher of the great locomotive almost in front of the woman.

"What's the matter?"

"The track around the curve is all covered with trees. I came to warn you."

Just ahead there was a curve, a sharp turn, so sharp that, after an obstruction upon it had come into the engineer's view, no human power could have prevented a calamity. The woman was Mrs. Emily Branson. From her house near the track she saw the wind hurl several huge trees across the rails. She was alone with her two little children.[55]

A quote from the woman and then a paragraph about the grateful passengers, giving the names of the ones familiar to New Yorkers, follow, and that's the end. The short item, with its sense of immediacy and drama, has no real impact on most *Tribune* readers; it's merely a brief, real tale of a woman who left her children alone to save a train from crashing.

It also was common, particularly in the Sunday papers, to publish short articles almost entirely in dialogue whose only purpose was to capture a moment that revealed aspects of human behavior. For instance, under the head "Dear Delightful Woman!" and a subhead that read "Troublesome Some-Times, But Always Delightful," the *Sun* depicted an exchange between "two dear, delightful, bright-eyed, red-cheeked girls" and a "phlegmatic" theater ticket seller over the costs of tickets and whether they could afford it. Somewhat sexist and condescending, this inconsequential exchange is pure fluff, yet it appeared at the top of page three along with several typical news stories, including two short items on the state legislature. There is only one apparent reason for writing the article: to illustrate the Victorian view that females, although charming, are just about helpless when it comes to getting along on their own in the city or dealing with money. It reinforces a stereotype and is designed to entertain the reader, eliciting a smile and a knowing nod from male readers. But despite being factually flaccid and short on quality and imagination, the article is typical of attempts to recreate an actual, everyday scene (two women buying theater tickets) for the purpose of illustrating an idea or viewpoint (a common opinion of women) that doesn't inform readers—except in the manner that fiction informs readers—but entertains them. Of course, the roots of such actual moments depicted were firmly planted in the penny papers.

Occasionally, a journalist takes a moment and goes beyond such superficial depictions, as Crane did in his first acknowledged urban sketch, "The Broken-Down Van," which ran in the Sunday *Tribune* in 1892. Appearing under a standing *Tribune* head, "Travels in New York," Crane witnesses a furniture van or wagon breaking down and shows what happens as attempts are made to fix the wheel. Crane allows the reader to actually experience this single, relatively insignificant incident through his eyes as they sweep over and around the scene, revealing aspects of human nature and life in a poor section of the city through the conversation of van drivers and bystanders discussing what should be done. But he also portrays a part of urban life by describing people and interactions on the periphery, which is more important in the end than the fact that a nut came off a wagon wheel. Ultimately, this moment in time reveals "the physical details of poverty, vice, and exploitation," as Michael Robertson has convincingly explained.[56]

Closer to the turn of the century, depictions of immigrants and labor became increasingly sympathetic and more authentic, particularly when the writers were either immersed in the culture or actually a part of it, as had been the case with Hearn and Riis, for instance. Abraham Cahan was both immersed totally in the Jewish Lower East Side and a Lithuanian immigrant and his journalism consistently went beyond the superficial and stereotypical. A novelist as well as a journalist who became the highly influential editor of the *Jewish Daily Forward,* Cahan said that the most important question to ask about either journalism or literature is "does this feel like real life?" and that good journalism was novelistic in that it "unfolded the thousands and thousands of life stories in tenement homes."[57]

Cahan's writing did indeed feel like real life being lived by the Jews of the Lower East Side. But while Crane depicted the city's residents as almost helpless before the cruel and unforgiving urban forces, Cahan located his sketches more closely to the emotional center of his immigrants. Cahan wrote for a number of publications, including the Sunday *Sun,* the *Atlantic Monthly, Ainslee's Magazine, Century Magazine, Scribner's,* and *Harper's Weekly,* but before taking over the *Forward,* from 1897 to 1902 he was one of Lincoln Steffens's literary journalists at the *Commercial Advertiser,* where he brought "the spirit of the East side into our shop," according to Steffens.[58] Those *Commercial Advertiser* sketches and articles, along with some from other publications, are collected in *Grandma Never Lived in America: The New Journalism of Abraham Cahan.* With scene setting, imagery, dialogue, and dialect, Cahan's *Advertiser* writing brings to life customs, attitudes, values, and mannerisms of the Jewish immigrants, fully humanizing them with recognizable universal qualities as well as distinctive ethnic and religious characteristics presented with respect and understanding.

Any of the many sketches provide a good sense of Cahan's style and content, but particularly effective and striking is "Pillelu, Pillelu," which takes place at the intersection of two street marketplaces where women are buying food for Passover. It is a rich little tale that is place-specific and timely—the corner of Hester and Ludlow streets—but also impressionistic in its opening. Similar street scenes crowded with vendors and shoppers were pictured in many paintings, illustrations, and photographs from the period.[59] On this night, Cahan writes, "The sidewalks and the asphalt pavements were crowded with pushcarts, each with a torch dangling and flickering over it, and the hundreds of quivering flames stretched east and west, north and south, two restless bands of fire crossing each other in a blaze and losing themselves in a medley of fire, smoke, many-colored piles of fish and glimmering human faces." Yet the narrative also contains a touch of mystery with a hint of danger. Ironically, the intersection of the lighted streets "looked like a vast cross of flaring gold." As the vendors shout out their produce—"Prunes, prunes—they are huge diamonds and pearls, not prunes! Prunes, good women! Buy them and be blessed!"—there is a loud disturbance caused by a stranger described by a vendor as the Evil Visitation, but who is merely "a dashing young fellow in charge of fortune-telling mice and parrots," poorly dressed and speaking in broken English and Yiddish. The scene moves from mystery to comedy as the "wizard" gives two young women fortunes provided by "Mousie" but when one fortune turns out to be for a Catholic, the women chase off the fortune-teller, and the story ends with the cry of the market: "Carrots, carrots. Fish, living fish."[60] Especially revealing of the situation, outlook, and mind-set of just-arrived immigrants, many of the sketches are located at the Barge Office, which was a temporary receiving station. Particularly compelling and representative are "Can't Get Their Minds Ashore," "What About the Baby," and "Wilhelmina Had Neither Money Nor Friends."[61]

Cahan's sketches of poignant immigrant adaptation to America reveal the mix of innocence and hope, of wonder and bewilderment, of the newly arrived. They are original renderings of experience, or what Rischin has called "the most informative evocations of the newcomers' initial reactions to their new country to appear in the daily press and the whole literature of immigration." Or as Evensen, a journalism historian has written, one recognizes in "Cahan's cultural canvas chronicles of fitful adaptation, the modern paradox of people seeking community even at the loss of self."[62]

Cahan's treatment of immigrants as individuals with inherent dignity and familiar aspirations would have fit smoothly with Lewis Hine's photographs of new immigrants taken between 1904 and 1909.[63] The immigrants Cahan wrote about with care and respect are evident in Hine's photos, where they also were depicted with care and respect. Not only did Hine document the arrivals themselves, but also the daily processing of immigrants at Ellis Island, providing crucial visual documentation of a real and symbolic moment of American history. But Cahan's friend and *Commercial Advertiser* colleague, Hutchins Hapgood, also wrote about the Jewish immigrants and the Jewish ghetto with respect, with the assistance of Cahan, who showed him around the East Side and introduced him to its people, cafes, and hangouts.

Hapgood enjoyed roaming the streets and watching and listening in parks and cafes, gathering material for his *Commercial Advertiser* sketches, which were collected and published as *The Spirit of the Ghetto: Studies of the Jewish Quarter in New York* in 1902. Because of these "studies" but especially his books on labor, radical politics, and an array of "types" from the Bowery, Filler called

Hapgood "the sociologist of the muckraking movement."[64] But it is with Hapgood's attempt to get inside the labor movement, his nonfiction 1907 book, *The Spirit of Labor,* and with Upton Sinclair's 1906 novel, *The Jungle,* that we see two additional attempts to go beyond the facts to illuminate conditions, document life being lived, and depict struggling immigrant workers as deserving human beings. Both writers relied on close observation and direct participation in the worlds and working-class cultures they depicted; both moved to Chicago and immersed themselves in working-class life, gathering material.

Although Hapgood's book is nonfiction, he carefully selected his main character, a labor leader he identified only after closely following the Chicago labor movement by attending meetings and frequenting saloons where workers and labor leaders gathered. His tale is straightforward and often consists of long sections of quotes and parts of conversations with little description or elaboration, more of a presentation of evidence gathered than an imaginative telling that creates meaning. To a certain extent, Hapgood represents an almost pure belief in the ability to faithfully, accurately, and perfectly document reality by doing what a photographer does: "find this thing already existing, and then photograph it," as he wrote a few years later. The writer would do this, according to Hapgood, by simply recording the words of his subjects by efficiently using the most basic tool of the newspaper reporter: the interview. He put it this way: "The newspaper had laid the foundation for a general interest in every section of humanity. Every class of people now feels that there is a chance to express itself. All that is wanting, is for our authors to pick up the material that abounds, forget their romantic and historical conventions, and impersonally reflect, with understanding, the drama of real life."[65] Sinclair's mostly fictional descriptive narrative is solidly grounded in actuality based on observation, but in contrast to Hapgood's nonfiction tale, it contains fully developed scenes, dialogue, and plot development. But the authenticity weakens in the last third of the story. Although what Sinclair had observed was shaped by his imagination and tempered with imagery and symbolic significance, the story's end becomes unrealistically idealistic and didactic.

Regardless of their shortcomings, these books by Hapgood and Sinclair have value as cultural documents of a time and place. They are not simply two additional writer-crusaders in the muckraking movement. Their publications and those of Riis and Flynt are documents of the movement and certainly of the Progressive Era, representative of the journalistic reformist tendency, and more specifically a part of the more than half-century-long depiction of immigrants and workers and the urban landscape in which most of them were warehoused. But they also are part of the persistent, evolving attempt to show life being lived.

EIGHT

◈

DOCUMENTING TIME AND PLACE

In January 2005, I was picking my way through a small pile of out-dated newspapers during a stay in Florida and a "Special Report" in the *St. Petersburg Times* grabbed my attention with its photos, colorful layout, and unusual headline: *A Husband for Vibha.* I soon discovered that the three-part series had three "chapters"— "An American Girl," "The Match Game," and "The Boy Next Door"—and it was about a well-known Indian cultural tradition, the arranged marriage, clashing with the expectations of a young Indian American woman, Vibha. Significantly, it was written by another Indian American woman, Babita Persaud.

Persaud's topic wasn't new. I had read about traditional Indian ways pushing against the desires of Indians who had grown up or lived for a long time in the United States in a wonderful short story collection, Jhumpa Lahiri's *Interpreter of Maladies,* which won the Pulitzer Prize for fiction in 2000. At least one of Lahiri's tales involved an arranged marriage. In addition, Chitra Banerjee Divakaruni, another Indian American author, published a collection of short stories in 1995 called *Arranged Marriage.* Divakaruni's 1999 novel, *Sister of My Heart,* also involved cultural clashes, including the arranged marriage of one of the two main characters. The Lahiri and Divakaruni stories are examples of realistic fiction, or writing that deals with real-life problems in a believable plot that involves characters, scenes, and settings that actually could exist. Howells and Alden would champion these tales, and Abraham Cahan would recognize the immigrant issues depicted, the conflict between Old and New World values, and the struggle to adapt yet maintain identities formed by distinctive cultural practices and rituals. But Cahan and Hapgood would also be pleased and impressed with Persaud's account of the same issues, one that features a character who actually does exist, a University of South Florida graduate student who grew up in Florida and who was "an American girl who was Indian too." Here's the opening of the first installment, "An American Girl," a scene-setting lead that introduces both the story's main characters and the issue that is the source of tension between parents and daughter:

> Vibha Dhwahan fidgeted in the back seat of the family car, her body wrapped in a beaded Indian tunic. Up front, her father drove. Her mother sat beside him, complaining about a book someone had borrowed.
>
> Vibha tuned out. Her mind was filled with images, photo after photo of the eligible bachelors her parents had shown her—the kind of young men they thought their daughter should marry, if only she would let them arrange it.
>
> "When is Vibha getting married?" her mother chimed almost daily.
>
> In the white Monte Carlo, they were headed down Interstate 4 toward Orlando, 30 miles from their Deltona home. Vibha looked out the window and watched the traffic flowing past: families

bound for Disney World, truckers barreling toward Tampa, teenagers looking for something to do on a Saturday.

Vibha's parents were taking her to see a Hindu priest. He would use astrology to predict when she might get married.

She never guessed that she would be the kind of woman to even consider an arranged marriage. In her mid 20s, strong-minded, a feminist, she hoped one day to sit at the head of a boardroom table.

Born in India, Vibha came to the United States with her parents at age 2. She grew up in Florida, an American girl who was Indian too.

Now she was at the University of South Florida, savvy enough to organize a charity basketball game, poised enough to stand before her peers with a microphone and talk about the importance of community involvement.

Vibha looked at her mother and father in the front seat. The couple, who treated driving as a collaborative venture, were debating a lane change. Thirty years ago, they were like her, alone, until their families put them together. Was an arranged marriage to be her destiny too?

Vibha adjusted the long shawl draped over her shoulders and stared out the window.[1]

Persaud spent three years following Vibha and her family in their quest for a husband for Vibha, and Persaud's story naturally moves with that plotline: Will Vibha find a match? Who will he be? Resolution doesn't come until the last part of the final segment, "The Boy Next Door," but as the story unfolds, characters and themes are fully developed, especially the challenge of cultural adaptation, and stereotypes fall by the wayside as misconceptions about arranged marriages are slowly corrected and the practice clarified. Overall, it's a solid work of literary journalism.

More recently, readers of a March 2010 issue of the *New Yorker* magazine learned about squid fishing and eating in Southern California in a "Talk of the Town" sketch that had its share of facts but also had a light, whimsical tone. Here's the beginning of Dana Goodyear's "Postcard from California, Squidding":

> "I'm Schmitty. This is Poke, a.k.a. Squidmaster, a.k.a., Mr. Bates."
> Poke: "Schmitty here we call Shipwreck."
> Poke, a commercial lobsterman from Long Beach, wearing camouflage overalls and rubber boots, was squatting in a pool of lamplight outside Davey's Locker Sportfishing, in Newport Beach, one recent night, fiddling with his tackle: a forty-to-sixty-pound-cast rod and a twelve-ounce, twenty-five-dollar, glow-in-the-dark, medievally barbed lure, heavy enough to drop three hundred feet to where the jumbo squid were feeding. "You got to fight the monsters with the monsters," Poke said. Not that they are wily prey. "They're dumb," he said. "Like a blonde or a doorknob."

In the same issue, another "Talk of the Town" piece, "On Parade, Lovefest" by Ian Frazier, gives readers a glimpse of a city event:

> On a Saturday morning so cold that the coffee spills on the sidewalks of Rogers Avenue, in Flatbush, were glistening light-brown rinks, and the ice in the gutters had turned to grit-covered iron, and the wind whistled though the intersection where Rogers and Church Avenues meet, the West Indian-American Day Carnival Association held a solidarity and prayer march called Haiti We Love you. All New York was invited to show support for the people of Haiti in a twenty-block march up Rogers Avenue, to begin at eleven o'clock. At eleven-seventeen, seventeen would-be marchers were warming up nearby in the nave of Holy Cross Ro-

man Catholic Church (services in English, Spanish, and Creole). "Our police permit to march is for twelve o'clock. Cold, rain, snow—nothing don't stop us," said Hazel Beckles, as she stood on the corner in an impressive fur hat with ear flaps and a high-visibility green vest identifying her as an organizer of the march. Her cell phone rang, and she said, "Yes, I am doing fine here—filled with God's cold!"

These two sketches are the typical length of a "Talk of the Town" piece, or about eight-hundred words each. Of course, this issue of the magazine also had several lengthy, in-depth articles, including "Strangers on the Mountain," with a double-page full color illustration of a confrontation between a park ranger and two Ramapough Mountain Indians who live in the hills of northern New Jersey within site of the Manhattan skyline. The confrontation is described in the article's scene-setting lead. The author, Ben McGrath, uses the incident to explore the history and nature of the "mountain people" and their relationship with surrounding communities.[2]

Such writing and reporting reverberates back to and through the nineteenth century to the observations of a Foster or a Whitman, but also to the mix of observation and immersion of a Hearn. It also moves forward to the in-depth investigative reporting of the twentieth century, to the brief snatches of life and the passing scene found in newspaper and magazine columns, and to the richly detailed narratives of literary journalists and nonfiction writers. The Goodyear "postcard" is similar to a nineteenth-century "letter" from California, perhaps sent by Twain, while the sketch on the march for Haiti compares to the "slices" of New York—and other cities—that blossomed through much of the 1800s. The McGrath article discloses the racism and marginalization of a misunderstood minority living in woods surrounded by suburban development and at the edges of the New York metropolitan area, and the Persaud series brings to life and humanizes an aspect of the immigrant experience, just as so much writing did in the late 1800s and early 1900s. Real people, real events, real places, all depicted through use of varied literary techniques and from material based on observation, interviews, and immersion. All these examples illustrate the enduring quest to document actuality. Persaud, Goodyear, Frazier, and McGrath, like Foster, Hearn, Cahan, Crane, Hapgood, Riis, Flynt, and so many others, are *cultural reporters* who craft renderings of American life that are documents that reveal, as Raymond Williams has said, "this felt sense of the quality of life at a particular time and place."[3] And that is just how Francis X. Clines described his own urban sketches.

Writing in the preface to his 1980 collection of three years' worth of *New York Times* articles, *About New York: Sketches of the City,* Clines explained that together the sketches were "a story of time and place" and "the story of the city's ordinary people, how they come to live and die in the city and make peace with it or not." He added that his aim was "simply try to describe what life looked like and felt like for this instant, to document the obvious truth that each human being is precious in his or her slot of time."[4] Clines's "roaming" the city, as he put it, as well as his writing, clearly makes him a direct descendant of Foster, as well as a close cousin of Gay Talese, whose articles were collected in *New York: A Serendipiter's Journey,* published in 1961. While all the writers considered in this book would easily nod in agreement with Clines's explanation, Cahan and Rebecca Harding Davis would also vigorously agree with the notion that "each human being is precious in his or her slot of time," and so would most literary journalists writing today.

The nineteenth-century writers and editors also would admire Talese's method of observing his subjects "in revealing situations, noting their reactions and the reactions of others to them," and they would fully understand his endorsement of nonfiction writing that brings "the reader into close proximity to real people and places."[5] Talese made it very clear in the preface to a new edition of his early work of literary journalism, *The Bridge,* that when he decided to write about the building of the Verrazano-Narrows Bridge in the early 1960s that he was specifically intent on documenting the exploits and lives of the workers who "risked their lives" to "ascend to high and dangerous places," yet were generally ignored. Looking back forty years after the bridge was built, Talese said he was gratified that he had succeeded in "establishing their rightful place in the history of this grand undertaking."[6] He brought readers closer to the men in hard hats and scuffed work boots.

But it is Talese's flaneur-like sketches, *A Serendipiter's Journey,* that especially connect to several of the urban writers considered here. Most of the book's sketches first appeared in the *New York Times,* just as Foster's *Slices* first ran in the *Tribune,* and the book's photographs work with the text just as first illustrations and then photographs did in the nineteenth century, enhancing authenticity. Talese walked the street, cast his gaze over the spectacle, and recorded what he saw and heard, creating a cultural document of the city around 1960, including a sampling of city voices, such as that of the bootblacks, some of them as young as Twain's bootblacks when he strolled New York's streets:

> "SHINE, mistah?"
>
> "Shine, mistah?"
>
> "Hey, mistah, shine?"

> This is what you hear along New York's sidewalks when the sun is shining and when the city's roving bootblacks are lined up like buzzards for business—sometimes lurking in corners, sometimes perched at the curb, sometimes wandering through the crowds whispering *"shine, shine"* like a peddler of dirty postcards.

His look at buses and bus drivers even has a tone similar to Foster's "The Omnibuses," as well as similar information. Just as Foster related the different classes of riders at different times of the day, so does Talese: "At 9 A.M. the bus is filled with secretaries and receptionists and the smell of perfume. At ten o'clock, there are executive secretaries (who'll work until six) and white-collar workers not yet ready to splurge on cabs and also the first waves of the busman's chief *bête noire*—lady shoppers."[7]

Thus, what is evident from the nineteenth century through the twentieth century and recently is a continuity of motivation and purpose and the firm desire to capture with words observed life. The paradigm of actuality, expanded and refined, persists.

For much of the nineteenth century and the first couple decades of the twentieth century, journalism was just one cultural form trying to observe, reflect, present, and report the daily lives and happenings of actual or recognizable people in real regions, cities, towns, and neighborhoods, in the process giving us not Reality or Truth—although many writers and artists claimed such—but versions of reality, pieces and parts of a time and place. For much of the twentieth century, journalism in various forms, including radio, television, and documentary filmmaking, has remained the most persistent cultural form embracing the real and actual. Daily journalism, which throws up a dizzying array of material from the present in its news reports, columns, commentary, and feature stories, including the articles on the Hmong and Somali communities cited in this book's preface, has been the most accessible realistic form, especially when joined to the Web. While it certainly expresses aspects of time and place, it often is, however, too superficial. In-depth investigative reporting and literary journalism, however, provide depth and heft to capturing actuality, and both are, as has been demonstrated, deeply rooted in journalism's emergence as a late nineteenth-century expression of and vehicle for realism. But while investigative reporting, the scion of muckraking, exposes aspects of society, particularly its problems, challenges, and wrongdoing, literary journalism more clearly, fully, and distinctly renders and depicts life being lived.

A continuity of motivation and purpose is evident in the writing but also in the declarations of the writers. As with Clines and Talese, the language writers use to describe what they do and why they do it is strikingly familiar and similar to the contentions and calls of nineteenth-century writers and editors. They confirm that unending determination to try to depict the real and actual. John McPhee, for instance, has described his work as "Real people and places," while Lounsberry, writing in the nonfiction collection she edited with Talese emphasizes that what distinguishes the writing in that collection is that it is "based on facts, on material chosen from (and remaining a verifiable part of) the real world."[8] Babita Persaud says that the idea for "A Husband for Bibha" did not come from beat coverage or the news but from "life—my life."[9] Not only are some of the same words used to describe technique and purpose, but so also are references to the primacy of observation. Katherine Boo of the *Washington Post* insists that to accurately capture people, "watching them live" is essential. Anne Hull of the *Post* notes the "art of watching"; Ted Conover emphasizes the necessity "to bear witness to them [people he writes about] in some way," while Sims says Conover "bears witness to the common life."[10]

Even the titles of any number of books suggest the ongoing journalism-realism discourse. In addition to the Talese-Lounsberry anthology, other examples include *To Tell the Truth: Practice and Craft of Nonfiction* (2009) or *Telling True Stories* (2007), both of which are guides to nonfiction writing. Although different in content and intent, with claims to its continuing impact and influence frequently overstated, *The New Journalism*—in which Tom Wolfe called for journalists to document society and its manners and ways since, he claimed, there was no longer a vibrant realistic fiction to do it—frequently serves as an originating point for a reconsideration of just how writers might render society and culture. However, these books, including *The New Journalism,* as well as the many articles and book-length works of literary journalism, are a realization of both Hutchins Hapgood's 1905 call for "A New Form of Literature" that would be the "story of life" and consist of "real" tales and characters, and Charles Godfrey Leland's 1862 plea for a "steam-engine whirling realism" that deals with the "Actual of life."[11]

But saying that continuity exists and that purpose and intent are similar if not the same as they were a hundred years ago does not mean that differences do not exist over time. As society and culture have changed, so have its forms of expression. After all, journalism in the nineteenth and early twentieth centuries was at the center of a print culture that was learning how to portray American society and everyday life. Yet more works of extremely sophisticated literary realism, much of which can be considered journalistic, are being written in the early twenty-first century than a hundred years ago.[12] Even as new media emerge and forms of communication converge, people remain curious about one another and how we live. New and old media still are showing people to people, still trying to make sense of actuality, still feeding that national need to know and understand, as well as the desire to just curiously look and see.

Just as Jacob Riis latched onto photography to help him lend authenticity to his observations, so today those who wish to document observed life to its fullest can turn to digital technology. For instance, a multimedia package built around "A Husband for Vibha" can still be accessed online. While the series that appeared in the newspaper read more like a photo-illustrated novella, the online materials produce a very different experience, integrating images, voices, and text, making the mix even more immediate and grounded in the present than the original newspaper presentation. At least four different versions of Mark Bowden's "Black Hawk Down: A Story of Modern War" are available: the original *Philadelphia Inquirer* series; the *Inquirer*'s online multimedia package that includes video, photographs, the complete text, analysis of each segment or chapter, and Q&A with Bowden; the best-selling book, *Black Hawk Down;* and the movie based on the book.[13] The focus on actuality that arose in the 1800s as part of a cultural-wide move to depict and document reality remains the prime mover of journalism and literary journalism, whether in newspapers, magazines, books, or as part of online multimedia packages. Then and now such writing or presentations give us windows that never provide a complete view of reality; sometimes the view can be a murky one that suggests reality's incomprehensibility. Nevertheless, meaning-making occurs in the very act of observing, writing, and illustrating. Whether in 1895 or 2005, such accounts are still telling us something about who we were or who we are and they remain cultural documents of a time and place.

NOTES

PREFACE

1. Erin Carlyle, "Minneapolis Somali community facing dark web of murders," *City Pages,* November 12, 2008.

2. MacLeish, "Poetry and Journalism."

3. "The Recording Tendency and What It Is Coming To," *Century* 53 (Feb. 1897): 634–35.

CHAPTER ONE

1. Twain, *The Autobiography of Mark Twain,* 125–26.

2. Wallace Stegner, introduction to Bret Harte, *The Outcasts of Poker Flat and Other Tales,* viii. Similarly, another literary scholar says Harte "was no literary realist . . . save in the very broadest sense of the term," which seems to be the consensus. Scharnhorst, *Bret Harte,* 25.

3. Stegner perceptively observes: "Harte's geography seems vague because he did not know the real geography of the Sierra well, and didn't feel that he needed to. His characters seem made because they *were* made, according to a formula learned from Dickens: the trick of bundling together apparently incompatible qualities to produce a striking paradox." Stegner, introduction to *The Outcasts of Poker Flat,* ix.

4. Shi, *Facing Facts: Realism in American Thought and Culture 1850–1920.* Another valuable recent book that intersects at several points with *Journalism and Realism* is Underwood, *Journalism and the Novel: Truth and Fiction, 1700–2000.*

5. Emerson, "The American Scholar," in *Essays and Lectures,* 69.

6. Scharnhorst, ed., *Bret Harte's Calilfornia: Letters to the Springfield Republican and Christian Register, 1866–67.*

7. Boyer, *Scholarship Reconsidered,* 18–19.

CHAPTER TWO

1. Crane, "The Men in the Storm," in *Tales, Sketches, and Reports: The Works of Stephen Crane, VIII,* ed. Fredson Bowers, 315–22; Sinclair, *The Jungle.* Shin's painting is at the Corcoran Gallery of Art and is in a number of books, including an exhibition book. Zurier, Snyder, and Mecklenburg, *Metropolitan Lives: The Ashcan Artists and Their New York,* 12, 69.

2. For instance, see Bell, *The Problem of American Realism,* and Kaplan, *The Social Construction of American Realism.* For a wide-ranging and largely traditional overview of realism as a movement, see Smith, ed., *American Realism,* which includes "A Historical Overview of American Realism," 10–35. In the introduction, Smith declares that, "Realism in one form or another now stands as one of the most important and enduring movements in American literary history," 8. Chapters consist of selections from books by scholars who have helped define realism and naturalism over the past forty years, with an Alfred Kazan chapter going back to the 1940s.

See also Barrish, *American Literary Realism, Critical Theory, and Intellectual Prestige, 1880–1995,* especially his discussion of "Realist Dispositions," 3–7.

3. Shi, *Facing Facts: Realism in American Thought and Culture 1850–1920,* 163, 86. Among various works that acknowledge or demonstrate the broad cultural influence of realism as observed life, perhaps the most thorough, impressive, and well-documented is Shi's.

4. "The Artists' Fund Society, Fourth Annual Exhibition," *The New Path* 1 (December 1863): 94; Introductory, *The New Path* 1 (May 1863): 3.

5. Benjamin T. Spencer, Introduction in Charles Godfrey Leland, *Sunshine in Thought,* ix.

6. Leland, *Sunshine in Thought,* 4.

7. Ibid., 95–96.

8. Leland, "To Readers and Correspondents," *Graham's* 51 (July 1857): 82; *Graham's* 50 (May 1857): 468–69.

9. Emerson, "Conduct of Life," *Emerson: Essays and Lectures,* 952, 1062.

10. James, *Pragmatism,* 97.

11. *Kindred Spirits* came into prominence in 2005 when it was purchased from the New York Public Library by Wal-Mart heiress Alice L. Walton for $35 million. In 2007, it was the center of special exhibits at the National Gallery of Art and at the Brooklyn Museum. It can be viewed at a number of online sites, as well as most books dealing with either the Hudson River School or American landscape painting, including: Wilton and Barringer, *American Sublime: Landscape Painting in the United States, 1820–1880;* Cooper, *Knights of the Brush: The Hudson River School and the Moral Landscape.*

12. In Noyes, *English Romantic Poetry and Prose,* 1125.

13. Cole, "Essay on American Scenery," in *American Art, 1700–1960: Sources and Documents,* ed. John Walker McCoubrey, 102. First published in *American Monthly Magazine* 1 (January 1936): 1–12. Also reprinted in Benton and Short, *Environmental Discourse and Practice: A Reader,* 87–90.

14. Bryant, *Funeral Oration, Occasioned by the Death of Thomas Cole, Delivered Before the National Academy of Design, New York, May 4, 1848.* Available at http://books.google.com and at http://www.catskillarchive .com/cole/wcb.htm. The New York Historical Society sponsored an exhibit from October 2000 to February 2001 titled "Intimate Friends: Thomas Cole, Asher Durand, William Cullen Bryant." An article in the online publication *Resource Library* (http://www.tfaoi.com) describes Bryant as "friend and muse to Cole and Durand" and based on research by the exhibit curators claims that the three "were crucial in the formation of the 19th-century American artistic taste and attitudes toward the natural world." One of the more popular poems of the early nineteenth century was Bryant's "Thanatopsis," which was rendered on canvas by Durand with his 1850 "Scene from Thanatopis," which is very similar in tone and style to Cole's landscapes.

15. Pearce, *The Continuity of American Poetry,* 206. Mott, *American Journalism,* 258.

16. Ed Folsom, ed., "'This Heart's Geography Map': The Photographs of Walt Whitman," Special Issue of *Walt Whitman Quarterly Review*

4 (2–3, Fall–Winter 1986–87): 70. See also *Thomas Eakins* (Washington, D.C.: Simthsonian Institution Press, 1993), 109–11.

17. Matthiessen, *American Renaissance: Art and Expresssion in the Age of Emerson and Whitman,* 604; Homer, *Thomas Eakins: His Life and Art,* 213.

18. Shi, *Facing Facts,* 97.

19. Matthiessen, *American Renaissance,* 603.

20. Emerson, *The Early Lectures of Ralph Waldo Emerson,* 361–62. Emerson emphasizes the importance of a poet knowing the real world in its totality, of being one "who announces news—the only teller of news, of news that never get old," 356–57. Whitman covered Emerson delivering a version of this talk, "The Poet," for the *New York Aurora* on March 5, 1842, and wrote about it for the paper two days later. "Suffice it to say," Whitman wrote, "the lecture was one of the richest and most beautiful compositions, both for its matter and style, we have ever heard anywhere, at any time." Whitman, *The Collected Writings of Walt Whitman: The Journalism,* 44.

21. Whitman, *The Uncollected Poetry and Prose of Walt Whitman,* vol. 2, 69. In the same notebook verse, Whitman said, "that all the things seen are real." 69.

22. Whitman, *Complete Poetry and Selected Prose,* 41, 42.

23. Whitman, *Complete Poetry and Selected Prose,* 31.

24. Canby, *Walt Whitman: An American,* 57. The relationship between Whitman's poetry and journalism was acknowledged before Canby and continues today. Hyatt Waggoner, for instance, describes Whitman's poetry as seemingly "journalistic restatement." Waggoner, *American Poets from the Puritans to the Present,* 159. Shelley Fisher Fishkin has probably provided the fullest examination of the relationship between Whitman's journalism and poetry. Fishkin, *From Fact to Fiction: Journalism and Imaginative Writing in America,* 13–51.

25. Zurier, Snyder, and Mecklenburg, *Metropolitan Lives,* 63, 8.

26. Rosebault, *When Dana Was the Sun,* 145.

27. Leland, *Sunshine in Thought,* 96.

28. Schiller, *Objectivity and the News: The Public and the Rise of Commercial Journalism,* 95.

29. Mindich, *Just the Facts: How "Objectivity" Came to Define American*

Journalism, 14. See especially ch. 4, 103–6, for a discussion of realism in American culture.

30. Mott, *American Journalism,* 224.

31. Ibid., 222.

32. See Ibid., 223–24, for an example of a full "Police Office" police report from a July 1834 issue of the *Sun.*

33. Reprinted in Cray et al., 31.

34. Historians and scholars have made a number of claims regarding the role and impact of New York's penny papers. Some claims, such as Susan Thompson's contention that the advent of the penny papers "created a new movement in civilization," may strike some as extravagant. See Thompson, *The Penny Press,* 192–93; and Thompson and Michael Bucholz, "The Penny Press, 1833–1861," in *The Media in America: A History,* ed. Wm. David Sloan, 126. Others go in the opposite direction and insist the originality and influence of the penny papers is a myth created by scholars of various perspectives. See Nerrone, "The Mythology of the Penny Press," with criticism by Michael Schudson, Dan Schiller, Donald L. Shaw, and John J. Pauly, *Critical Studies in Mass Communication* 4 (December 1987): 376–422. Still others fall somewhere in between. In dispute is not just the genuine nature and impact of the penny papers, but also what was responsible for the rise of the penny papers. Was their birth and eventual dominance primarily due to economic forces, including industrialization? Social and cultural forces? Or was it the drive, genius, and entrepreneurial instincts of individuals such as Bennett, Benjamin Day of the *Sun,* and Horace Greeley of the *Tribune*? Most seem to agree that a mix of those forces allowed the penny press to emerge and grow. Although much has been written about the penny press, Thompson's is the only book-length work and contains significant verifiable detail, if occasionally short on cultural interpretation. The Schiller and Mindich books contain important details and interpretations of the penny press but Mindich's account is especially vital because the book explores the myth and reality of the concept of objectivity more completely than has been done previously. Schudson's *Discovering the News: A Social History of the American Newspapers,* has become a standard work in any consideration of nineteenth- and early twentieth-century journalism, including the penny papers and objectivity, while Stevens's *Sensationalism*

and the New York Press and Dicken-Garcia's *Journalistic Standards in Nineteenth-Century America* provide insight and perspective on the penny papers and the press generally during the century. Dicken-Garcia shows clearly how journalism was part of and influenced by larger forces in society and convincingly demonstrates how societal values were evident in press performance and standards. The antebellum press also is the focus of Huntzicker, *The Popular Press, 1833–1865.*

35. Carey, *Communication as Culture: Essays on Media and Society,* 21.

36. Quoted in Carlson, *The Man Who Made the News,* 150.

37. Although certainly Poe-like, most of Poe's tales and poems, with a few exceptions, were published in the 1840s. Bennett's tone and style, however, are distinctly romantic and perhaps a bit Gothic.

38. Tucher, *Froth and Scum: Truth, Beauty, Goodness, and the Ax Murder in America's First Mass Medium,* 68. Roggenkamp, *Narrating the News: New Journalism and Literary Genre in Late Nineteenth-Century American Newspapers and Fiction,* 74. For a comparison of the penny papers' coverage of the Jewett murder to the crime pamphlet literature, especially the timeliness and immediacy of the newspaper coverage see Cohen, *The Murder of Helen Jewett: The Life and Death of a Prostitute in Nineteenth-Century New York,* 25–26.

39. Rowson, *Charlotte Temple,* 5.

40. Davidson, Introduction, *Charlotte Temple,* xii.

41. Beginning in the 1830s and 1840s, counternarratives started to emerge from such authors as Catherine Sedgwick, although seduction narratives with the woman succumbing to the man and dying as a result remained a staple in men's fiction. Baym, *Woman's Fiction: A Guide to Novels by and about Women in America, 1820–1870,* ch. 3.

42. Tucher, *Froth and Scum,* 1, 3.

43. Cohen, *The Murder of Helen Jewett,* 322.

44. Tucher, *Froth and Scum,* 60, 64. Tucher also notes that "the rhetoric of egalitarianism complemented and upheld the classic myth of the poor oppressed victim, producing for working-class readers a clear and comprehensible explanation of who was to blame for evil." 74.

45. Roggenkamp, *Narrating the News,* 1.

46. Ibid., 74. See Schiller, *Objectivity and the News.* Schiller examines the *National Police Gazette* to illustrate his thesis.

47. Quoted in Tucher, *Froth and Scum,* 54.

48. Patricia Cline Cohen, "The Helen Jewett Murder: Violence, Gender, and Sexual Licentiousness in Antebellum America," *NWSA Journal* 2, 3 (Summer 1990): 376.

49. David Anthony. "The Helen Jewett Panic: Tabloids, Men, and the Sensational Public Sphere in Antebellum New York," *American Literature* 69, 3 (September 1997): 488.

50. Cohen, *The Murder of Helen Jewett,* 219. Cohen quotes extensively from the letters of Jewett and Robinson. Although Jewett's letters are, as Cohen points out, "sexually assertive," they also strike one as being rather typically manipulative in the manner of love letters and not in the manner of a prostitute to a favored client.

51. The penny papers would again get swept up in trying to make sense of the murder of a woman; for instance, in 1841 with the never-solved brutal death of Mary Rogers. Historian Amy Gilman Srebnick has shown how the woman's death became a "source of mystery and romance" through extensive newspaper coverage that then led to a number of book-length accounts, including novels. This case was the basis for Poe's early work of detective fiction, "The Mystery of Marie Roget." Srebnik shows how this case illustrates "the relationship between gender and culture (especially between women and cities)." Not unlike the Jewett murder, it became a story of urban culture, social class, and female sexuality. Srebnick, *The Mysterious Death of Mary Rogers: Sex and Culture in Nineteenth-Century New York,* xv, xiv.

52. Crouthamel, *Bennett's New York Herald and the Rise of the Popular Press,* 25.

53. Longstreet. *Augustus Baldwin Longstreet's Georgia Scenes Completed: A Scholarly Text.* In the introduction, editor David Rachels calls Longstreet's pieces "realistic sketches," xxiii. He also says that when Longstreet bought the newspaper, which like most newspapers in the South was primarily an impersonal information sheet, he personalized the new *State Rights' Sentinel,* "moving it beyond the neoclassical editorializing that dominated the pages of its competitors," a move not unlike that of the penny papers, xxiv.

54. Longstreet, *Georgia Scenes,* 3–4.

55. Ibid., xxv, xxvii.

56. Ibid., xlv–xlvi.

57. Ibid., xlviii.

58. Ibid., xlvii–xlix. Longstreet probably met many of his characters and experienced some of the incidents while serving first as a circuit judge and then as a Methodist minister.

CHAPTER THREE

1. Whitman, *The Collected Writings of Walt Whitman: The Journalism,* ed. Herbert Bergman, "The Penny Press," 1 (March 26, 1842), 74. Bergman has collected two volumes of Whitman's journalism. Volume 1 consists of almost six-hundred pieces of Whitman's journalism (articles, editorials, and essays) from 1834 to 1846 from twenty different publications.

2. The concept of the flaneur has typically been traced to Paris and specifically to the writings of Charles Baudelaire and later through Walter Benjamin's interpretation of Baudelaire in *The Arcades Project*. Literary scholar Dana Brand, however, makes a convincing case for its London roots and he defines and explores an American version that appears in the works of Poe, Hawthorne, and Whitman, with discussion as well of some nonfiction and journalism, including that of George Foster. See Brand, *The Spectator and the City in Nineteenth Century American Literature*. See especially chapter 3, "The Flaneur in America," and chapter 8, "'Immense Phantom Concourse': Whitman and the Urban Crowd." Brand's opening chapter, "The Flaneur and Modernity," fully discusses the context and definition of the term, which is a development of modernity and the accompanying birth of the modern city. Brand uses Baudelaire's phrase, "the painter of modern life" or an artist who embraces "modern subjective experience" to explain the concept of flaneur (4–5). Throughout his book, Brand contests Walter Benjamin's (and therefore Baudelaire's) presentation of the flaneur as specifically local (Parisian) and brief. For a focus on the flaneur in Paris, see Ferguson, *Paris as Revolution: Writing the Nineteenth Century City,* especially chapter 3, "The Flaneur: The City and Its Discontents." Ferguson includes a rather striking quote from Auguste

de Lacroix: "Art, science, and literature owe their progress more or less to the flaneur" (80).

3. Whitman, *The Collected Writings of Walt Whitman,* Bergman, Introduction, xliii–lxx (hereafter cited as Whitman, *The Collected Writings*).

4. Fishkin, *From Fact to Fiction: Journalism and Imaginative Writing in America,* 17.

5. Whitman, *The Collected Writings,* "The New York Press," March 29, 1842, 81.

6. Ibid., 100.

7. Ibid., "New York Boarding Houses," March 18, 1842, 61.

8. Ibid., "Life in a New York Market," March 16, 1842, 55.

9. Ibid., 55–56.

10. Ibid., 57.

11. Ibid., "The Clerk from the Country," March 24, 1842, 72.

12. Fishkin, *From Facts to Fiction,* 19–22.

13. Whitman, *The Collected Writings,* "Scenes of Last Night," April 1, 1842, 90.

14. Fishkin, *From Facts to Fiction,* 22.

15. Whitman, *The Collected Writings,* 90.

16. Ibid., 91. This type of positive exclamation at the end of an article that deals with a rather sad topic was not unusual for Whitman. For example, in "An Afternoon at the Blind Asylum," written for the *Brooklyn Eagle,* June 9, 1846, he visits a home for the blind and describes the "piteous sight" and particularly is overcome by the blind children, innocent but "wilted and withered." But he concludes that he spent "the most agreeable hours there," after noting that he could see how when they sang hymns that in "their unearthly smiles" they were connecting with God and that "perhaps the Kind God vouchsafes them to *imagine* the beauties of *His* dwelling place, though they cannot see the firmament," 407–9.

17. Fishkin, *From Fact to Fiction,* 22.

18. Ibid., 26.

19. Ibid., 22.

20. Crane's urban journalism has been collected in *Tales, Sketches, and Reports,* which is volume 8 of *The University of Virginia Edition of the Works of Stephen Crane.*

21. Whitman, *The Collected Writings,* "New Publications," *Brooklyn Eagle,* March 9, 846, 272.

22. Whitman, *The Collected Writings,* "The New York Press," March 29, 1842, 81. It was the "best," according to Whitman, because "it is bound to no party, but fearless, open, and frank in its tone—brilliant and sound, pointed without laboring after effect, ardent without fanaticism, humorous without coarseness, intellectual without affectation—and altogether presents the most entertaining mélange of latest news, miscellaneous literature, fashionable intelligence, hits at the times, pictures of life as it is, and every thing else that can please and instruct—far beyond any publication in the United States."

23. George G. Foster, *New York Naked* (New York: De Witt and Davenport, 1854), 12.

24. Historian Stuart M. Blumin's "George G. Foster and the Emerging Metropolis," is the best and most recent source on Foster's work and life and is the introduction to his collection of Foster's urban writing: Blumin, ed., with an Introduction, *New York by Gas-Light and Other Urban Sketches by George G. Foster.* This collection contains all the *Gas-Light* sketches as well as four of Foster's *Slices* sketches (out of thirty-four total), and four sketches from *Fifteen Minutes Around New York* (out of thirty-two total). All citations of sketches from *Gas-Light* will be from the Blumin collection.

25. Blumin, *New York by Gas-Light,* 34–35. In *New York Naked,* Foster says when he started writing the *Slices* sketches at the *Tribune,* he tried to produce "more finished" work than "the daily paragraphs" he had done to that point, 16.

26. Foster, *New York Naked,* 14.

27. Ibid., 16. Foster also claimed that the idea itself became popular and that shortly after the "Slices" began appearing, "we had 'Hudson in Patches,' 'Wisconsin in Chunks,' and 'Mississippi in Gobs'—and all sorts of states, cities and provinces, in all sorts of aliquot quantities."

28. Blumin, Introduction, *New York by Gas-Light,* 38.

29. Ibid., 40.

30. Foster, *New York in Slices,* 9.

31. Ibid., 40.

32. Ibid., 40–41.

33. Foster, *Fifteen Minutes Around New York*, 27–28.

34. Foster, *New York in Slices*, 40.

35. Foster, *New York by Gas-Light*, 85.

36. Foster, *New York in Slices*, 65.

37. Ibid., 32.

38. Ibid., 31.

39. Foster, *New York by Gas-Light*, 174.

40. Foster, *Fifteen Minutes Around New York*, 40

41. Ibid., 27.

42. Foster, *New York in Slices*, 66–67.

43. Foster, *Fifteen Minutes Around New York*, 77–80.

44. Foster, *New York by Gas-Light*, 178–88.

45. Foster, *New York in Slices*, 4.

46. Foster, *New York by Gas-Light*, 69–70.

47. Ibid., 73–74.

48. Blumin, Introduction, *New York by Gas-Light*, 60.

49. Foster, *New York in Slices*, 4.

50. Foster, *New York by Gas-Light*, 191.

51. Ibid., 191–92.

52. Ibid.,189, 190, 191.

53. Ibid., 192.

54. Foster, *Fifteen Minutes Around New York*, 19. In the final sketch in *Fifteen Minutes*, "A Saturday Night Ramble," Foster concludes by admonishing the city's affluent class: "The truth is, that the condition, both moral and physical, in which such a city as New York permits its poor to exist, is utterly disgraceful—not to the poor, for they deserve only our deepest pity, but to the community—the powerful, enlightened, wealthy community—which permits its unfortunate children, who know nothing but how to work, to become thus horribly degraded. Are our readers weary of hearing this repeated? But it must be repeated and reiterated, until government and the wealthy know and feel its truth, and see clearly their bounden duty to that portion of their fellow creatures who are not able, in the sharp and selfish competition of keener brains, to take care of themselves," III.

55. Foster, *New York in Slices,* 19.

56. Ibid., 20.

57. Ibid.

58. Ibid., 22.

59. Ibid.

60. Ibid., 23.

61. Ibid., 24.

62. Brand, *The Spectator and the City in Nineteenth Century American Literature,* 74.

63. Blumin, Introduction, *New York by Gas-Light,* 1.

64. Thea Holme, Introduction in Charles Dickens, *Sketches by Boz: Illustrative of Every-Day Life and Every-Day People,* vii.

65. Foster, *New York in Slices,* 22–23. The "Willis" Foster mentions is Nathaniel Parker Willis, best known for his poetry, essays, travel writing, and magazine editing, particularly of *Town and Country,* but who also had written a number of sketches of life around him. Although Willis was interested in writing about fashion and taste and especially in depicting scenes and capturing conversation among high society, his sketches, especially those sent from Europe to the *New York Mirror* in the 1830s, were marked by vividness of description, an impressionistic style that focused on real people and events, and the conversation or "chit-chat" of people in private social settings, which brought him accusations of bad taste for doing so. His sketches, in the form of letters to the *Mirror,* ran from 1832 to 1836 under the heading "First Impressions of Europe" and were collected and published under the title *Pencillings by the Way* in 1844. In the book's preface, he said he had "indulged" himself "in a freedom of detail and topic which is usual only in posthumous memoirs." Willis, *Pencillings by the Way,* iii. For a perceptive biography of Willis that places him within a broad cultural context that focuses on the "modern ethos of sentiment and personality," see Baker, *Sentiment and Celebrity: Nathaniel Parker Willis and the Trials of Literary Fame.*

66. Blumin, Introduction, *New York by the Gas-Light,* 11.

67. Ibid., 53.

68. Thomas Bender, "The Culture of the Metropolis," *Journal of Urban History* 14 (August 1988): 494.

CHAPTER FOUR

1. Rebecca Harding Davis, *Life in the Iron Mills,* 11.

2. Ibid.,11, 12.

3. For a fresh, perceptive investigation of depictions of class in the works of several writers, including Davis, Crane, and Whitman, see Dow, *Narrating Class in American Fiction.* Whitman, with a focus on *Leaves of Grass,* is considered in chapter 1, while Davis and Crane are paired in chapter 2, focusing on Davis's *Life in the Iron Mills* and Crane's novel *Maggie.* Dow acknowledges how writers have struggled with finding language that represents "a reality lived by others in the face of readership often far from such realities," which is an underlying premise in this book (Dow, 219). But what is significant about Dow's study is that it demonstrates how such works are ultimately subjective and his central thesis is that the concept of "class" in writing from Whitman through James Agee has been consistently dynamic and discursive.

4. Davis, *Life in the Iron Mills,* 69.

5. Mott, *A History of American Magazines,* 173.

6. Elizabeth Ammons, Introduction, in *"How Celia Changed Her Mind" and Selected Stories,* ed. Rose Terry Cooke, xxix–xxx.

7. Rose, *Rebecca Harding Davis,* 13.

8. Davis, *Life in the Iron Mills,* 65.

9. Rose, *Rebecca Harding Davis,* 142. See also, 133–34.

10. Davis, *Life in the Iron Mills,* 13–14.

11. Davis, *Margret Howth: A Story of To-day,* 3.

12. Ibid., 5–6.

13. Ibid., 6. Davis's claim that there is value in the common and everyday is similar to Norman Sims's contention that literary journalists by "paying attention to the "normal rounds of life . . . confirm that the crucial moments of everyday life contain great drama and substance." Sims, *The Literary Journalists,* 3.

14. Davis, *Margret Howth,* 7.

15. Harris, *Rebecca Harding Davis and American Realism,* 9. Harris makes a strong case that Davis wasn't just writing from "compassion" but from a "well-developed literary theory."

16. Davis, *Margret Howth,* 101–2.

17. Ibid., 102.

18. Harris briefly discusses this, noting that *Waiting for the Verdict* is "a psychological study of miscegenation, an issue most Americans wished to ignore at the time." *Rebecca Harding Davis and American Realism,* 133.

19. "Rebecca Harding Davis," author unknown, in Rebecca Harding Davis, *Waiting for the Verdict.*

20. Harris, *Rebecca Harding Davis and American Realism,* 3.

21. Mott, *A History of American Magazines,* 309–10.

22. Rose, *Rebecca Harding Davis,* 133. See also Harris, *Rebecca Harding Davis and American Realism,* 233.

23. Harris, *Rebecca Harding Davis and American Realism,* 233.

24. *Scribner's Monthly* 8 (Sept 1874): 541.

25. "By-Paths in the Mountains," *Harper's New Monthly Magazine* 61 (July–Sept.) 1880): 167–85, 353–69, 532–47; "Here and There in the South," *Harper's New Monthly Magazine,* 75 (July–Nov. 1887), 235–46, 431–43, 593–606, 747–60, 914–25.

26. Rose, *Rebecca Harding Davis,* 111–12; Harris, *Rebecca Harding Davis and American Realism,* 208–9.

27. Rose, *Rebecca Harding Davis,* 112.

28. Ibid., 112.

29. Harris, *Rebecca Harding Davis and American Realism,* 223–24.

30. Rose, *Rebecca Harding Davis,* 112. Rose also points out that the travel pieces were popular. Davis wrote a children's version of "By-Paths in the Mountains" for *Youth's Companion,* "Vacation Sketches among the Alleghenies," June 1882: 243, and she wrote an essay for the *Atlantic* prompted by her "Here and There in the South" trip called "Some Testimony in the Case," November 1885: 602–8.

31. Davis, "Here and There in the South," *Harper's New Monthly Magazine* 75 (July–November 1887): 914–25.

32. See Sims, *True Stories: A Century of Literary Journalism,* especially 45–53; Twain is the first writer considered in Connery, ed., *A Sourcebook of American Literary Journalism: Representative Writers in an Emerging Genre*; in Connery, see Jack A. Nelson, "Mark Twain," 41–53; one of the earliest discussions of a "literary journalism" that also included Twain can be found in Ford, "Foreword," *A Bibliography of Literary Journalism in America.*

33. Sims, *True Stories,* 53.

34. This has been pointed out by a number of Twain scholars. For a perceptive summing up, see Fishkin, ed., Foreword, all volumes of *The Oxford Mark Twain,* xii.

35. "The New Chinese Temple," August 23, 1864, in Branch, ed., *Clemens of the Call: Mark Twain in San Francisco,* 82–83. Contains 198 of Twain's sketches and reports for the *Call.*

36. "Runaway," July 14, 1864, in Branch, *Clemens of the Call,* 43–44.

37. Ibid., 22.

38. Ibid., 5.

39. Ibid., "Original Novelette," July 4, 1864, 128–29.

40. "Roughing It Lecture," Lecture Season, 1871–72, in *Mark Twain Speaking,* ed. Paul Fatout, 60.

41. Such "letters" were a common form of writing in nineteenth-century newspapers. Very generally, they were reports or articles about places outside a newspaper's circulation area, often from another part of the state, region, or country. For instance, while Twain was at the *Call,* the paper ran "Letter from Santa Catalina Island" in Southern California, from the paper's "Regular Correspondent" there. But many letters were from faraway places, with the correspondents describing, say, familiar European cities and sites, or exotic islands and less-familiar continents, none of which most readers had ever seen and might not ever see, except through the eyes of the travel correspondent. Such personal and subjective writing consisted of facts, impressions, and descriptions, much like feature writing or magazine writing today. Many such midcentury travel accounts were overly exuberant about the foreign sites visited and provided good fodder even for twenty-one-year-old Sam Clemens, who wrote a parody of such letters under the name Thomas Jefferson Snodgrass for the *Keokuk (Iowa) Post* in 1856.

42. Bridgman, *Traveling in Mark Twain,* 1.

43. Day, ed., *Mark Twain's Letters from Hawaii,* 68–69.

44. Ibid., 30–32.

45. Ibid., 197.

46. Ibid., 137.

47. Ibid., 160.

48. Mark Twain, "Forty-Three Days in an Open Boat: Compiled from

Personal Diaries," *Harper's New Monthly Magazine* 34 (December 1886): 104–13. Although pleased to have this narrative appear in the prestigious *Harper's,* the magazine's index listed the author as Mark "Swain."

49. Walker and Dane, eds., *Mark Twain's Travels with Mr. Brown,* 83.

50. Ibid., 84.

51. Ibid., 106–7.

52. Ibid., 187–89.

53. Ibid., 223.

54. Ibid., 224.

55. McKeithan, ed., *Traveling with the Innocents Abroad: Mark Twain's Original Reports from Europe and the Holy Land,* 4; Twain, *The Innocents Abroad,* 51.

56. McKeithan, *Traveling with the Innocents Abroad,* 16; Twain, *The Innocents Abroad,* 55.

57. McKeithan, *Traveling with the Innocents Abroad,* 45; Twain, *The Innocents Abroad,* 164. For comparisons of the reports and the book see Leon T. Dickinson, "Mark Twain's Revisions in Writing *The Innocents Abroad,*" *American Literature* 19 (May 1947): 139–57; and Calder M. Pickett, "Mark Twain as Journalist and Literary Man: A Contrast," *Journalism Quarterly* (Winter 1961): 59–66. Pickett incorrectly cites the Genoa priest description as being from the *Alta* report dated September 8, 1867, but it was dated July 16.

58. Twain, *The Innocents Abroad,* v.

59. Bridgman, *Traveling in Mark Twain,* 15.

60. Twain, *The Innocents Abroad,* 190–93.

61. David E. E. Sloane, "Afterword," *The Innocents Abroad,* 2. Sloane later compares Twain's account with that of Louisa Griswold, who also was on the trip. Sloane says her *A Woman's Pilgrimage to the Holy Land; or Pleasant Days Abroad* (Hartford: J. B. Burr and Hyde, 1871), published two years after *Innocents,* has a "prevailing dullness" when compared to *Innocents.* He calls Griswold a "literalist" who treats what she sees as "isolated components" of the tour while Twain provides context and meaning. Noting her "bland and unappealing" account of a mosque, Sloane says, "when Twain enters a mosque, we can anticipate delicious particularizations of overwrought architectural details, caustic asides about the sincer-

ity of the attending clerics, and an engaged, role-playing narrator. Twain will involve us," 11.

62. Nelson, "Mark Twain," in Connery, *A Sourcebook of American Literary Journalism,* 42. Nelson connects Twain to Norman Mailer's *Armies of the Night,* but also notes that Thompson's work has "strange modern echoes of Twain," and he says Thompson trying to get press passes at the race track in "The Kentucky Derby Is Decadent and Depraved" is "reminiscent of Twain wandering through the bazaars of Turkey or Florence."

63. Nelson, "Mark Twain," in Connery, *A Sourcebook of American Literary Journalism,* 50.

64. Gerber, 39.

65. Twain, Prefatory, *Roughing It.*

66. "A True Story, Repeated Word for Word as I Heard It," *Atlantic Monthly,* 34 (November 1874): 591–94.

67. "Recent Literature," *Atlantic Monthly* 36 (December 1875): 750–51. Howells's comments were part of a review of *Mark Twain's Sketches,* which included "A True Story."

CHAPTER FIVE

1. *Harper's Weekly* 12 (July 25, 1868), "New England Factory Life," 471; "New England Factory Life—'Bell-Time,'" 472.

2. Andrea G. Pearson, "*Frank Leslie's Illustrated Newspaper* and *Harper's Weekly*: Innovation and Imitation in Nineteenth-Century American Pictorial Reporting," *Journal of Popular Culture* 23 (4): 81–82.

3. Brown, *Beyond the Lines: Pictorial Reporting, Everyday Life, and the Crisis of Gilded Age America,* 41.

4. *Harper's Weekly,* January 3, 1857; *Frank Leslie's Illustrated Newspaper,* December 15, 1855. Another New York illustrated publication, the *Illustrated News,* was started in 1859 but it was gone by 1864 when it merged with a fashion magazine, *Mirror of Fashion.*

5. *Frank Leslie's Illustrated Newspaper,* June 21, 1856, 17–18.

6. Pearson, "*Frank Leslie's Illustrated Newspaper* and *Harper's Weekly,*" 83.

Pearson makes a strong case for first *Leslie's* and then *Harper's* building credibility around the accuracy of their illustrations, thus creating a trust in the visual even before photographs came to be accepted and trusted as a mirror of reality.

7. *Frank Leslie's Illustrated Newspaper,* June 21, 1856, cover.

8. Ibid., Feb. 21, 1857, 181.

9. Ibid., "Our Present Number—Triumphant Success," Feb. 21, 1857, 189. In addition to the illustrations mentioned, there were sketches of a doorknob with the caption, "Handle of the door of the attic room," a large dagger with the caption, "The dagger found in Mrs. Cunningham's bureau," and the heart mentioned in the editorial with the caption, "Doctor Burdell's heart, showing the two wounds."

10. *Frank Leslie's Illustrated Newspaper,* Feb. 25, 1871, cover. Reproduced in Brown, *Beyond the Lines,* 69. Brown's study is a fully detailed look at the role and impact of *Leslie's,* connecting the publication's visual depictions to American social issues and social history.

11. *Frank Leslie's Illustrated Newspaper,* April 26, 1873, 102. Quoted in Brown, *Beyond the Lines,* 33.

12. Gambee, *Frank Leslie and His Illustrated Newspaper, 1855–1860,* 40. Joseph Becker, who went to work for *Leslie's* when he was nineteen and stayed for forty-one years, becoming one of the publication's "special artists," in 1905 reflected on his career and said he was regularly assigned to illustrate "important" events because he had become "the regular pictorial reporter." Quoted in Brown, *Beyond the Lines,* 131. Gambee's 1964 booklet, part of his dissertation, takes a detailed look at a typical *Leslie's* issue for each year, 1855–60.

13. Hudson, *Journalism in the United States, from 1690 to 1872,* 705.

14. Griffin, *Homer, Eakins, and Anshutz: The Search for American Identity in the Gilded Age,* 51.

15. A selection of thirteen Brooklyn Bridge illustrations with detailed captions that provide context can be found in John Grafton, *New York in the Nineteenth Century: 321 Engravings from Harper's Weekly and Other Contemporary Sources,* 27–39.

16. Trachtenberg, "Photography: The Emergence of a Keyword," in *Photography in Nineteenth Century America,* ed. Martha A. Sandweiss, 19.

17. Grafton, *New York in the Nineteenth Century.*

18. Thompson, *The Image of War: The Pictorial Reporting of the American Civil War,* 16.

19. Ibid., 24.

20. Roger Butterfield, "Pictures in the Papers," *American Heritage* 13 (June 1962): 43. Quoted in David Park, "Picturing the War: Visual Genres in Civil War News," *Communication Review* 3 (1999): 289. Park notes similarities between landscape paintings and early battlefield illustrations. See 291–94. Also, Brown, citing Thompson, discusses a shift from "the romanticism of early engravings, where combatants assumed the classic poses of academic painting" to "less lyrical compositions." See Brown, *Beyond the Lines,* 56–57.

21. *Harper's Weekly,* June 3, 1865, 339; *Frank Leslie's Illustrated Weekly* quoted in Pearson, 90.

22. Listed in the editorial were: Alfred Waud, Theodore R. Davis, William Waud, Robert Weir, Andrew McCalum, and A. W. Warren.

23. During the sixteen years or so that Homer supported himself through publication illustrating, he depicted a relatively wide range of events and topics, although before and after the war many of them dealt with middle- and upper-class men and women enjoying various activities. Several of his street scenes for *Ballou's,* such as "View in South Market Street, Boston" in 1857, connect Homer to the general attempt to depict city life. For a broad view of Homer's publication work, including wood-engraved illustrations for *Ballou's,* see the exhibition book for the Brooklyn Museum of Art's exhibit on Homer's illustrations: Kushner, Gallati, and Ferber, *Winslow Homer: Illustrating America.* Of particular interest is Gallati's essay, "Narrative Strategies in Winslow's Art," 9–26.

24. Simpson, *Winslow Homer Paintings of the Civil War,* 28. Simpson may be overstating the case just a bit.

25. *Harper's Weekly,* July 12, 1862, 439.

26. Ibid., June 14, 1862, 376–77.

27. Of course, Homer did do some battlefield sketches, including the standard cavalry charge. "The War for the Union, 1862—A Cavalry Charge," *Harper's Weekly,* July 5, 1862, which is strikingly similar in tone, theme, and general depiction to "Washington Rallying the Troops at Monmouth," a painting done in 1854 by Emanuel Leutze. The two are juxtaposed in Simpson, *Winslow Homer Paintings,* 74–75. Many of

Homer's illustrations dealt with camp life. Simpson's book, an excellent exhibition catalog done in conjunction with an exhibition of Homer's Civil War paintings, contains *Harper's Weekly* illustrations as well as the paintings. Simpson was curator of the exhibit.

28. Gallati, "Narrative Strategies in Winslow Homer's Art," in Kushner, Gallati, and Ferber, *Winslow Homer: Illustrating America,* 11.

29. Simpson, *Winslow Homer Paintings,* 123.

30. Ibid., 125.

31. Ibid.

32. Ibid., 13, 14. Gallati argues that the more precise image of the shooter as well as the presence of the canteen in the *Harper's* illustration creates "a hint of narrative interplay" and "promotes a narrative process in the viewer." Gallati, "Narrative Strategies in Winslow Homer's Art," 11.

33. Simpson, *Winslow Homer Paintings,* 14.

34. Ibid., 14.

35. Sheldon, *Hours with Art and Artists,* 136.

36. For examples, see Brown, *Beyond the Lines,* 90, and Grafton, *New York in the Nineteenth Century,* 162–63.

37. *Frank Leslie's Illustrated Newspaper,* August 16, 1873, cover.

38. Brown, *Beyond the Lines,* 89–90.

39. *Frank Leslie's Illustrated Newspaper,* August 16, 1873, 363.

40. See Brown, *Beyond the Lines* for discussions of how depictions of types created and reinforced social attitudes toward the poor, toward workers, and regarding race and class, especially chapter 3, "Constructing Representation, 1866–77"; chapter 4, "Balancing Act, 1866–77"; and chapter 5, "Reconstructing Representation, 1866–77." See also *Harper's Weekly,* September 5, 1868, for a typical drawing of a Five Points man. Three men, Democrats who oppose the Reconstruction Act, are shown stepping on and holding down a young black man. One figure represents big money, another represents the South, and both of these figures have normal facial features. The third, wearing a hat with Five Points on it, is not quite fully human, with apelike features, a club in his hand, and a whiskey bottle in his pocket.

41. For a discussion of and examples of wood engravings—and publication illustrations—made from photographs during the war see Car-

lebach, *The Origins of Photojournalism in America,* chapter 3, "Photographs of War."

42. Of course, as time passed, the reading public became more interested in the war. For instance, from 1884 to 1887, *Century Magazine* published a series of articles and illustrations that documented and reassessed the war, with many of the articles written by military and political leaders, and illustrations made from photographs, wartime sketches, and visits to battle sites. That series was collected and expanded into a four-volume set, *Battles and Leaders of the Civil War.* In 1974, *American Heritage* published images from that series and from the *Century* collection of images, which it had acquired. See Sears, ed., *The American Heritage Century Collection of Civil War Art.* Included in the *American Heritage* collection are sketches by Edwin Forbes, who was a war artist for *Frank Leslie's Illustrated Newspaper.* Forbes put together two books of his war illustrations, *Life Studies of the Great Army* (1876) and *Thirty Years After: An Artist's Memoir of the Civil War* (1890). Louisiana State University Press reissued *Thirty Years After* in 1993; see also Dawson, ed., *A Civil War Artist at the Front: Edwin Forbes' Life Studies of the Great Army.*

43. Edgar Allan Poe, "The Daguerreotype," in *Classic Essays on Photography,* ed. Alan Trachtenberg, 37. The essayist Nathaniel Parker Willis writing in 1839, probably before he even saw a photograph or daguerreotype, said "Talk no more of 'holding the mirror up to nature'—she will hold it up to herself, and present you with a copy of her countenance for a penny." But Willis also found the idea of a permanent fixed image troubling, yet he was remarkably prescient: "What would you say to looking in a mirror and having the image fastened!! As one looks sometimes, it is really quite frightful to think of it; but such a thing is possible—nay, it is probable—no, it is certain. What will become of the poor thieves, when they shall see handed in as evidence against them their own portraits, taken by the room in which they stole, and in the very act of stealing!" Willis quoted in Trachtenberg, "The Emergence of a Keyword," 30.

44. Poe, "The Daguerreotype," 38.

45. Trachtenberg, *Reading American Photographs,* 14.

46. Oliver Wendell Holmes, "The Stereoscope and the Stereograph," *Atlantic Monthly* 3 (June, 1859): 439, 438.

47. Trachtenberg, "The Emergence of a Keyword," 18.

48. Ibid. Trachtenberg refers to this as "the camera as the eye of God."

49. Trachtenberg, *Reading American Photographs,* 33.

50. Holmes, "Doings of the Sunbeam," *Atlantic Monthly* 12 (July 1863): 9.

51. Walt Whitman, "Visit to Plumbe's Gallery," *Brooklyn Eagle,* July 2, 1846, in *The Collected Writings of Walt Whitman,* 448–49.

52. Holmes, "The Stereoscope and the Stereograph," 744.

53. *New York Times,* October 20, 1862, 5; quoted in Marianne Fulton, *Eyes of Time: Photojournalism in America,* 19.

54. Holmes, "Doings of the Sunbeam," 11.

55. Ibid., 11–12.

56. The illustration and the three photos are juxtaposed in Fulton, *Eyes of Time,* 22–23. For a juxtaposition of a wood engraving made from a Timothy O'Sullivan photograph see Carlebach, *The Origins of Photojournalism,* 80–81. The illustration appeared on the cover of *Frank Leslie's Illustrated Newspaper* in 1864. The sketch presents a wider, more expansive view of the event, a gathering outdoors of General Grant with his generals, providing a vista in the background not present in the photo. Whether that makes the illustration "picturesque" and less realistic, as Bruce Catton has maintained, is highly questionable. See Catton's "Foreword" in Sears, *The American Heritage Century Collection of Civil War Art,* especially 9–10.

57. Gardner, *Gardner's Photographic Sketch Book of the Civil War,* plate 37. First published in 1866 as *Gardner's Photographic Sketch Book of the War.*

58. Stapp, "'Subjects of strange . . . and of fearful interest': Photojournalism from its Beginnings in 1839," in Fulton, *Eyes of Time,* 27, 28. Images in Barnard, *Photographic Views of Sherman's Campaign,* provide additional perspectives of the distinctive ability of photographs to document reality. These photos were privately published by Barnard, who accompanied Sherman's march through the South. Particularly striking are scenes of bombed-out and burned destruction in Charleston, Columbia, and Atlanta.

59. G. F. Muller, "The City of Pittsburgh," *Harper's New Monthly Magazine* 53 (December, 1880): 57.

60. Ibid., 56.

61. Ibid., 57, 57–58.

62. See Griffin, *Homer, Eakins, and Anshutz,* plate 2, Thomas Anshutz, "The Ironworkers' Noontime." Also in Griffin is Anshutz's "Steamboat on the Ohio," 1896, plate 4, which captures a river idyll, with boys swimming nude in the Ohio while a steamboat approaches, but at the same time pricks the river myth by showing fire, smoke, steam, and smokestacks filling the opposite riverbank and the sky.

CHAPTER SIX

1. Hearn, *Period of the Gruesome: Selected Cincinnati Journalism of Lafcadio Hearn,* 5, 3.

2. When Hearn arrived in Cincinnati he had no money or place to stay and for a while slept wherever he could find a spot: haylofts, floors, corners of cold rooms. He did menial tasks that paid pennies till he finally was recommended for a job by a printer friend. Even after getting a regular income as a journalist, he tended to live among or near the people he wrote about. Supposedly, he was asked to leave the *Enquirer* when it was discovered that he was living with a mulatto woman. Hughes says Hearn claimed to be married to the woman but such a marriage was not recognized by Ohio law. Hearn, *Period of the Gruesome,* 4.

3. "Pariah People," Aug. 22, 1875, in Hearn, *Period of the Gruesome,* 184–85. Also in Hearn, *Children of the Levee,* 32–48. The Library of America's Literary Classics of the United States published a selection of Hearn's writing, including his journalism, in 2009. A good selection of the range of Hearn's writing published between 1874 and 1905 is collected in *Selected Writings of Lafcadio Hearn.* Hughes provides some biographical background, especially about Hearn's life as a journalist, but see also Elizabeth Stevenson's biography *Lafcadio Hearn.*

4. "Pariah People," Hearn, *Period of the Gruesome,* 186–87.

5. "The Tannery Horror," November 12, 1874, in Hearn, *Period of the Gruesome,* 140.

6. "Violent Cremation," November 9, 1874, in Hearn, *Period of the Gruesome,* 109–10. The editor who hired Hearn at the *Enquirer* assigned him to the tanyard murder, played the story up in a sensational

fashion, and then fired Hearn for living with a mulatto woman, was a young John A. Cockerill, who would go on to oversee some rather sensational coverage as well as Hearn-style human-interest reporting, first at Pulitzer's St. Louis *Post-Dispatch* and then at Pulitzer's New York *World*. When Cockerill let him go, Hearn took his reporting sources and writing style to the competing *Commercial*.

7. Hearn, *Children of the Levee*, 6, 7.

8. Ibid., "Introduction," 2–3.

9. Ibid., "Dolly of the Levee," 13.

10. Ibid., "Banjo Jim's Story," 23–24.

11. Hearn's West Indies sketches were published in 1890 as *Two Years in the French West Indies*. Some of the New Orleans journalism was published as *Creole Sketches*. While working as a reporter, Hearn also co-founded and wrote for *Ye Giglampz,* a satirical magazine that blended writing and illustrations but lasted only nine weeks. See Jon Christopher Hughes, "*Ye Giglampz* and the Apprenticeship of Lafcadio Hearn," *American Literary Realism* 25 (Autumn 1982): 182–99.

12. Quoted in Hudson, *Journalism in the United States, from 1690 to 1872, 679*.

13. Dana's declaration of principle and intent as new owner of the *Sun* ran on January 27, 1868, and is reprinted in Obrien, *The Story of The Sun,* 145–46. A Greenwood Press reprint edition was published in 1968. The most perceptive, and fullest, account of Dana's life and work as well as the significance of the *Sun* is Steele, *The Sun Shines for All*. Steele effectively places Dana and his newspaper within the cultural context of his time while investigating the play of Dana's pragmatism and ideals, especially his deep-rooted democratic faith. Steele's discussion of coverage of the Tompkins Square labor rally that was described as a "riot" of no-good workers and foreigners by all New York City papers except the *Sun* nicely symbolizes the pervasive negative stereotyping of immigrants and the working class, as well as society's fear of those workers.

14. Charles Dana, "The Modern American Newspaper," lecture delivered July 24, 1888, in Dana, *The Art of Newspaper Making,* 11–12.

15. Dana, "The Profession of Journalism," lecture delivered October 13, 1895, in *The Art of Newspaper Making,* 54.

16. Dana, "The Making of a Newspaper Man," lecture delivered January 11, 1894, in *The Art of Newspaper Making,* 103.

17. Steele, *The Sun Shines for All,* 83. Steele plays off William Taylor's description that the *Sun* had a "pastiche" quality typical of the Gilded Age commercial culture. It is just as likely, however, that it was due as well to the nature of a growing, crowded urban society with many subcultures.

18. Hearn, *Selected Writings of Lafcadio Hearn,* 146. Published as a book by Harper and Brothers in 1889.

19. Hearn, "A Winter's Journey to Japan," *Harper's New Monthly Magazine* 81 (November 1890): 861.

20. W. D. Howells, "'In Memoriam,' Editor's Easy Chair," *Harper's Monthly Magazine* 140 (December 1919): 133.

21. Henry Mills Alden, "Fifty Years of Harper's Magazine," *Harper's New Monthly Magazine,* 100 (May 1900): 955, 953. As with much of Alden's writing, this combination history and reflection did not have Alden's name on it but was "By the Editor."

22. Alden, "Fifty Years of Harper's Magazine," 952.

23. Ibid., 957–59.

24. Alden, *Magazine Writing and the New Literature,* vii.

25. Ibid., 68, 152.

26. Ibid., 153.

27. Ibid., 233.

28. Ibid., 243, 269, 270.

29. Ibid., 51–52.

30. Ibid., 54–55. Alden wrote that "it is in periodicals that this new literature has had its amplest opportunity and representation" of writing that "belongs distinctively to our own time," 178.

31. Ibid., 285.

32. Quoted in Eble, *William Dean Howells,* 93–94.

33. Howells, *Years of My Youth and Three Essays,* 122. *Years of My Youth* was first published by Harper and Brothers in 1916.

34. Howells, *My Literary Passions,* 127, 59. Howells also wrote that as a young man his "whole life was in books," *Years of My Youth,* 92.

35. Howells, *Years of My Youth,* 154, 153.

36. Howells, *Venetian Life,* 12. In 1906, Twain acknowledged having

read *Venetian Life* when it was published in 1866, three years before *The Innocents Abroad* was published.

37. Eble, *William Dean Howells,* 39.

38. Howells, *Their Wedding Journey,* 2, 1.

39. Ibid., 255, 111. When Isabel, the wife on the journey, reads to her husband something he had written years before when he had traveled to the same place, he describes it as a "sad farrago of sentiment" and says to Isabel, "Yes, life was then a thing to be put into pretty periods; now it's something that has risks and averages, and may be insured," 255.

40. Howells, *Criticism and Fiction and Other Essays,* 38, 51.

41. See Kaplan, *The Social Construction of American Realism,* especially the introduction and chapter 1, "The Mass Mediated Realism of William Dean Howells."

42. Howells, *Criticism and Fiction,* 274–75.

43. Crane, *Maggie: A Girl of the Streets,* 149.

44. Ibid., 150.

45. Ibid., 144.

46. Quoted in the introduction, Garland, *Crumbling Idols: Twelve Essays on Art,* xxi. *Crumbling Idols* was first published in 1894 in Chicago by Stone and Kimball.

47. Garland, *Crumbling Idols,* 52, 53–54, 64. Garland also described local color this way: "Local color in fiction is demonstrably the life of fiction. It is the native element, the differentiating element. It corresponds to the endless and vital charm of individual peculiarity. It is the differences which interest us; the similarities do not please, do not forever stimulate and feed as do the differences. Literature would die of dry rot if it chronicled the similarities only, or even largely," 49.

48. Garland, "Up the Cooly," *Main-Travelled Roads,* 78, 129.

49. Lawrence J. Oliver, "Brander Matthews' Re-visioning of Crane's *Maggie,*" *American Literature* 60 (December 1988): 657.

50. Quoted in Mott, *A History of American Magazines, 1885–1905,* 403.

51. B. O. Flower, "Mask or Mirror," *Arena* 45 (August 1893). The shift to realism lagged in drama and theater compared to other forms of cultural expression. Many believed as Flower, but audiences preferred melodrama with familiar touches of sentimentality and plays that favored "an idealized, simplified, and neatly wrapped fantasy." Richardson,

American Drama From the Colonial Period Through World War I: A Critical History, 155. See especially ch. 7, "The Development of Realism." Besides Howells's plays, those of Steele MacKaye, Bronson Howard, and William Gillette contained distinctly realistic aspects, but James A. Herne and his plays *Margaret Fleming* (1890), *Shore Acres* (1892), and *Sag Harbor* (1899) are particularly strong examples of realism. The full blossoming of realism in American drama would come later with works by Clifford Odets, Eugene O'Neill, Thornton Wilder, Tennessee Williams, and Arthur Miller, to name the most prominent. See Demastes, ed., *Realism and the American Dramatic Tradition.* See also Smith, *Plays in American Periodicals, 1890–1918.*

52. Footnote in Flower, "Mask or Mirror," 304.

CHAPTER SEVEN

1. In his review of *Maggie,* Frank Norris referred to Crane's story as a "picture of the other half," but criticized it for consisting of "scores of tiny flashlight photographs, instantaneous, caught, as it were, on the run." Norris's review was published in *The Wave,* a San Francisco publication, and reprinted in Crane, *Maggie: A Girl of the Streets, An Authoritative Text,* ed. Thomas A. Gullason, 151.

2. Crane, *Maggie,* 151. Norris, who was twenty-six at the time of his review (Crane was twenty-five), was greatly influenced by the work of French realist/naturalist Emile Zola's work, which emphasized environmental influences on human behavior and living conditions, as did Crane. Crane died in 1900 at twenty-nine, Norris died in 1901 at thirty-two.

3. Hapgood, *Types from City Streets,* 24. First published 1910.

4. "Sentiment in the Bowery," *New York Sun,* February 4, 1894, 7.

5. Hapgood, *A Victorian in the Modern World,* 140.

6. O'Higgins, "The Italian Quarter and Its Resorts," *New York Commercial Advertiser,* February 10, 1900.

7. "The Inspecter's Museum," *The Evening Sun,* May 16, 1890, 6. Another example is "Young Ladies in the Tombs," *Sun,* April 3, 1890, 3. The Tombs, of course, is the New York City jail. For another contrasting view of the Bowery, see Julian Ralph, "The Bowery," *Century Magazine,*

93 (December 1891): 227–37. Ralph was a highly respected reporter who worked for several New York City newspapers covering many of the major news events from 1875 on and had a reputation for thoroughness and smoothly integrating extensive detail. His "Bowery" article, while not as lively or colorful as some, is full of detailed observations so that it would fit well with "studies" of life on the Lower East Side. He also was a regular contributor to *Harper's Monthly* and many of his sketches, mixing fiction and nonfiction, were collected in *People We Pass: Stories of Life Among the Masses of New York City* (New York: Harper and Brothers, 1896). See Thomas B. Connery, "Julian Ralph: Forgotten Master of Descriptive Detail," *American Journalism* 2 (1985): 165–73.

8. Riis, *How the Other Half Lives: Studies Among the Tenements of New York,* 49. The 1890 edition contained thirty images, fifteen illustrations made from photographs, and fifteen weak photographs lacking contrast and tone. The Dover edition, cited here, greatly expands on the original, from thirty images to one hundred.

9. "Tenement Life In New York," *Harper's Weekly* 23 (March 22, 1879): 226. The other articles appeared on March 29 and April 5. Both the content and illustrations focused on a specific building—Bottle Alley, Gotham Court, and Rag-pickers' Court—each of which Riis later photographed. A full-page sketch titled "Ragpicker's court, Mulberry Street" on p. 265 of the April 5 issue has often been reproduced to illustrate tenement conditions.

10. In the preface to the Dover Edition of *How the Other Half Lives,* Charles A. Madison says that "what Riis saw in the late 1870's and 1880's was the cankered fruit of decades of callous exploitation and neglect by rapacious landlords in connivance with venal and vapid politicians," vi.

11. Riis, *The Making of an American,* 132–33.

12. "Pestilence in Nurseries. Summer Sufferings of Dwellers in Tenement Houses," *New York World,* June 11, 1883—Tribune and Associated Press Bureau. Quoted in Daniel Czitrom, "Jacob Riis's New York," in Yochelson and Czitrom, *Rediscovering Jacob Riis: Exposure Journalism and Photography in Turn-of-the-Century New York,* 21–23. Czitrom's take on Riis as a journalist is insightful and fully captures the cultural context from Riis's arrival in America in 1870 through the publication of *How the Other Half Lives;* Yochelson's investigation

of Riis's photos, "Jacob A. Riis, Photographer 'After a Fashion,'" is equally perceptive. Together they are essential reading for anyone interested in Riis and the significance of and influences on his best-known book.

13. Yochelson and Czitrom, *Rediscovering Jacob Riis,* 23. Czitrom also says that "a large fraction of Riis's police journalism turned on explorations of the anonymity and randomness of big-city life," 13. Crane's urban sketches also tend to deal with the same two themes.

14. Riis, *Out of Mulberry Street: Stories of Tenement Life In New York City,* preface. Interestingly, Riis also makes a claim that sounds similar to one occasionally made by nonfiction writers and literary journalists more recently: "In the few instances in which I have taken the ordering of events into my own hands, it is chiefly their sequence with which I have interfered. The facts themselves remain as I have found them."

15. Riis, *Out of Mulberry Street,* "'T Was Liza's Doings," 47; "A Dream of the Woods," 73; "Nigger Martha's Wake," 106.

16. Riis, *The Making of an American,* 132.

17. Quoted in Yochelson and Czitrom, *Rediscovering Jacob Riis,* 97. The quote is from the only existing stenographic record of a Riis slide lecture, this one given in Washington, D.C., in 1891.

18. "How the Other Half Lives: Studies Among the Tenements," *Scribner's* 6 (December 1889): 643–62.

19. Yochelson and Czitrom, *Rediscovering Jacob Riis,* 105.

20. Riis, *How the Other Half Lives,* 100.

21. Ibid., 107. Riis's follow-up to *Other Half* was *Children of the Poor.* In the book's preface, Riis said, "The Two books are one. One supplements the other." A few of the book's pieces are human-interest sketches or descriptive narratives that approach literary journalism. See, for example, "The Story of Kid McDuff's Girl," 87.

22. "A Hunger-Stricken Horde," *New York Tribune,* January 5, 1894, 7.

23. "In Poverty's Realm," *New York Press,* February 6, 1894, 3.

24. Letter to *Leslie's Weekly* editor, 1895, in Stallman and Gilkes, *Stephen Crane: Letters,* 78. Letter to Lily Brandon Munroe, 1894, 31. In the same letter, Crane said, "If I had kept to my clever, Rudyard-Kipling style, the road might have been shorter, but, ah, it wouldn't be the true road," 32.

25. Crane, "Howells Discussed at Avon-By-The-Sea," *Tales, Sketches, and Reports,* 507.

26. Crane, "The Men in the Storm," *Tales, Sketches, and Reports,* 317.

27. "Bells A-Jingling All Day Long," *New York Sun,* February 14, 1894, 2.

28. Crane, "Men in the Storm," *Tales, Sketches, and Reports,* 316–21.

29. Crane, "An Experiment in Misery," *Tales, Sketches, and Reports.* The version that Crane revised for book publication appears on 283; the *Press* version, along with the headline and subheads is from 861–64 in "The Text: History and Analysis" section. The first subhead on "Experiment in Luxury," 293–301 and 864, is "The Experiences of a Youth Who Sought out Croesus."

30. Robertson, *Stephen Crane, Journalism, and the Making of Modern American Literature,* 98.

31. Crane, "An Experiment in Misery," 863.

32. Bremner, *The Discovery of Poverty in the United States,* 142.

33. Riis, *How the Other Half Lives,* 61.

34. Ibid., 64.

35. Ibid., 67.

36. Richard Harding Davis, "Confiding Crooks," *Philadelphia Press,* December 18, 1887, 10.

37. Bremner discusses Flynt's work in a sociological context in *The Discovery of Poverty in the United States,* 142. Louis Filler treats Flynt as a muckraker in Filler, *Crusaders for American Liberalism,* 67. Filler devotes an entire chapter to Flynt with the title "Cigarette," which was Flynt's hobo name.

38. London was only about eighteen when he tramped, moving west to east, which wasn't so much an experiment as London just hitting the road. For a while, he joined Kelly's Army, the western arm of Coxey's Army, and his tramping included spending thirty days in jail. London's own undercover experiment, in the slums of London, *The People of the Abyss,* was published in 1903.

39. Flynt, *Tramping with Tramps: Studies and Sketches of Vagabond Life.*

40. Josiah Flynt, "Club Life Among Outcasts," *Harper's Monthly* 90 (April 1895): 712. This article ran with six illustrations and six illustrated

headshots that capture distinguishing facial features of supposedly typical tramps.

41. Flynt, *Tramping with Tramps,* Author's Note, ix.

42. Flynt would conduct another undercover investigation, joining a railroad police force as a patrolman in the summer of 1899. He said he wanted to come into contact with tramps and criminals as a representative of the law and the result was a number of articles in *Harper's Weekly* and *Munsey's Magazine,* as well as others, and distribution through McClure's Syndicate. Flynt then revised the articles and they were published as *Notes of an Itinerant Policeman.* Books for Libraries Press reprinted the book in 1972.

43. Wyckoff, *A Day with a Tramp and Other Days,* 5.

44. Czitrom says Wingate's articles "seem to constitute an uncanny blueprint for *How the Other Half Lives,*" but argues that Riis didn't steal Wingate's idea, rather Wingate "pointed toward a new kind of activist journalism that Riis would fully develop on his own," *Rediscovering Jacob Riis,* 70.

45. Campbell, *Prisoners of Poverty: Women Wage-Workers, Their Trades and Their Lives,* Preface. A reprint was published by Greenwood in 1970, and the full text of the original is available online.

46. Campbell, *The Problem of the Poor: A Record of Quiet Work in Unquiet Places.*

47. Campbell, *Darkness and Daylight; or, Lights and Shadows of New York Life. A Pictorial Record of Personal Experiences by Day and Night in the Great Metropolis,* vii–xi. In touting Campbell's qualifications as well as validation of the book's authenticity, the publisher writes: "Her interest in missions and her labors among the lower classes have brought her face to face with squalor and misery among the hopelessly poor, as well as with degraded men and women in their own homes; while her ready sympathy gained for her access to their hearts, and thus gave her a practical insight into their daily life possessed by few. Who but a woman could describe to women the scenes of sin, sorrow, and suffering among this people that have presented themselves to her womanly eye and heart?" vii. To a certain extent, this publication was somewhat ironically playing off the urban guidebooks that were popular in the 1870s and after. See,

for example, McCabe, *Lights and Shadows of New York Life; Or, The Great City. A Work Descriptive of New York In All Its Various Phases.*

48. Dreiser, *Newspaper Days,* 52. Here is Riis's declaration regarding facts: "Ours is an age of facts. It wants facts, not theories, and facts I have endeavored to set down in these pages," *Children of the Poor,* preface.

49. The "nonessentials" statement is from Shuman, *Steps Into Journalism,* 79.

50. Steffens, *The Autobiography of Lincoln Steffens,* 241–43. Steffens is a particularly appropriate representative figure of the ascension of the real. Not only did he cover the usual mix of daily news stories in his career but he was a practitioner of both of the major journalistic strains that came to characterize the paradigm of actuality: literary journalism and muckraking. In fact, after experimenting at the *Commercial Advertiser* with his storytelling approach to journalism, he made his name as a highly influential muckraker at *McClure's,* which published some of the most effective exposés of the movement, and he joined with his muckraking colleagues at *McClure's,* Ida Tarbell and Ray Stannard Baker, to create *The American Magazine* in 1906. His urban reform articles were published as *The Shame of the Cities* in 1904.

51. "Literature and Journalism in 1896," *New York Commercial Advertiser,* January 1, 1897.

52. Although this study has not focused on the very popular, sensational, and innovative *Journal* and *World* of Hearst and Pulitzer, their competitive race to top one another led to an emphasis on storytelling, crusades, and a range of features, and also exemplified the cultural expression of the real and actual. The best recent look at the "yellow" papers can be found in Campbell, *Yellow Journalism: Puncturing the Myths, Defining the Legacies;* see also Campbell, *The Year That Defined American Journalism: 1897 and a Clash of Paradigms.*

53. Garland, *Crumbling Idols,* 13–14; "Newspapers and Fiction," *Scribner's Magazine* 40 (July 1906): 122.

54. "Naughty Protectory Boys," *New York Times,* February 5, 1894, 3.

55. "A Train Saved By A Woman," *New York Tribune,* August 2, 1890, 1.

56. Robertson, *Stephen Crane,* 85; for a consideration of "The Broken-Down Van" within a literary journalistic context over time, see Connery, ed., Introduction, "Discovering a Literary Form," *A Source-*

book of American Literary Journalism, 5–12; for a consideration of another Crane newspaper report on an urban incident, "When Man Falls, A Crowd Gathers," as well as an overview of literary journalism's turn-of-the-century roots, see Connery, "A Third Way to Tell the Story," *Literary Journalism in the Twentieth Century,* ed. Norman Sims.

57. Quoted from the *Jewish Daily Forward,* December 21, 1903, by Bruce J. Evensen, "Abraham Cahan." Connery, *A Sourcebook of American Literary Journalism,* 95. Reviewing Cahan's novel *Yekl* in 1896 in the Sunday *World,* Howells called Cahan a "new star of realism" rendering the "truest" pictures of East Side life. Quoted in Cahan, introduction, *Grandma Never Lived in America,* ed. Moses Rischin, xxi.

58. Steffens, *Autobiography of Lincoln Steffens,* 317.

59. See, for instance, the double-page spreads of the intersection of Ludlow and Essex streets in the Lower East Side in 1900 as well as a very familiar 1900 Mulberry Street photo of the busy, crowded street market just below the tenements in Burns and Sanders, *New York: An Illustrated History,* 240–41, vi–vii.

60. Cahan, "Pillelu, Pillelu!" in *Grandma Never Lived in America,* 56–59.

61. Ibid., 113, 120, 127.

62. Ibid., xxxiii; Evensen, in Connery, *A Sourcebook of American Literary Journalism,* 97. Rischin also says Cahan was "the direct ancestor" of the new journalists of the 1960s, specifically mentioning two writers from that period, Tom Wolfe and Norman Mailer. Certainly, Cahan's journalism can be assessed and characterized as literary journalism and therefore an ancestor of the new journalists of the 1960s, who also were writing literary journalism. But Cahan would have far more in common with a Gay Talese or a Bob Greene, or even certain works of Joseph Mitchell rather than a Wolfe or Mailer.

63. Hine's photographs, especially his photos documenting child labor as well as some of his more than two hundred photos of immigrants, are readily available in various books and catalogs, including online. See, for instance, the exhibition book, Rosenblum, Rosenblum, and Trachtenberg, *America and Lewis Hine: Photographs 1904–1940.* See also Guimond, *American Photography and the American Dream,* chapter 3, "Lewis Hine and American Industrialism," 55.

64. Filler, *Crusaders for American Liberalism*, 118. As with many declarations of Filler, this is an exaggeration, but it nevertheless reveals again how someone who closely observes society and writes about it can defy categorization, while at the same time emphasizing that what is being written and read is so "real" that it is social scientific.

65. Hapgood, *A Victorian in the Modern World*, 194, and Hapgood, "A New Form of Literature," *Bookman* 21 (1905): 424. For a more complete discussion of Hapgood and his work, see Connery, "Hutchins Hapgood and the Search for a 'New Form of Literature,'" *Journalism History* 13:1 (1986): 2–9.

CHAPTER EIGHT

1. Colon, ed., *Best Newspaper Writing 2005*, 87. The Persaud series ran in the *Times* on December 19, 22, and 26, 2005, and won an ASNE (American Society of Newspaper Editors) Distinguished Writing Award for Diversity Writing in the Narrative category. The series and an interview with Persaud appears in the *Best Newspaper* collection of ASNE winners on pages 85–134.

2. *New Yorker*, March 1, 2010, 23–24, 25, 50–59.

3. Williams, *The Long Revolution*, 47.

4. Clines, *About New York: Sketches of the City*, vii.

5. Talese, Preface, *Fame and Obscurity*, 9. Talese, "Origins of a Nonfiction Writer," in Talese and Lounsberry, eds., *Writing Creative Nonfiction: The Literature of Reality*, 5.

6. Talese, *The Bridge*, ix–x.

7. Talese, *New York: A Serendipiter's Journey*, 39, 32.

8. McPhee quoted in Sims, "The Art of Literary Journalism" in *Literary Journalism: A New Collection of the Best American Nonfiction*, 17. Lounsberry, Anthology Introduction, *Writing Creative Nonfiction: The Literature of Reality*, vii.

9. Colon, *Best Newspaper Writing*, 125.

10. Boo and Hull are quoted in *Telling True Stories: A Nonfiction Writers' Guide*, ed. Mark Kramer and Wendy Call, 15, 40. Conover and Sims

quotes in "The Art of Literary Journalism," Sims and Kramer, *Literary Journalism,* 13, 14.

11. Hapgood, "A New Form of Literature," 424, 425. Leland, *Sunshine in Thought,* 4.

12. For an excellent overview and discussion of contemporary literary journalism's place and status and its changing relationship with magazines see Sims, *True Stories,* chapter 7.

13. The "A Husband for Vibha" website is http://www.sptimes.com/2004/webspecialso4/indianwoman. The BlackHawk Down website is http://inquirer.philly.com/packages/somalia/sitemap.asp.

BIBLIOGRAPHY

Alden, Henry Mills. "Fifty Years of Harper's Magazine." *Harper's New Monthly Magazine* 100 (May 1900): 947–62.

———. *Magazine Writing and the New Literature.* New York and London: Harper and Brothers, 1908.

Ammons, Elizabeth. Introduction to *"How Celia Changed Her Mind" and Selected Stories,* by Rose Terry Cooke. New Brunswick, N. J.: Rutgers University Press, 1986, ix–xxxv.

Anthony, David. "The Helen Jewett Panic: Tabloids, Men, and the Sensational Public Sphere in Antebellum New York." *American Literature* 69 (September 1997): 488.

Baker, Thomas N. *Sentiment and Celebrity: Nathaniel Parker Willis and the Trials of Literary Fame.* New York and Oxford: Oxford University Press, 1999.

Banta, Martha. "The Three New Yorks: Topographical Narratives and Cultural Texts." *American Literary History* 7 (Spring, 1995): 28–54.

Barnard, George N. *Photographic Views of Sherman's Campaign.* New York: Dover Publications, 1977.

Barrish, Phillip. *American Literary Realism: Critical Theory and Intellectual Prestige, 1880–1995.* Cambridge: Oxford University Press, 2001.

Baym, Nina. *Woman's Fiction: A Guide to Novels by and about Women in America, 1820–1870.* Ithaca and London: Cornell University Press, 1978.

Bell, Michael Davitt. *The Problem of American Realism.* Chicago: University of Chicago Press, 1993.

Bender, Thomas. "The Culture of the Metropolis." *Journal of Urban History* 14 (August 1988): 494.

Benton, Lisa M., and John Rennie Short. *Environmental Discourse and Practice: A Reader.* Oxford: Blackwell, 2000.

Berthoff, Werner. *The Ferment of Realism: American Literature, 1884–1919.* New York: Free Press, 1965.

Blumin, Stuart M. "George G. Foster and the Emerging Metropolis." Introduction. In *New York by Gas-Light and Other Urban Sketches,* ed. Stuart M. Blumin. Berkeley and Los Angeles: University of California Press, 1990, 1–61.

Borus, Daniel. *Writing Realism: Howells, James, and Norris in the Mass Market.* Chapel Hill: University of North Carolina Press, 1989.

Boyer, Ernest L. *Scholarship Reconsidered.* Princeton, N.J.: Carnegie Foundation for the Advancement of Teaching, 1990.

Boynton, H. W. "The Literary Aspect of Journalism." *Atlantic* 93 (June 1904): 845–51.

Branch, Edgar M., ed. *Clemens of the Call: Mark Twain in San Francisco.* Berkeley and Los Angeles: University of California Press, 1969.

Brand, Dana. *The Spectator and the City in Nineteenth Century American Literature.* Cambridge: Cambridge University Press, 1991.

Bremner, Robert H. *The Discovery of Poverty in the United States.* New Brunswick and London: Transaction Publishers, 1992.

Bridgman, Richard. *Traveling in Mark Twain.* Berkeley and Los Angeles: University of California Press, 1987.

Brown, Joshua. *Beyond the Lines: Pictorial Reporting, Everyday Life, and the Crisis of Gilded Age America.* Berkeley and Los Angeles: University of California Press, 2002.

Bryant, William Cullen. *Funeral Oration, Occasioned by the Death of Thomas Cole, Delivered Before the National Academy of Design, New York, May 4, 1848.* New York: D. Appleton and Company, 1948.

Burns, Ric, and James Sanders. *New York: An Illustrated History.* New York: Alfred A. Knopf, 1999.

Butterfield, Roger. "Pictures in the Papers." *American Heritage* 13 (June 1962): 287–321.

Cady, Edwin H. *The Light of Common Day: Realism in American Fiction.* Bloomington: Indiana University Press, 1971.

Cahan, Abraham. *Grandma Never Lived in America.* Edited by Moses Rischin. Bloomington: Indiana University Press, 1985.

Cameron, James E. *Mark Twain: Unsanctified Newspaper Reporter.* Columbia and London: University of Missouri Press, 2008.

Campbell, Helen. *Darkness and Daylight; Or, Lights and Shadows of New York Life. A Pictorial Record of Personal Experiences by Day and Night in the Great Metropolis.* Hartford, Conn.: The Hartford Publishing Company, 1895.

———. *Prisoners of Poverty: Women Wage-Workers, Their Trades and Their Lives.* Boston: Roberts Brothers, 1887.

———. *The Problem of the Poor: A Record of Quiet Work in Unquiet Places.* New York: Fords, Howard and Hulbert, 1882.

Campbell, W. Joseph. *The Year That Defined American Journalism: 1897 and a Clash of Paradigms.* New York: Routledge, 2006.

———. *Yellow Journalism: Puncturing the Myths, Defining the Legacies.* Westport, Conn.: Praeger, 2001.

Canby, Henry Seidel. *Walt Whitman: An American.* Boston: Houghton Mifflin Company, Riverside Press Edition, 1943.

Carey, James W. *Communication as Culture: Essays on Media and Society.* Boston: Unwin Hyman, 1989.

Carey, John, ed. *Eyewitness to History.* Cambridge, Mass.: Harvard University Press, 1987.

Carlebach, Michael L. *The Origins of Photojournalism in America.* Washington and London: Smithsonian Institution Press, 1992.

Carlson, Oliver. *The Man Who Made the News.* New York: Duell, Sloan, and Pearce, 1942.

Carter, Everett. *Howells and the Age of Realism.* Philadelphia: Lippincott, 1954.

Clines, Francis X. *About New York: Sketches of the City.* New York: McGraw-Hill Book Company, 1980.

Cohen, Daniel A. "The Beautiful Female Murder Victim: Literary Genres and Courtship Practices in the Origins of a Cultural Motif, 1590–1850." *Journal of Social History* 31 (Winter 1997): 277–306.

Cohen, Patricia Cline. "The Helen Jewett Murder: Violence, Gender, and Sexual Licentiousness in Antebellum America." *National Women's Studies Association Journal* 2, 3 (Summer 1990), 374–89.

———. *The Murder of Helen Jewett: The Life and Death of a Prostitute in Nineteenth-Century New York.* New York: Alfred A. Knopf, 1998.

Cole, Thomas. "Essay on American Scenery." In *American Art, 1700–*

1960: Sources and Documents, ed. John Walker McCoubrey. Englewood Cliffs, N.J.: Prentice-Hall, 1965.

"Confessions of a Literary Journalist." *Bookman* 26 (December 1907):
370–76.

Connery, Thomas B. "A Third Way to Tell the Story: American Literary
Journalism at the Turn of the Century." In *Literary Journalism in
the Twentieth Century,* ed. Norman Sims, 3–20. New York: Oxford
University Press, 1990.

———. "Discovering a Literary Form." In *A Sourcebook of American
Literary Journalism: Representative Writers in an Emerging Genre,* ed.
Thomas B. Connery, 3–37. New York: Greenwood, 1992.

———. "Hutchins Hapgood and the Search for a 'New Form of Literature.'" *Journalism History* 13:1 (1986): 2–9.

Cooper, James F. *Knights of the Brush: The Hudson River School and the
Moral Landscape.* New York: Hudson Hills Press, 2000.

Corkin, Stanley. *Realism and the Birth of the Modern United States: Cinema,
Literature, and Culture.* Athens: University of Georgia Press, 1996.

Crane, Stephen. *Maggie: A Girl of the Streets.* Norton Critical Edition. Edited by Thomas A. Gullason. New York and London: W. W. Nor-
ton, 1979.

———. *Stephen Crane: Letters.* Edited by R. W. Stallman and Lillian
Gilkes. New York: New York University Press, 1960.

———. *Tales, Sketches, and Reports: The Works of Stephen Crane, VIII.*
Edited by Fredson Bowers. Charlottesville: University Press of
Virginia, 1973.

Cray, Ed, Jonathan Kotler, and Miles Beller, eds. *American Datelines: One
Hundred and Forty Major News Stories from Colonial Times to the Present.* New York: Facts on File, 1990.

Crouthamel, James L. *Bennett's New York Herald and the Rise of the Popular
Press.* Syracuse: Syracuse University Press, 1989.

Dana, Charles. *The Art of Newspaper Making.* New York: Arno Press Reprint Edition, 1970, originally published by D. Appleton, 1895.

Davis, Michael. *The Problem of American Realism.* Chicago and London:
University of Chicago Press, 1993.

Davis, Rebecca Harding. *Life in the Iron Mills.* Biographical Interpretation
by Tillie Olsen. Old Westbury, N.Y.: Feminist Press, 1972.

——. *Margret Howth: A Story of To-day.* New York: Feminist Press, 1990.

——. *Waiting for the Verdict.* Upper Saddle River, N.J.: Gregg Press, 1968, first published in 1867 by Sheldon and Company.

Dawson, William Forrest, ed. *A Civil War Artist at the Front: Edwin Forbes' Life Studies of the Great Army.* New York: Oxford University Press, 1957.

Demastes, William W. *Realism and the American Dramatic Tradition.* Tuscaloosa and London: University of Alabama Press, 1996.

Dicken-Garcia, Hazel. *Journalistic Standards in Nineteenth-Century America.* Madison: University of Wisconsin Press, 1989.

Dickens, Charles. *Sketches by Boz: Illustrative of Every-Day Life and Every-Day People.* Introduction by Thea Holme. Oxford and New York: Oxford University Press, 1957.

Dickinson, Leon T. "Mark Twain's Revisions in Writing *The Innocents Abroad." American Literature* 19 (May 1947): 139–57.

Dow, William. *Narrating Class in American Fiction.* New York: Palgrave Macmillan, 2009.

Dreiser, Theodore. *Newspaper Days.* New York: Horace Liveright, 1922.

——. *Selected Magazine Articles of Theodore Dreiser: Life and Art in the American 1890s.* Edited by Yoshinobu Hakutani. London and Toronto: Associated University Presses, 1985.

Eble, Kenneth E. *William Dean Howells.* Second edition. Boston: Twayne, 1982.

Emerson, Ralph Waldo. *The Early Lectures of Ralph Waldo Emerson.* Edited by Robert E. Spiller and Wallace E. Williams. Cambridge, Mass.: The Belknap Press of Harvard University Press, 1972.

——. *Essays and Lectures.* New York: Library of America, 1983.

Emery, Michael, Edwin Emery, and Nancy Roberts. *The Press and America: An Interpretive History of the Mass Media,* 9th ed. Boston: Allyn and Bacon, 2000.

Evening Sun, "The Inspector's Museum," May 16, 1890, 6.

Ferber, Linda S., and William H. Gerdts, *The New Path: Ruskin and the American Pre-Raphaelites.* New York: Schocken Books and the Brooklyn Museum, 1985.

Ferguson, Priscilla Parkhurst. *Paris as Revolution: Writing the Nineteenth Century City.* Berkeley: University of California Press, 1994.

Filler, Louis. *Crusaders for American Liberalism.* Yellow Springs, Ohio: Antioch Press, 1964.

Fishkin, Shelley Fisher, ed. Foreword, all volumes of *The Oxford Mark Twain.* New York and London: Oxford University Press, 1996.

———. *From Fact to Fiction: Journalism and Imaginative Writing in America.* Baltimore and London: Johns Hopkins University Press, 1985.

Flower, B. O. "Mask or Mirror." *Arena* 45 (Aug. 1893): 304–13.

Flynt, Josiah. "Club Life Among Outcasts." *Harper's Monthly* 90 (April 1895): 712–22.

———. *The Little Brother: A Story of Tramp Life.* Upper Saddle River, N.J.: The Gregg Press, 1968. First published by Century, 1902.

———. *Notes of an Itinerant Policeman.* Boston: L. C. Page, 1900.

———. *Tramping with Tramps: Studies and Sketches of Vagabond Life.* New York: Century, 1901.

Folsom, Ed, ed., "'This Heart's Geography Map': The Photographs of Walt Whitman." *Walt Whitman Quarterly Review,* Special Issue 4 (Fall–Winter 1986–87).

Ford, Edwin H. *A Bibliography of Literary Journalism in America.* Minneapolis: Burgess, 1937.

Foster, George G. *Fifteen Minutes Around New York.* New York: De Witt and Davenport, 1854.

———. *New York by Gas-Light and Other Urban Sketches by George G. Foster.* Edited by Stuart M. Blumin. Berkeley and Los Angeles: University of California Press, 1990.

———. *New York Naked.* New York: De Witt and Davenport, 1854.

Fulton, Marianne. *Eyes of Time: Photojournalism in America.* New York: Little, Brown, 1988.

Gambee, Budd Leslie, Jr. *Frank Leslie and His Illustrated Newspaper, 1855–1860.* Ann Arbor: University of Michigan Department of Library Science Studies 8, 1964.

Gardner, Alexander. *Gardner's Photographic Sketch Book of the Civil War.* New York: Dover, 1959.

Garland, Hamlin. *Crumbling Idols.* Cambridge, Mass.: Harvard University Press, 1960.

———. *Main-Travelled Roads.* New York: Harper and Brothers, 1891.

Gerber, John C. *Mark Twain.* Boston: Twayne Publishers, 1988.

Glazener, Nancy. *Reading for Realism: The History of a Literary Institution*. Durham, N. C.: Duke University Press, 1997.

Grafton, John. *New York in the Nineteenth Century: 321 Engravings from Harper's Weekly and Other Contemporary Sources*. New York: Dover, 1977.

Griffin, Randall C. *Homer, Eakins, and Anshutz: The Search for American Identity in the Gilded Age*. University Park, Penn.: Pennsylvania State University Press, 2004.

Guimond, James. *American Photography and the American Dream*. Chapel Hill and London: University of North Carolina Press, 1991.

Hapgood, Hutchins. "A New Form of Literature." *Bookman* 21 (1905): 423.

———. *The Spirit of the Ghetto*. Urbana and Chicago: University of Illinois Press, 2004.

———. *The Spirit of Labor*. New York: Dufield, 1909.

———. *Types From City Streets*. New York: Funk and Wagnalls, 1910.

———. *A Victorian in the Modern World*. New York: Harcourt, Brace, 1939.

Harris, Sharon M. *Rebecca Harding Davis and American Realism*. Philadelphia: University of Pennsylvania Press, 1991.

Harte, Bret. *Bret Harte's California*. Edited by Gary Scharnhorst. Albuquerque: University of New Mexico, 1990.

———. *The Outcasts of Poker Flat and Other Tales*. Introduction by Wallace Stegner. New York and Toronto: New American Library, 1961.

Hartsock, John C. *A History of American Literary Journalism: The Emergence of a Modern Narrative Form*. Amherst: University of Massachusetts Press, 2000.

Hearn, Lafcadio. "A Winter's Journey to Japan." *Harper's New Monthly Magazine* 81 (November 1890): 861.

———. *Children of the Levee*. Edited by O. W. Frost. Lexington: University of Kentucky Press, 1957.

———. *Creole Sketches*. Edited by Charles W. Hutson. Boston and New York: Houghton Mifflin, 1924.

———. *Period of the Gruesome: Selected Cincinnati Journalism of Lafcadio Hearn*. Edited by Jon Christopher Hughes. Lanham, N. Y., and London: University Press of America, 1990.

————. *Selected Writings of Lafcadio Hearn.* Edited by Henry Goodman, with an Introduction by Malcolm Cowley. New York: Citadel Press, 1949.

————. *Two Years in the French West Indies.* New York: Harper and Brothers, 1890.

Hine, Lewis. *America and Lewis Hine: Photographs 1904–1940.* Edited by Walter Rosenblum, Naomi Rosenblum, and Alan Trachtenberg. New York: Aperture, 1977.

Holmes, Oliver Wendall. "Doings of the Sunbeam." *Atlantic Monthly* 12 (July 1863): 1–15.

————. "The Stereoscope and the Stereograph." *Atlantic Monthly* 3 (June 1859): 738–48.

Homer, William Innes. *Thomas Eakins: His Life and Art.* New York: Abbeville Press Publishers, 1992.

Howells, William Dean. *Criticism and Fiction and Other Essays.* Edited by Clara Marburg and Rudolf Kirk. New York: New York University Press, 1959.

————. *Impressions and Experiences.* Freeport, N.Y.: Books for Libraries Press, 1972, first published in 1896.

————. "In Memoriam." Editor's Easy Chair. *Harper's Monthly Magazine* 140 (December 1919): 133.

————. *My Literary Passions.* New York: Krause Reprint of Harper and Brother 1895 edition, 1952.

————. "Recent Literature." *Atlantic Monthly* 36 (December 1875): 750–51.

————. *Their Wedding Journey.* Boston: James R. Osgood, 1872.

————. *Venetian Life.* Boston: Houghton, Mifflin, 1885.

————. *Years of My Youth and Three Essays.* Introduction by David J. Nordloh. Bloomington: Indiana University Press, 1975.

Hudson, Frederic. *Journalism in the United States, From 1690 to 1872.* New York: Harper and Brothers, 1873.

Hughes, Helen MacGill. *News and the Human Interest Story.* Chicago: University of Chicago Press, 1940.

Hughes, Jon Christopher. "*Ye Giglampz* and the Apprenticeship of Lafcadio Hearn," *American Literary Realism* 25 (Autumn 1982): 182–99.

Huntzicker, William E. *The Popular Press, 1833–1865.* Westport, Conn.: Greenwood Press, 1999.

James, William. *Pragmatism.* Cambridge, Mass.: Harvard University Press, 1975.

Kaplan, Amy. *The Social Construction of American Realism.* Chicago: University of Chicago Press, 1988.

Kerrane, Kevin, and Ben Yagoda. *The Art of Fact: A Historical Anthology of Literary Journalism.* New York: Scribner, 1997.

Kolb, Harold H., Jr. *The Illusion of Life: American Realism as a Literary Form.* Charlottesville: University of Virginia Press, 1969.

Kramer, Mark, and Wendy Call. *Telling True Stories.* New York: Plume, 2007.

Kummings, Donald D., ed. *A Companion to Walt Whitman.* Malden, Mass. and Oxford: Blackwell Publishing, 2006.

Kushner, Marily S., Barbara Dayer Gallati, and Linda S. Ferber. *Winslow Homer: Illustrating America.* New York: George Braziller, 2000.

Leland, Charles Godfrey. *Sunshine in Thought.* Gainesville, Fla.: Scholars' Facsimiles and Reprints, 1959, first published 1862.

Longstreet, A. B. *Augustus Baldwin Longstreet's Georgia Scenes Completed: A Scholarly Text.* Edited by David Rachels. Athens and London: University of Georgia Press, 1998.

Lutz, Tom. *Doing Nothing: A History of Loafers, Loungers, Slackers, and Bums in America.* New York: Farrar, Straus and Giroux, 2006.

MacLeish, Archibald. "Poetry and Journalism." The Gideon Seymour Memorial Lecture. University of Minnesota, October 12, 1958.

Martin, Jay. *Harvests of Change: American Literature, 1865–1914.* Englewood Cliffs, N. J.: Prentice-Hall, 1967.

Matthews, Brander. *Outlines in Local Color.* New York: Harper and Brothers, 1898.

———. *Vignettes of Manhattan.* New York: Harper and Brothers, 1894.

Matthiessen, F. O. *American Renaissance: Art and Expression in the Age of Emerson and Whitman.* London, New York, Oxford: Oxford University Press, 1941.

McCabe, James D., Jr. *Lights and Shadows of New York Life; Or, The Great City. A Work Descriptive of New York In All Its Various Phases.* Philadelphia, Cincinnati, Chicago, St. Louis: National Publishing Company, 1872.

Mindich, David T. Z. *Just the Facts: How "Objectivity" Came to Define American Journalism.* New York: New York University Press, 1998.

Moers, Ellen. *Two Dreisers.* New York: Viking Press, 1969.

Mott, Frank Luther. *A History of American Magazines.* Cambridge, Mass.: Harvard University Press, 1938.

———. *American Journalism.* New York: Macmillan, 1962.

Muller, G. F. "The City of Pittsburgh." *Harper's New Monthly Magazine* 53 (December 1880): 46–68.

Nerrone, John C. "The Mythology of the Penny Press." *Critical Studies in Mass Communication* 4 (December 1987): 376–422.

New York Commercial Advertiser, "Literature and Journalism in 1896," January 1, 1897.

New York Press, "In Poverty's Realm," February 6, 1894, 3.

New York Sun, "Bells A-Jingling All Day Long," February 14, 1894, 2.

———, "Sentiment in the Bowery," February 4, 1894, 7.

New York Times, "Naughty Protectory Boys," February 5, 1894, 3.

New York Tribune, "A Hunger-Stricken Horde," January 5, 1894, 7.

———, "A Train Saved By A Woman," August 2, 1890, 1.

Noyes, Russell, ed. *English Romantic Poetry and Prose.* New York: Oxford University Press, 1950.

Obrien, Frank M. *The Story of The Sun.* New York: D. Appleton, 1928.

Oliver, Lawrence J. "Brander Matthews' Re-visioning of Crane's *Maggie.*" *American Literature* 60 (December 1988): 657.

Panzer, Mary. *Mathew Brady and the Image of History.* Washington and London: Smithsonian Institution, 1997.

Park, David. "Picturing the War: Visual Genres in Civil War News." *Communication Review* 3 (1999): 287–321.

Pearce, Roy Harvey. *The Continuity of American Poetry.* Princeton, N. J.: Princeton University Press, 1961.

Pearson, Andrea G. "*Frank Leslie's Illustrated Newspaper* and *Harper's Weekly:* Innovation and Imitation in Nineteenth-Century American Pictorial Reporting." *Journal of Popular Culture* 23 (4): 81–111.

Persaud, Babita. "A Husband for Vibha." In *Best Newspaper Writing 2005,* ed. Aly Colon, 85–134. Washington, D.C.: The Poynter Institute for Media Studies and CQ Press, 2006.

Philadelphia Press, "Confiding Crooks," December 18, 1887, 10.

Pickett, Calder M. "Mark Twain as Journalist and Literary Man: A Contrast." *Journalism Quarterly* (Winter 1961): 59–66.

Pizer, Donald, ed. *Documents of American Realism and Naturalism.* Carbondale and Edwardsville: Southern Illinois University Press, 1998.

———. *Realism and Naturalism in Nineteenth Century American Fiction.* Carbondale: Southern Illinois University Press, 1966.

Poe, Edgar Allan. "The Daguerreotype." In *Classic Essays on Photography,* ed. Alan Trachtenberg. New Haven, Conn.: Leetes Island Books, 1980, 37–38.

Price, Kenneth M., and Susan Belasco Smith, eds. *Periodical Literature in Nineteenth-Century America.* Charlottesville and London: University Press of Virginia, 1995.

Quirk, Tom, and Gary Scharnhorst, eds. *American Realism and the Canon.* Newark: University of Delaware Press, 1994.

Rahv, Philip. "The Cult of Experience in American Writing." *Essays on Literature and Politics 1932–1972.* Edited by Arabel J. Porter and Andrew Dvosin. Boston: Houghton Mifflin, 1978.

Ralph, Julian. "The Bowery." *Century Magazine* 93 (December 1891): 227–37.

———. *People We Pass: Stories of Life Among the Masses of New York City.* New York: Harper and Brothers, 1896.

"The Recording Tendency and What It Is Coming To," *Century* 53 (Feb. 1897): 634–36.

Richardson, Gary A. *American Drama From the Colonial Period Through World War I: A Critical History.* New York: Twayne Publishers, 1993.

Riis, Jacob A. *Children of the Poor.* New York: Charles Scribner's Sons, 1892.

———. *How the Other Half Lives: Studies Among the Tenements of New York.* New York: Dover Publications, 1971.

———. *The Making of an American.* New York: Macmillan, 1927.

———. *Out of Mulberry Street: Stories of Tenement Life In New York City.* New York: Century, 1898.

Robertson, Michael. *Stephen Crane, Journalism, and the Making of Modern American Literature.* New York: Columbia University Press, 1997.

Roggenkamp. Karen. *Narrating the News: New Journalism and Literary Genre in Late Nineteenth-Century American Newspapers and Fiction.* Kent and London: Kent State University Press, 2005.

Rose, Jane Atteridge. "A Bibliography of Fiction and Non-Fiction by Rebecca Harding Davis." *American Literary Realism* 22 (Spring 1990): 67–86.

———. *Rebecca Harding Davis.* New York: Twayne Publishers, 1993.

Rosebault, Charles. *When Dana Was the Sun.* New York: Robert M. McBride, 1931.

Rowson, Susanna Haswell. *Charlotte Temple.* Edited with an introduction by Cathy N. Davidson. New York and Oxford: Oxford University Press, 1986.

Ryan, Ann M., and Joseph B. McCullough. *Cosmopolitan Twain.* Columbia and London: University of Missouri Press, 2008.

Sandweis, Martha A. *Photography in Nineteenth-Century America.* New York and Fort Worth: Henry Abrams and Amon Carter Museum, 1991.

Scharnhorst, Gary. *Bret Harte.* New York: Twayne Publishers, 1992.

Schiller, Dan. *Objectivity and the News: The Public and the Rise of Commercial Journalism.* Philadelphia: University of Pennsylvania Press, 1981.

Schudson, Michael. *Discovering the News: A Social History of American Newspapers.* New York: Basic Books, 1978.

Scribner's Magazine. "Newspapers and Fiction," July (1906): 122.

———. "The Point of View: The Newspaper and Fiction," 40 (1960): 122–24.

Sears, Stephen W., ed. *The American Heritage Century Collection of Civil War Art.* New York: American Heritage Publishing, 1974.

Sheldon, George W. *Hours with Art and Artists.* New York and London: Garland Publishing, 1978. Originally published in 1882.

Shi, David E. *Facing Facts: Realism in American Thought and Culture, 1850–1920.* New York: Oxford University Press, 1995.

Shuman, Edwin L. *Steps Into Journalism.* Evanston Ill.: Correspondence School of Journalism, 1894.

Siegel, Adrienne. *The Image of the American City in Popular Literature*

1820–1870. Port Washington, N.Y., and London: Kennikat Press, 1981.

Simpson, Marc. *Winslow Homer Paintings of the Civil War.* The Fine Arts Museums of San Francisco: Bedford Arts, 1988.

Sims, Norman, ed. *Literary Journalism in the Twentieth Century.* Evanston: Northwestern University Press, 2008. First published by Oxford University Press, 1990.

———, ed. *The Literary Journalists.* New York: Ballantine Books, 1984.

———. *True Stories: A Century of Literary Journalism.* Evanston: Northwestern University Press, 2007.

Sims, Norman, and Mark Kramer, eds. *Literary Journalism: A New Collection of the Best American Nonfiction.* New York: Ballantine Books, 1995.

Sinclair, Upton. *The Jungle.* Foreword by Eric Schlosser, Introduction by Ronald Gottesman. New York: Penguin Books, 2006.

Smith, Christopher, ed. *American Realism.* San Diego: Greenhaven Press, 2000.

Smith, Susan Harris. *Plays in American Periodicals, 1890–1918.* New York: Palgrave Macmillan, 2007.

Snyder, Louis L., and Richard B. Morris, eds. *A Treasury of Great Reporting.* 2nd revised edition. New York: Simon, 1962.

Srebnick, Amy Gilman. *The Mysterious Death of Mary Rogers: Sex and Culture in Nineteenth-Century New York.* New York and Oxford: Oxford University Press, 1995.

Steele, Janet E. *The Sun Shines for All.* Syracuse: Syracuse University Press, 1993.

Steffens, Lincoln. *The Autobiography of Lincoln Steffens.* New York: Harcourt, Brace, 1931.

Stevens, John D. *Sensationalism and the New York Press.* New York: Columbia University Press, 1991.

Stevenson, Elizabeth. *Lafcadio Hearn.* New York: Macmillan, 1961.

Sundquist, Eric, ed. *American Realism: New Essays.* Baltimore: Johns Hopkins, 1982.

Talese, Gay. *The Bridge.* New York: Walker and Company, 2003. First published in 1963.

———. *Fame and Obscurity.* New York: Dell Publishing, 1981.

————. *New York: A Serendipiter's Journey.* With photographs by Marvin Lichtner. New York: Harper and Brothers, Publishers, 1961.

Talese, Gay, and Barbara Lounsberry. *Writing Creative Nonfiction: The Literature of Reality.* New York: Harper Collins College Publishers, 1996.

"Tenement Life In New York," *Harper's Weekly* 23 (March 22, 1879): 224, 226–27; (March 29, 1879): 245, 246; (April 5, 1879): 265, 266–67.

Thompson, Susan. *The Penny Press.* Northport, Ala.: Vision Press, 2004.

Thompson, Susan, and Michael Bucholz. "The Penny Press, 1833–1861." In *The Media in America: A History,* ed. William David Sloan, 126. Northport, Ala.: Vision Press, 2008.

Thompson, William Fletcher, Jr. *The Image of War: The Pictorial Reporting of the American Civil War.* New York: Thomas Yoseloff, 1959.

Trachtenberg, Alan, ed. *Classic Essays on Photography.* New Haven, Conn.: Leete's Island, 1980.

————. *The Incorporation of America: Culture and Society in the Gilded Age.* New York: Hill and Wang, 1982.

————. "Photography: The Emergence of a Keyword," In *Photography in Nineteenth Century America,* ed. Martha A. Sandweiss. New York: Harry N. Abrams, 1991, 16–46.

————. *Reading American Photographs.* New York: Hill and Wang, 1989.

Tucher, Andie. *Froth and Scum: Truth, Beauty, Goodness, and the Ax Murder in America's First Mass Medium.* Chapel Hill and London: University of North Carolina Press, 1994.

Twain, Mark. "A True Story, Repeated Word for Word as I Heard It." *Atlantic Monthly* 34 (November 1874): 591–94.

————. *The Autobiography of Mark Twain.* Edited by Charles Neider. New York: Harper and Brothers, 1959.

————. "Forty-Three Days in an Open Boat: Compiled from Personal Diaries." *Harper's New Monthly Magazine* 34 (December 1886): 104–13.

————. *The Innocents Abroad.* The Oxford Mark Twain. Edited by Shelley Fisher Fishkin. New York and Oxford: Oxford University Press, 1996.

————. *Mark Twain's Letters from Hawaii.* Edited by Grove A. Day. Honolulu: University of Hawaii Press, 1966.

———. *Mark Twain Speaking.* Edited by Paul Fatout. Iowa City: University of Iowa Press, 1976.

———. *Mark Twain's Travels with Mr. Brown.* Edited by Franklin Walker and G. Ezra Dane. New York: Alfred A. Knopf, 1940.

———. *Roughing It.* The Oxford Mark Twain. Edited by Shelley Fisher Fishkin. New York and Oxford: Oxford University Press, 1996.

———. *Traveling with the Innocents Abroad: Mark Twain's Original Reports from Europe and the Holy Land.* Edited by Daniel Morley McKeithan. Norman: University of Oklahoma Press, 1958.

Underwood, Doug. *Journalism and the Novel: Truth and Fiction, 1700–2000.* Cambridge: Cambridge University Press, 2008.

Waggoner, Hyatt H. *American Poets from the Puritans to the Present.* New York: Dell Publishing, 1968.

Whitman, Walt. *The Collected Writings of Walt Whitman: The Journalism.* Edited by Herbert Bergman. New York: Peter Lang, 1998.

———. *Complete Poetry and Selected Prose.* Edited by James E. Miller Jr. Boston: Houghton Mifflin, Riverside Editions, 1959.

———. *The Uncollected Poetry and Prose of Walt Whitman.* Edited by Emory Holloway. New York: Peter Smith, 1932.

Williams, Raymond. *The Long Revolution.* New York: Harper and Row, 1966.

Willis, Nathanial Parker. *Pencillings by the Way.* New York: Morris and Willis, 1844.

Wilmerding, John, ed. *Thomas Eakins.* Washington, D.C.: Smithsonian Institution Press, 1993.

Wilson, Christopher P. *The Labor of Words: Literary Professionalism in the Progressive Era.* Athens: University of Georgia Press, 1985.

Wilton, Andrew, and Tim Barringer. *American Sublime: Landscape Painting in the United States, 1820–1880.* Princeton, N.J.: Princeton University Press, 2002.

Wolfe, Tom. *The New Journalism.* New York: Harper and Row, 1973.

Wyckoff, Walter A. *A Day with a Tramp and Other Days.* New York: Scribner's Sons, 1901.

———. *The Workers, An Experiment in Reality: The East.* New York: Charles Scribner's Sons, 1897.

————. *The Workers, An Experiment in Reality: The West*. New York: Charles Scribner's Sons, 1898.

Yochelson, Bonnie, and Daniel Czitrom. *Rediscovering Jacob Riis: Exposure Journalism and Photography in Turn-of-the-Century New York*. New York and London: New Press, 2007.

Zboray, Ronald J., and Mary Saracino Zboray. *Literary Dollars and Social Sense: A People's History of the Mass Market Book*. New York and London: Routledge, 2005.

Ziff, Larzer. *The American 1890s: Life and Times of a Lost Generation*. New York: Viking, 1966.

Zurier, Rebecca, Robert W. Snyder, and Virginia M. Mecklenburg. *Metropolitan Lives: The Ashcan Artists and Their New York*. Washington, D.C.: National Museum of American Art, 1996.

INDEX

flaneurs, 55, 57, 69, 222n2; Foster, 40,
53, 94; Hearn, 136; Howells, 156;
Twain, 88, 94
Flower, B. O., 163–64, 240n51
Flynt, Josiah, 10, 186–89, 191, 244n37,
245n42; as cultural reporter, 208;
Progressive Era and, 202
"Forest Hymn, A" (Bryant), 19
"Forty-Three Days in an Open Boat"
(Twain), 92–93
Forum magazine, 160
Foster, George G., 49–52, 78, 119,
136, 175, 207; as cultural reporter,
208; Dickens as influence on, 69,
70; as flaneur, 40, 53, 94; reputation
among historians, 9–10; slang ex-
pressions and, 195; "underground"
of city and, 62–63; Whitman and,
52, 53–55, 57, 60, 64. See also *Fifteen
Minutes Around New York* (Foster);
New York by Gas-Light (Foster); *New
York in Slices* (Foster)
Foster, Hannah, 31
Frank Leslie's Illustrated Newspaper,
106
Frazier, Ian, 206–7, 208
Froth and Scum (Tucher), 31

Galaxy, 84, 114
gamblers/gambling, 3, 62, 112, 142
Gardner, Alexander, 127–29
*Gardner's Photographic Sketch Book of
the Civil War* (Gardner), 127–28,
129
Garland, Hamlin, 15, 145, 157, 159–64,
194; lecture on Howells and real-

ism, 179; local color fiction and,
162, 240n47
Gas-Light sketches. See *New York by
Gas-Light* (Foster)
gender, 9, 33, 78
"General Dash at the Ferries, A"
(Foster), 55
Georgia Scenes (Longstreet), 35–37,
221n53
Gettysburg, Battle of, 127
Gibson, William Hamilton, 103
Gilded Age, The (Twain and Warner),
149
"Girl of the Year, The" (Wolfe),
100
Goodyear, Dana, 206, 207
gossip, 34
Graham's Monthly, 17
Grandma Never Lived in America (Ca-
han), 198
Grant, Ulysses S., 160
Greeley, Horace, 219n34
"Green River" (Bryant), 19
Griswold, Louisa, 230n61
Guernsey, Alfred H., 151

"Halt of the Wagon Train" (Homer),
116, 117
Hapgood, Hutchins, 166–67, 200–202,
204, 208, 212
Harper and Brothers, 36, 151
Harper's Magazine (*Harper's New
Monthly Magazine*), 147–48, 151
Harper's Monthly, 10, 79, 103, 151;
Alden as editor, 150, 152; Davis and,
81; Flynt and, 187; Garland and,

Thomas B. Connery is a professor of communication and journalism and former dean of the College of Arts and Sciences at the University of St. Thomas in St. Paul, Minnesota, the editor of *A Sourcebook of American Literary Journalism,* the coauthor of *Writing Across the Media,* and one of the founding editors of the scholarly journal *Literary Journalism Studies.*

Roy Peter Clark is a senior scholar at the Poynter Institute and the author of fourteen books on journalism and writing, including *Writing Tools: 50 Essential Strategies for Every Writer, Free to Write: A Journalist Teaches Young Writers, Coaching Writers: Editors and Reporters Working Together Across Media Platforms,* and *The Values and Craft of American Journalism.*